T0097924

Full Swing

The Minority Quarterback
Court Vision
To the Hoop
The Gospel According to Casey (with Jim Kaplan)
How to Talk Jewish (with Jackie Mason)
Hank Greenberg: Hall-of-Fame Slugger
Hank Greenberg: The Story of My Life (editor)
Pitchers Do Get Lonely
The Man Who Robbed the Pierre
Red: A Biography of Red Smith
Carew (with Rod Carew)
The DuSable Panthers
Maxwell Street
Beyond the Dream
Rockin' Steady (with Walt Frazier)
Oscar Robertson: The Golden Year

Full Swing

HITS, RUNS AND ERRORS
IN A WRITER'S LIFE

~~~~~~~~~~~~~~~~

Ira Berkow

Ivan R. Dee

CHICAGO

www.ivanrdee.com

The paperback of this book carries the ISBN 1-56663-755-4.

Library of Congress Cataloging-in-Publication Data:
Berkow, Ira.
Full swing : hits, runs and errors in a writer's life / Ira Berkow.
p. cm.
Includes index.
ISBN 1-56663-689-2 (cloth : alk. paper)
1. Berkow, Ira. 2. Sportswriters–United States–Biography. I. Title.
GV742.42.B47A3 2005
070.4'49796'092–dc22
2005023919

For my mother, father, and brother

Contents

Prologue 3

1 Who Wrote the Poem? 15

2 Look to the Curtain 37

3 Thunderstruck 52

4 Try Again 69

5 Who Moved the Spike? 89

6 You Can't Write That 113

7 Steamy 139

8 Good News and Bad News 160

9 Full of the Devil 177

10 It Must Have Cost You a Fortune 193

11 It's Our Show Biz 217

12 Me and Koufax 233

13 The Comedy Poorhouse 244

14 Blue Skies 260

Acknowledgments 275

Index 277

"In fully extended power swing, hands
(arrow) move the bat through hitting area as
the hips are opened up. Hands still lead,
arms extend, thus increasing arc of swing to
bring fat part of bat up into pitch."
—From a diagram in *The Science of Hitting*
by Ted Williams and John Underwood

"If you will tell me why the fen / appears
impassable, I then / will tell you why I think
that I / can cross it if I try."
—From "I May, I Might, I Must"
by Marianne Moore

"The heart is half a prophet."
—Yiddish proverb

Full Swing

Prologue

I WAS BORN in January, which meant that I must have been conceived the previous April, in the springtime of 1939. Springtime, if you listen to the songs and read the sonnets, is a time that stirs a young man's fancy. I've always imagined that such fancy is shared by young women, too. And I'd like to believe that my parents, then in their early twenties, were equally blithe-spirited participants in that long-ago romantic interlude on the West Side of Chicago. It's difficult to picture one's parents in the throes of such private moments, but facts must be countenanced.

Other widely appreciated aspects of spring are, of course, renewal and rebirth, or, in my case, just plain inception.

And somewhere in that mix, in America, to be sure, is the return of the sound of the crack of the bat. Baseball.

I doubt that my parents had baseball in mind when engaged in their amorous pursuit. And surely they had no idea that their eventual offspring (who was distinguished as a toddler for hair so curly that some mistook him for a girl, or miniature kin to Harpo Marx) would grow up to write about sports, often about baseball, as well as a wide variety of other subjects, from politics to entertainment to the law to the underworld–sometimes all even related to sports–for a national as well as an international audience.

Many springs passed from the one in 1939, and, regularly at that time of year, I found myself traveling to Florida to cover the training of major league baseball clubs. My parents, both retired, would rent a condominium in Hallendale, Florida, where they'd go from December to March to escape the brutal winters of Chicago, where they lived the rest of the year. On one of my visits, a sweet March morning in 1983, we went for breakfast at a nearby coffee shop that they frequented. The place was located directly across Hallandale Boulevard from the Gulfstream Race Track, and many stable hands, jockeys, agents, and others who worked with horses also ate there.

My parents were friendly with the owner of the coffee shop, a balding, middle-aged, genial man who greeted us at the door.

My mother introduced us. "This is my son," she said.

"Nice to meet you," he said.

"He's a writer," my mother said proudly.

The man looked me over–6 feet, 190 pounds.

"A rider?" he said. "Kinda big to be a rider."

"No, not 'rider,'" my mother corrected, with emphasis: "wriTer."

The owner still gazed at me. He wasn't sure he believed this, either.

"Well," I said with a smile, trying to be helpful, "it all depends on who you ask."

It's true. One person's writer is another person's, well, horse's ass, perhaps. And it's probably harder to be a writer even than to look like one.

My father said nothing. He had an instinct that I always found remarkable, often to do or say the right thing at the right time. I think he figured I could handle this one by myself. If I needed him, he was invariably there.

And both he and my mother had greatly supported my foray into the strange craft of writing–strange because neither of them had much knowledge of that world.

Looking back, even to that point, I had had a circuitous journey as a writer, and that would continue to be so. Saul Bellow, who came from a similar area in Chicago as I did, once said that in the early part of his career as a novelist "I was restrained, controlled, demonstrating that I could write 'good.' I didn't understand that if you came from the streets of Chicago, to write 'good' was to write in a foreign language." If little else, I could identify with this esteemed Nobel Prize-winner the steep climb of trying to write well and to say something of value, to say it fresh, with sinew, with logic, with insight, with emotion, with humor, from the vantage point of my varied and, as I saw it, uncommon experiences.

And little could I have imagined when I began this professional passage out of college the worlds I would enter, the people I would meet, the lessons I would learn.

I found myself one evening, for example, in the Clinton White House.

I had been invited there for a screening of an HBO documentary about women's achievements in sports, "Dare to Compete," on Monday night, March 9, 1999. This was the night after Monica Lewinsky appeared on the "Barbara Walters Show" and talked of her liaison with the president.

I spoke with the president about his number one sports hero, Henry Aaron, whom, Clinton said, he admired for the skill and dignity of his play. The two of us, along with Donna DeVarona, the onetime Olympic gold medal swimmer, were chatting in a corner of the state dining room when Eleanor Holm (now Eleanor Holm Whalen), who won an Olympic gold medal for the 100-meter backstroke in the 1932 Olympics, walked over. Holm, now eighty-six, had been interviewed for the documentary about a year earlier in her home in Miami. Attractive enough to have turned down an offer to be in the Ziegfeld Follies, she had also been one of the Janes in a 1938 Tarzan movie, *Tarzan's Revenge.* This followed after a controversial decision by the imperious Avery Brundage, head of the American Olympic team in 1936, affecting Holm, then Mrs. Arthur Jarrett.

At the White House in 1999, I looked on as two Olympic gold medal winners in swimming, Eleanor Holm and Donna DeVarona, flanked President Clinton.

Brundage had thrown her off the team because she was seen drinking champagne on the boat with Olympic teammates on the way to the Berlin Olympics. ("I've never made any secret of the fact that I like a good time and that I am particularly fond of champagne," she said at the time. She asked for another chance and was denied it.)

Her hair now was white and cut short, but she wore a colorful dress, a pair of bright eyes shown through her glasses, and she had a white, effervescent smile. She exuded vitality, even at her age.

"Mr. President," she said, "I'm Eleanor Holm."

"I know," he said, "I remember you from the film."

"Mr. President," she said, "you know, you are one good-looking dude."

Clinton smiled, almost shyly. "Well, thank you, Eleanor. I'm flattered. And Eleanor, I have to say, watching the film, that when

I saw you sitting on that yellow couch in your home, I thought, 'I'd like to be on that couch with you.'"

I don't remember Holm's response. What I do remember is that DeVarona and I exchanged glances. Did he really say that? At this time of all times?

Was Clinton shameless, or crass, or just innocent and trying to offer a compliment? I thought it was a telling clue to the man, one who couldn't pass up an attempt to charm a woman, even an octogenarian, and add at least a dash of sensuality to it. Such a character trait, as I perceived it, led directly to some of his troubles.

As a reporter, I knew the story wasn't finished. I later approached Eleanor and asked what she thought of Clinton's remark, that he'd like to have been on that couch with her? "Oh," she said, with a sparkle in her eyes, "I guess I'm just his type."

In the midst of the Watergate furor in 1974, when burglars under apparent direction from the White House broke into Democratic National Headquarters in Washington, D.C.–it ended, of course, with Nixon resigning the presidency–I wrote a series for Newspaper Enterprise Association (NEA), a national feature syndicate where I worked before joining the *New York Times*, about some of the major figures in the scandal. Although sportswriting has always been prominent in my life in journalism, I have regularly embarked on a variety of general assignments, from newspaper and magazine stories to books. This was such an instance. I hoped to interview Judge John Sirica, the judge who had the power of sentencing for the Watergate burglars, and who in effect broke open the case with confessions from some of them by threatening severe jail terms.

But Judge Sirica was not doing interviews. I learned this when I called his office and reached an assistant. I asked if Sirica went to lunch. Yes, but he would not go to lunch with a reporter. I decided to give Sirica a try anyway. I arrived at his office on the second floor of the U.S. District Courthouse in Washington at about ten o'clock. The assistant said Sirica wouldn't see me. I waited for more than two hours. At a little past noon the judge came out of his office. At sixty-nine, in June 1973, he still had thick wavy dark hair, a somewhat flattened nose–perhaps a remnant from his days as an amateur boxer–and looked natty in a grey suit. I walked over and introduced myself. He was wary. I said, "Judge, I have just one question."

"What's that?" he said. NEA hardly had the cachet of the *New York Times* or a local newspaper so I had to try to make myself interesting at first impression since I might never get a second.

"How did it come about," I said, "that Jack Dempsey was the best man at your wedding?" The fact was not widely known.

Sirica had been married some thirty years, I had read, and former world heavyweight boxing champion Jack Dempsey, of all people, was the best man.

Sirica looked at me and smiled. "Come into my office, young man," he said.

And we chatted for nearly two hours. He didn't reveal inside dope about the Watergate proceedings, but he did tell me about his life, which helped me understand how and why he made his judicial decisions. He was the child of immigrant Italian parents who felt deeply about the opportunities that America held out, and of which he was a prime example, being of a mother and father who spoke broken English and rising to the federal bench. It's almost an American cliché, this rags-to-riches tale, but it was real, it was emotional, and he was going to do everything in his considerable power not to let even the President of the United States subvert our Constitution.

Sirica was, in his eyes, akin to the dream of Holden Caulfield in *The Catcher in the Rye*, in which he was saving not just little kids from harm in the rye but his entire beloved nation. I felt this intensely as I sat across from this honorable, resolute man in his chambers, and it naturally brought to mind thoughts of my own family history, of Jewish grandparents already with families coming from small towns or villages in Romania and Russia, enduring hardships in "The Promised Land" to seek the advertised fruits of the New World. My parents, as it happened, were each the baby of their families and were born in Chicago.

At Ellis Island, where my grandparents with several of the people who would become my uncles and aunts first entered this country shortly after the turn of the twentieth century, a museum to the immigrant experience has been established. I visited there and was struck by one of the inscriptions on a wall:

"When I was in the Old Country I heard that in America, the streets were paved with gold. When I got here, I found that not only were the streets not paved with gold, they weren't even paved. And I was expected to pave them."–Italian immigrant, anonymous.

And so he and millions of others like him, such as those members of my own family, sweated and strove on these often unyielding shores and in its teeming cities.

As a writer I also discovered that the best in a field, any field, must have a passion for his work. I recall meeting Ted Williams for the first time, and his talking about batting with–and this is the best word I can find to describe it–pure lust. It was in the visitor's dugout in Yankee Stadium, and Williams was the fifty-year-old manager of the Washington Senators. The "Splendid Splinter," as he was called in his playing days, now wore a jacket even in warm weather to cover his considerable belly. He jumped off the bench and began demonstrating his swing without benefit of a bat. "From the hips, from the hips!" he said in that deep, ardent baritone. "It's that little magic move at the plate."

I thought of this in 1975 when I interviewed Willie Sutton, the notorious bank robber. Willie was then seventy-five and out of prison, for the final time, since 1969. A New York police commissioner had called him the Babe Ruth of bank robbers. With his disguises and his daring, he had captured the public's imagination like no criminal since Jesse James.

Sutton had robbed nearly a hundred banks and stolen close to a million dollars. We had breakfast in the Dorset Hotel in

Manhattan. "I couldn't stop robbing banks," he told me, his pouch-eyed, crinkly face brightening in the telling. "It was a compulsion. I loved it. I was more alive when I was inside a bank, robbing it, than at any other time in my life. I enjoyed everything about it so much that one or two weeks later I'd be looking for another job. But to me the money was the chips, that's all. The winnings. Me looking at a bank was like some other guy looking at a beautiful woman. Irresistible."

Irresistible. I like that. It covers my feeling about writing. Once I started, there was nothing else I wanted to do. Auto mechanic was out: I couldn't fix a flat tire. Accounting was out: I didn't care which side of the ledger was the debit and which was the credit. And, unlike Willie Sutton, I didn't quite have the guts of a burglar. Especially when it came to banks.

In my wallet, when I went to that breakfast at the coffee shop with my parents in Hallendale—and despite the skepticism of the proprietor—was an element of proof of my membership in a writing fraternity. It was my Baseball Writers' Association of America card, the appearance of which is, for better or worse, yet another rite of early spring for those who cover teams and games—occasionally, like me, or on the beat.

Many people envy those journalists who receive this annual card which, as it states on the front, entitles the bearer "to press courtesies of the clubs of the National and American Leagues of professional baseball clubs. . . ." In other words, with this wallet-sized card you can get into any major league baseball game in the world free of charge. Of course, some card-holders have to work once inside the ballpark, but that's another matter.

Sportswriters, though, often approach the card's arrival with a certain amount of dread, if not trembling. For they know it is a living symbol of the end of the game—the game, as it were, of life. Few people in any profession or walk of life have as clear an indication of where one stands in relation to the eventual embrace of the Maker.

You see, printed at the top right-hand corner of my tan card that year, 1983–the color of the card changed every year, perhaps to make it more palatable, I don't know–was the number 142. (It happens that I've saved the cards from that point forward.)

Twenty-two years later, in 2005, my number was down to 20. The number is related to seniority in the Baseball Writers' Association. It means that of the now eight hundred or so members of the group, only nineteen writers have been in it longer than I have. Each year the number is lower as, in the mind's eye, the jaws of eternity widen. I know some writers who refuse to tell their numbers, fearing they would seem old, never mind the bald pate and sluggish stride.

The year before, in 2004, I was number 22. The meager decline may mean–in my imagination, anyway–that time is slowing for me. The drops in the previous three years had been the smallest I'd ever experienced in my journey through the dugouts and clubhouses of the nation. I began as a twenty-five-year-old baseball writer for the *Minneapolis Tribune* in 1965, when, according to Jack Lang, the retired but longtime secretary-treasurer of the Baseball Writers' Association, there were about eight hundred members. Although baseball team expansion has increased the number of teams, there has been a commensurate decline of newspapers.

There is no record of the exact number I started at, but Lang assured me it had to be close to 800. So in the previous 39 years, some 780 newspaper baseball writers or columnists who cover baseball have either retired or expired.

Here follows one man's march to cliff's end–from 1983 the numbers dwindle thusly: 142 (in 1983), 130, 121, 105, 100, 91 (down to double digits beginning in 1988), 86, 78, 71, 62, 56, 49 (broke the half-century mark in 1994), 45, 40, 36, 32, 31, 29 (broke 30 in 2000), 28, 24, 23, 22, and 20.

I once asked a writer who had attained card number 1 what that was like.

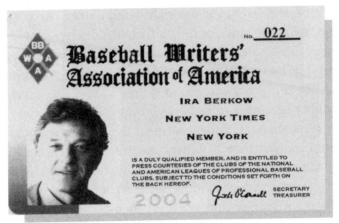

*My annual card from the Baseball Writers' Association of America,
No. 022 in 2004. My first card was issued when I began as a
sportswriter with the* Minneapolis Tribune *in 1965–it was around
No. 800 out of about eight hundred members. Every year, as other
members die, or in some cases retire, the number shrinks.*

"Better than the alternative," he replied.

Roger Angell, truthfully but mystically, has written in the
New Yorker:

"Since baseball time is measured in outs, all you have to do
is succeed utterly; keep hitting, keep the rally alive, and you have
defeated time. You remain young forever."

There has never been a game, of course, that went on forever
(the major league record is twenty-six innings), though some,
even those that go nine innings, *feel* as though they are going on
forever–with all the posturing and scratching of the pitcher and
the diggings-in of the batter seemingly searching for buried treas-
ure. But the baseball writer eschews this for a focus on the drama,
the beauty, the ambience, the strategies of the contest, and the
people in the game.

I've seen the inevitable diminishment of skills, the careers
gradually drawing to termination. Even the "immortals," as those
enshrined in Cooperstown are known, have not been spared, including those I covered as players, from Mickey Mantle to Catfish

Hunter to Waite Hoyt, and those whom I covered as managers or coaches, from Ted Williams to Joe DiMaggio to Casey Stengel.

And so, at some point, for superstars as well as journeymen, the writer must consider baseball players and his own baseball card not morbidly but objectively: there must be a conclusion.

A few years ago my father, Harold, lay in a Chicago hospital bed with severe heart congestion. The doctor took me aside and told me that my father had maybe a month or so to live. Should he tell him? I said yes, that my dad could take the truth, and, also, I could never successfully lie to him or deal in subterfuge. I learned that a long time ago. He could see right through it.

With my father now propped up on a pillow, the doctor related the news to him as gently as he could, and then departed.

I sat alone at my father's bedside. My mother, whose mind now had difficulty with comprehension, was home. I looked at the man who had just been given a literal death sentence. "How do you feel, Dad?" I asked.

"I'm eighty-seven years old," my father said to me. "Like I told Ma, nobody lives forever. No, I'm not scared and I'm not depressed. I tried to live a full and good life, tried to do the right thing. I hope I have."

I told him, yes—yes he had, and then I got emotional.

My dad, through his glasses, looked at me and said, "Don't cry for me . . . Argentina." And I laughed through my tears.

I hope I feel the same way, can deal with the dire circumstances in the same manner as my dad—are courage and grace overstatements? perhaps not—when the number on my baseball card is about to reach 0.

This book is about what I learned and whom I learned it from as I made my sometimes staggered way through life, with a particular emphasis on the forty years of my career as a writer.

No one taught me more than my father, who himself grew up an orphan during the depression on Chicago's difficult streets, and who was such a positive force through my life. He wasn't always right. He made mistakes that he tried to steer me away from.

And we did disagree. But more often than not his words hit the target, which I especially realized as I grew older.

I am reminded of the famous line attributed to Mark Twain, who said he left home as a boy of fourteen because his father was so dumb, but returned seven years later and "was astonished at how much he had learned in those years." I think most children can empathize.

My father's doctor, Edwin J. Smolovitz, was devastatingly correct. My father lived only another four weeks, dying on January 23, 2002, two weeks after my sixty-second birthday.

In the end, he taught me how to die, just as in so many ways he had taught me how to live.

1

~~~~~~~~~~~~~~~~~

Who Wrote the Poem?

IN THE LATE 1940S AND '50S I attended William Cullen Bryant Grammar School on the West Side of Chicago. Bryant was a red-brick, six-entranced school with inkwells in desks and streams of kids. Now it exists only in the mists of memory since it has been leveled to make way for something called urban renewal. At Bryant I was a good student and an avid reader. My juvenile tastes, however, did not tend toward William Cullen Bryant himself, the nineteenth-century New England poet, who wrote, as I ran across it several decades later: "The melancholy days are come, the saddest of the year, / Of wailing winds, and naked woods, / and meadows brown and sere"—which, more or less, describes the fate of his eponymous public school in Chicago, if you change "woods" and "meadows" for "city block" and "sere" for "gravel."

No, I read mostly biographies aimed at young audiences—books about Abraham Lincoln, Clara Barton, and a particular favorite, *Kit Carson: Boy of the Old West*—along with John R. Tunis's sports novels, especially *The Kid from Tomkinsville* and

Highpockets, which thrilled me with their galloping pace. I even skipped a grade at Bryant, going from fourth to fifth. (When, after morning recess on the day of the promotion, Miss Mele told me to report to the principal's office and didn't say why, I protested. "I didn't do anything this time," I said, for I occasionally had made a trek to that dreaded office for some infraction.) In high school, though, my grades were poor, since I concentrated primarily on playing sports, and success in the classroom was marked by the ability to manage, just barely, to stay eligible for the school teams. I read three books in my four years of high school. I have played arduous catch-up on reading ever since.

In an English class in my junior year at Sullivan High, however—it was October 1955, when I was fifteen—I did write something that drew the teacher's attention. It was in Miss Moody's English class. Miss Moody was a small woman with dyed red hair who wore circles of rouge marks on her cheeks. Every St. Patrick's Day she and Ralph Margolis, the football coach, used to dance the Irish jig on stage in the school auditorium. Coach Margolis was as hefty as Miss Moody was petite. It was quite a sight, and one wondered, given the weight of Coach Margolis, whether the wooden floor of the stage would hold.

But every Friday a rotating group of students was instructed to memorize a poem in Miss Moody's class, and to stand and read the poem aloud. The poem was supposed to be no shorter than twelve lines. One fellow in the class stood, rolled up his shirt-sleeves, and recited, glancing at his forearm with every line since the poem was inked on his arm. Somehow Miss Moody never noticed, though the rest of the class was falling into the aisles with muted laughter. Another guy tore a page out of our English textbook and taped it to the back of the guy sitting in front of him; he peered down and read it. Another fellow began, "You load sixteen tons, what do you get / Another day older and deeper in debt . . ." It was from the popular song of that year, "Sixteen Tons," by Tennessee Ernie Ford, but Miss Moody, sitting in the front of the classroom, wasn't aware of any of that, either.

Who Wrote the Poem?

Lenny Bretts never even bothered with a poem or even to raise his head that was crooked in the arm of his leather jacket as he slumbered on his desk, from the bell to start the class to the bell that ended it. Miss Moody ignored him. I believe she was content to let tough Lenny Bretts and his grease-thick ducktail lie undisturbed. As for me:

When the Dodgers finally won their first World Series, in the fall of 1955, at long last beating the Yankees, whom they'd lost the Series to in 1941, '47, '49, '52, and '53—and after a half-century of "wait till next years"—I was unaccountably moved to compose a poem about it, and their star pitcher Johnny Podres. I don't remember anyone else writing his or her own poem in the class, and why I did I have no idea. I wasn't a Dodgers fan, had never even been to Brooklyn. I had never written a poem for the class before—I had written some doggerel in grade school that was published in the school newspaper, the Bryant *Snoops*—and I never did it for the class again.

I rose and recited my poem—it was fourteen lines, as I recall, a kind of Herculean effort, being two lines more than required. I no longer have a copy of my poem, but I'm sure it had lines like "The Dodgers finally won the World Serious / And Brooklyn fans are going delirious." When I concluded, and was about to sit down, Miss Moody said, "You didn't give the name of the author who wrote the poem."

"I wrote the poem, Miss Moody," I replied proudly. "Wrote it myself."

She squinted through her sequined spectacles. She had me pegged as a troublemaker.

"If you don't tell me who really wrote the poem, I'm taking you right down to the office."

"Okay, okay, Miss Moody," I relented. "It was Charles Dickens. He wrote the poem." It was the only author's name that came immediately to mind.

"Very good," she said, smiling like a sleuth. "You may sit down."

As years passed into adulthood, I settled into a life with a wider range of interests, even to the point of reading authentic poetry.

As a boy, however, I had my heroes, which is part of the human condition, as I've come to understand it, going back at least to the days of Zeus and Homer. And for boys, especially when I was a kid, they are often sports stars. "Without heroes," Bernard Malamud wrote in his novel *The Natural*, "we are all plain people and don't know how far we can go." I don't think that's absolutely true, but there is some truth to it. We all have our influences, positive and negative, those we know who are part of our actual lives, like our parents, and those we hear about or read about or see in the flesh just beyond us, who may have legendary status, whom we admire and may wish to emulate for their performance, in any field. In the end, though, what is in *us*, in the deepest recesses of our minds and hearts, counts the most. Still, false gods—outstanding technicians but imperfect human beings—may serve a purpose for the rest of us. At best, as Malamud suggests, they set a bar for excellence, no mean thing.

And while as an adolescent I enjoyed reading books and magazine stories, sports and otherwise, I never dreamed of writing any of them. Even the image of a writer didn't exist in my mind. The stories were there in all their blood and body, in all their tumult and drama and adventures, but the writers were simply names on a page to which I paid little attention.

Growing up, I never knew a writer, and the books in our home were not of the highest literary caliber. As I recall, my mother read one book, *Marjorie Morningstar*, a novel by Herman Wouk about a Jewish girl who comes from a poor background and rises as an actress to national stardom. I'm certain my mother never harbored such pretensions of fame and fortune, but it may have been a welcome flight of fancy. My father, often drained from long hours at work, seemed to have little time to read, though he did go through the newspaper—he was one of the earliest subscribers to the *Chicago Sun-Times*. He also invested in *The Book of Knowledge,* a multi-volume encyclopedia that I turned to often and found fascinating. I remember reading about, and seeing pictures of, the density of the Milky Way and the twinkling stars going on forever and the unimaginable vastness of the universe, and growing dizzy from the very thought of this immensity.

I was born and lived on the West Side of Chicago, growing up mostly on Springfield Avenue in a two-bedroom apartment on the second floor in one of the three-story brick buildings that were so common there, until I was thirteen. It was a working-class, mixed racial and ethnic neighborhood called Lawndale, with black and Italian, Irish, Polish, Greek, Puerto Rican, and, most of all, Jewish immigrants or children of immigrants—my mother's parents were born in Russia, my father's in Romania. Not one of my grandparents could read or write in English. Along the main business street, Roosevelt Road, where I remember streetcars passing and sparking electricity from their trolley poles that reached up to the wires, I knew some small shopkeepers—the barber, the butcher, the dry cleaner (of course, he was my father)—some laborers, the precinct captain, a few con men, but no writers. I don't remember any professional men—lawyers, doctors, accountants.

There was a chiropractor, a short man with thick glasses, who lived with his family just below us on the first floor of our apartment building, where he did his business, but there seemed something nefarious about his operation. People seemed to come and go wearing shaded hats, and a little bent over as well. Sometimes I'd pass his door and hear moans coming from inside. An acrid, medicinal smell seeped through the doors. It was all unpleasant. He and his wife and daughter, a studious girl about my age who wore her hair as though she had just been frightened by something, kept to themselves. And that seemed fine to me.

Directly above us, on the third floor, lived a family with three kids whose breadwinner was a house painter. A florid-faced man, the husband and father spoke quickly, as though he was about to take flight. On some nights we'd hear from these upstairs neighbors something that resembled furniture moving. It turned out that the man was knocking his wife about, virtually from wall to wall. On more than one occasion my father called the police. The wife never pressed charges. My father once asked her why. "He's a good provider," she explained. When my father replied something to her, she had to turn to hear with her good ear. One of her husband's swats had permanently deafened the other one.

I don't remember anyone in the neighborhood having gone to college, let alone having graduated from a university. (The next generation, my generation, would be different, would have opportunities not readily available to, or taken by, the others.) After grammar school graduation, my family moved to the North Side, where I went to Sullivan High School. It was considered a step up from the West Side, the next level for the white migration as blacks moved in and soon fully occupied the old neighborhood. As a boy of thirteen, I wasn't happy with the move. My friends, some black, some white, still lived on the West Side, and for a time I continued to return there, until eventually and inevitably I made new friends in high school and in my new neighborhood of West Rogers Park. In my freshman year in high school I made the varsity baseball team as a pitcher, and though I played infrequently that season, my life took a new course.

I've had an interest in sports from as far back as I can remember, and played several of them with enthusiasm and sometimes with moderate skill. I was a sandy-haired kid of average size and average physical abilities. I played on the baseball and basketball teams at Sullivan, the northernmost high school in Chicago, making the starting varsity teams in both my junior and senior years, in 1955–1956 and 1956–1957. I followed sports to a normal degree for an American kid, I guess—knew some of the statistics, went to games. In pre–high school days my friends and I generally sneaked into any of the games that required the purchase of tickets, such as those of the Cubs, White Sox, Bears, and football Cardinals (scaling outfield walls, sliding down the vendors' iced beer chutes, and suffering a wet seat of the pants in the

The 1956–1957 Sullivan (Tigers) High School basketball team, in the Chicago Public League, with the starting five in the front row: from left, Berkow, Ian Levin, Bernie Kirsner, Stu Menaker, and Rob Sanders. Coach Art Scher is at far left.

process)—and tried to get autographs, but that ended for me by the eighth grade out of lack of interest.

When I first began following baseball, in 1948 when I was eight, I took a special attachment to Eddie Waitkus, the Cubs' smooth-fielding first baseman. In my neighborhood, and playing with older boys, I was more or less relegated to first base. Pitcher, shortstop, center field—the glamour positions—were forbidden to the youngest kid in the games. I even tried to imitate Waitkus's pet move, a comic little hop as he stretched to catch a peg to him from across the infield. (Many years later, in a bar with Mark Grace, then the Cubs' excellent first baseman, I mentioned his forebear Waitkus, whom he had never heard of, and demonstrated, right there, that little hop. Grace smiled, though I'm not sure he was especially taken by it, for he returned with not much comment to his beer.)

Waitkus was six feet tall, lean, with sharp Slavic features, as I recall from those long-ago days after games when my friends and I would wait at the clubhouse steps for the ballplayers as they descended, like tanned deities. They emerged in their dapper sport jackets, smelling of after-shave lotion, their hair slicked back, their shoes shined to an impressive gloss, and giving the impression to us kids that they were bigger than life. One of those players was Eddie Waitkus. And among the push and shove of the young idolators was, most probably, a teenage girl named Ruth Ann Steinhagen.

Waitkus was traded in 1949 to the Philadelphia Phillies, a kind of heartbreak for me. It turned out that Ruth Ann Steinhagen had a huge crush on Waitkus, had built a shrine in her bedroom to him, but understood, in her tortured mind, that she could never have him, and didn't want anyone else to have him, either (this was all later revealed in a psychological report on her). When the Phillies came to play the Cubs in the spring of 1949, she went to the Edgewater Beach Hotel on the North Side, with a rifle, gained access to his room, and shot him in the chest. It was in all the headlines and featured in the newscasts the next day. Waitkus's life hung in the balance. He pulled through, however, and, miraculously, returned the next season to play first base for the National League–winning Phillies' "Whiz Kids" team.

But the bullet that tore through the chest of Eddie Waitkus ripped a hole through my idea—a nine-year-old boy's fantasy notion—that sports was not a part of the real world and that sports heroes were greater than mere mortals. The rifle shot that exploded in that hotel room that night in Chicago, ten miles from where I lived, remained with me for the rest of my life.

⌐ By the time I was eleven years old I was selling women's nylon stockings, three pair for a dollar, on Maxwell Street, the Old World marketplace in the shadow of the Loop, where both my parents were born. They and their families had moved west from the Maxwell Street area in the late 1920s, and my family and I now resided some four miles from Maxwell Street, at the corner of Springfield Avenue and Roosevelt Road. Maxwell Street was a place where impoverished immigrants had been coming for more than half a century to try to make something of themselves, rising up sometimes literally by their shoestrings (selling a few, and gradually expanding the business). Some, like Supreme Court Justice Arthur Goldberg and clarinetist and band leader Benny Goodman and Admiral Hyman Rickover and world boxing champion Barney Ross and CBS chairman William Paley grew up there, or near there, and made national names for themselves. Another, it happened, was one Jacob Rubenstein, a neighbor of my mother's, whose father and my grandfather were drinking buddies. Jacob Rubenstein later changed his name to Jack Ruby. ("Jack," recalled my mother, "never was too right in the head.")

I once asked my Uncle Jerry, my mother's brother, to tell me more about the relationship between my grandfather and Jack Ruby's father. He said that together they had a homemade still in the Rubenstein apartment and made what they called bathtub gin in the early years of the depression.

"He was a great storyteller," my Uncle Jerry said. "We would sit and listen to him for hours. Sometimes he'd say things that would have shocked our mothers. His favorite saying was, 'Six-and-seven-eighths measurement.'"

I asked, "Why would he say that?"

"He was a carpenter."

"Yes, but why would—"

"You figure it out. He would laugh and say, 'It's six and seven-eighths.'"

↶ A boyhood friend of mine named Red Popowcer—his first name was Robert, or Bob, but no one called him that—was five years older. He taught me how to play baseball and was like an older brother. When I was about five or six, he also instructed me in the birds and the bees. I said babies came by the stork, and he explained that only stork babies came by the stork. Not only was Red funny and smart, he eventually played second base on an

American Legion team and was the first person I ever knew personally to wear a uniform on a baseball team. This was impressive, to say the least. Red's father worked on Maxwell Street on Sundays selling stockings. He followed his father there. I admired Red and was interested in doing what he did. Red also played the trumpet—which I did, too, briefly in high school. Red entered a talent show that was played on radio on Sunday mornings, the Morris B. Sachs Amateur Hour. He came in second on his Sunday morning, losing, in write-in votes, to a three-year-old tap dancer, who was not seen, mortifyingly for Red, but only heard.

Red got me a job on Maxwell Street too, selling stockings for a man who owned about twenty-five women's and men's socks stands on the nearly mile-long street.

Maxwell Street was packed on Sundays—no cars were allowed—with vendors and buyers, blues musicians, characters like the self-styled King of the Hobos and the man who walked around with a dancing chicken on his head and sold one egg for a dime and two eggs for a quarter. Bejeweled, storefront gypsies were ready to tell your fortune—and the romance and wealth that awaited you—for an agreed-upon price, payment before prophecy.

The odor of onions sizzling on the grills of hot dog stands wafted through the air and seemed to envelop passersby.

If you had a stand, you had to hawk your goods, in my case the women's stockings. I had to shout to the passing multitudes to promote them. "Wear 'em once and throw 'em away," I'd holler, "and you still got a bargain." Some people were suspicious that the merchandise, in that sleight-of-hand environment, was not of the best quality. Sometimes they were right. So, standing in back of my stand that consisted of four card tables and a sign tied to one table leg with heavy string, I had to assure the passing throng. So another of my come-ons was: "There's only one hole in these socks, and that's where you put your foot in!"

And, as the saying went, you had to have eyes in the back of your head. For while tending to a customer at one end of my stand, I had to be aware of someone trying to slide a box of my

Maxwell Street, Chicago's famous outdoor bazaar, circa 1955. (Chicago Historical Society)

nylons into a shopping bag or inside a coat. It was the kind of awareness—and peripheral vision—that not only would be an asset as a writer (what else is going on in a room where I'm reporting that might not meet my direct eye?) but also in the middle of a three-on-one fast break in basketball.

On Maxwell Street I hustled—I went into my own business, selling belts on the street, when I was sixteen—until I went away to school before my junior year in college, to Miami University in Oxford, Ohio, in 1959 at age nineteen. Among many other things, I learned on Maxwell Street never to count your money in public. I took it literally when I was a boy—some fellow workers, older than I, had been robbed by being careless—but I came to understand it also as a metaphor for keeping things private that ought not to be made public.

At day's end one late summer, with the sun beginning to sink behind the buildings, one of the older boys, a chunky redhead about nineteen or twenty, who also sold socks, was pulling his wagon down the street, on it piled the cardboard boxes of unsold goods. He was heading back to the basement where we got paid by the manager, a dour man named Morrie Kroan, who wore his cap so low one only saw a part of his eyes. The redhead had had a good day, selling over a hundred dollars' worth of stockings. Before arriving at the basement, he was stopped by a three-card monte guy, a skinny black man with an easy smile who looked a little older than the redhead. The hustler reeled the redhead into trying his luck, placing the cards on one of the redhead's boxes. The redhead, with a thick roll of bills in his pocket, thought he'd give it a shot or two. It had been a good day for him, and he felt flush. At about this time I rolled up beside him with my wagon and goods. I stopped to watch. The monte guy shuffled the three cards and tossed them face down, two reds and an ace of spades. Which one was the spade? The redhead lost, and he siphoned off part of his wad. Another shuffle. The redhead lost again, and again. Won, lost again. The wad dwindled. He began to sweat. I looked on, terrified for him. He won another, took heart, and tried again. Lost. Lost. Lost. The wad was gone, into the pocket of the three-card monte guy, and the redhead was in tears. The impression, as the redhead slowly but inevitably succumbed to the scam artist, had been that of a snake swallowing a rat whole. My heart sank for the redhead. He started genially but gradually lost control, out of fear and obsession.

We were paid 15 percent of the men's socks we sold, 20 percent for women's stockings, so the redhead was forced to work some six straight Sundays for free to make up for the money he owed Morrie. An older man, who worked there as well, advised me, "The smartest people are able to learn from other people's mistakes. It's not easy, but it's possible." In this regard, gambling so spooked me—I was then about fourteen years old—that I have never been tempted to engage in it. The memory remained so

Who Wrote the Poem?

First baseman Ira Berkow at age twelve in 1952, at a practice in Loyola Park, on the far North Side of Chicago, for the "Indians," a baseball team in the Thillens Little League. Teammates Barry Stein (left) and Harvey Cole are nearby.

vivid to me, the fear of loss for the redhead that had made my skin crawl that afternoon, resonated so deeply that this was one of those incidents in which I indeed learned from someone else's calamitous mistake. It was one reason why I stayed away not only from gambling but also, in later years despite the fashion, from drugs. As harmless as the moment might seem—"Here, try it, once, it's a kick"—the hook, I considered, could not be far off.

In many ways, the West Side neighborhood where I grew up had a catch-as-catch-can environment. It was a streetwise section of the city, and while honesty was a significant matter in my household—my mother and father considered it an article of faith—it wasn't always so among our neighbors, including some of my friends. At ages ten and eleven, when the boys I played ball with were all older, some four and five years older, I went along with them to steal into ball games at Wrigley Field and Comiskey Park and Soldier Field and Chicago Stadium, as well as committing petty thefts, such as pilfering baseballs and baseball bats from a hardware store in the neighborhood that sold sporting goods. I was never comfortable with it, but I did not refrain from using my bike and my services as a rider for a getaway vehicle. I feared my parents would find out, but they never did. By the time I was twelve, however, I was able to withstand the peer pressure, and stopped stealing.

One theft, though, was indelible to me. It occurred in the summer of 1952. I was twelve years old. Hank Sauer, the great Cubs slugger of the time, was the first man to be named most valuable player while on a team that finished in the second division—his Cubs finished fifth of eight National League teams. That was, yes, 1952, when Sauer was co-leader in the major leagues with 37 homers and led the majors with 121 runs batted in. He had a fine, 15-year major league career with four teams but was so popular in Chicago, where he played seven seasons, that he was called the Mayor of Wrigley Field. He was a large man, 6-3, 200 pounds, with a long, rugged, lined face but not an unkindly one; in another life he might have been a longshoreman who stood up to management thugs.

Two boys from the West Side—one fourteen (named Jerry), the other twelve (me)—had sneaked into Wrigley Field from a vendors' entrance early that summer day and made their way into the dugout.

There were no ushers, since the gates had not yet opened. Sauer came in from shagging balls in left field, tossed his glove on the dugout bench, and, scarcely noticing the two kids sitting there in the cool, sunny morning, went for batting practice.

The twelve-year-old took the glove and tried it on, pounding the pocket, thrilled to be inside a major leaguer's mitt—and not just any big leaguer, but Hank Sauer. The twelve-year-old handed the glove to his friend Jerry to check out. Without hesitation Jerry took the glove and slipped it under his sweater: "Let's get out of here!" he said. He leaped up and ran up the steep ramp leading from the dugout to under the stands.

"You crazy?" shouted the younger boy. "That's Hank Sauer's glove! Come back!" The older was flying, and then so did the younger boy.

Jerry was running to an exit. "Let's stay for the game," I said, in most naive fashion.

"Not on your life," said Jerry. And so, as an unwitting accomplice, I raced out of the ballpark with him to the elevated station about a block away.

Jerry was not a bad kid—he grew up to be a solid citizen—but temptation had got the best of him. It was Jerry's idea to change trains several times on the way home. "In case we're being followed," he said.

As I read in a magazine after that season ended, the incident had bewildered Sauer and brought an unsettling sense of loss. That moment of the theft would stay with me for years to come. I hoped one day to meet Hank Sauer to confess my guilt. Several decades later, in the midst of an earthquake in Candlestick Park in San Francisco, I finally did.

∽ My father had been unemployed and without enough money to take a streetcar from the hospital when I was born to where he lived in the apartment of my mother's parents. By the time I was in my teens, he owned and operated three dry-cleaning stores and a small factory, called a plant. In 1953 he sold the business and entered politics. Through patronage, in Richard J. Daley's Democratic party, my father was able to get me a city job in the summer of 1956. I became a temporarily assigned laborer in the 50th Ward for the Department of Streets and Sanitation (in Chicago, "Streets and San"). That is, I was a garbage collector. Officially, one had to be eighteen years old or older to hold such a job. I was sixteen, but this was Chicago, and, at 6 feet, 175 pounds, I was believed to be able to handle the hoisting of garbage drums as well as withstand the redolent fumes of the refuse. I worked at the job for four summers. It was a great learning experience, down to understanding what to do if, when shoveling out one of the concrete garbage boxes that were still used in the alleys in those days, a rat ran up your pants leg. It happened one morning to Fiori Calessi,

My identification card in the first of four summers as a garbage collector for the City of Chicago, when I was sixteen.

one of the two other laborers I was working with. The third worker, a black man of stature, Donald Groves, had the quickness of perception to grab at Fiori's knee so the rat couldn't run farther up his pants leg, and then whacked the rat with the shovel in his other hand, killing it in one menacing stroke. Fiori limped from the blow for several days after but never complained, given the other option he might have faced.

I was amazed at Groves's presence of mind. I, in that terrifying moment, had simply stood there, shovel in hand, mouth agape. It would be easy to classify various kinds of intelligence. A writer's intelligence, for example, might be different from a garbage collector's. In fact, I learned, intelligence doesn't fit so neatly into pigeonholes. Groves was also a writer. He had written several detective novels, though none of them had been published. He gave two of them to me to read, and I liked them. By this time I was in college and reading books, so he surely had presumed that literature was up my alley. I felt sad for him. I didn't know what it took to be published, but I thought his books were as good as many on the market. Still do. I wondered if it had anything to do with being black, for at that time there were very few black writers I knew of, Ralph Ellison and Richard Wright being two I had read. I remember him saying that Fiori, a dark-haired but balding man, who always talked about get-rich-quick schemes and saved what seemed half the stuff we collected to sell, would make a good subject for a novel. Fiori suspected his wife of cheating on him—he'd found a matchbox in her purse from a bar that raised his suspicions—and was seeking to track down the leads. He hired me at no charge to visit the bar one night and see if I could catch her. I went to the bar, but no woman of her description was there. Fiori then fired me. I was not insulted. I heard later that he got divorced.

As for Groves, I remember him fondly and can still picture him, a handsome, nicely built man, his baseball cap resting rather jauntily on his head, his work shirt tucked into his jeans, his alley boots a little worn at the heels, and with a ready, sometimes wry smile that obviously attracted some of the maids on our daily routes. During the two-hour lunch breaks—after the morning haul, the truck would take that long to go to the dump and return—he would often disappear with one of them, coming back looking refreshed in more ways than one.

When I first began work with Streets and San, I was lucky to be assigned to Groves's truck. I had just finished my sophomore year in high school. In fact, I felt equally lucky to be on the truck with Fiori and the driver, a huge, red-haired Irishman named Mahoney who was so fat he seemed wedged into the cab. I'd watch awestruck as he managed to climb in and out of it. When we took breaks, one or another of the guys would buy sodas, or pop as we called it in Chicago. I thought this was great, guys buying you drinks. Then one day, not long after I joined this group, Groves took me aside. "Ira, I'm telling you this because I like you," he said. I listened. "You see how Mahoney buys drinks, then Fiori, then me?" "Yes." "You have to carry your weight. You buy when it's your turn."

I was embarrassed at not having realized this. After all, though I was a kid, I was earning the same money they were getting.

I didn't grow up altogether in that moment, but it was a boost. And I always remembered that one of the great things I learned, I learned from a garbage collector. Not only to carry my own weight, but the way he said it: "I'm telling you this because I like you." With that, I was putty in his hands.

When I went away to college, I would often return and make a visit to the alleys, especially to see Groves, and walk an alley or two with him. One day, after I had been away for several months, I returned and went to the ward office to see which alley Groves was in. None, I was told. "He had a stroke," said the ward official. "He's in the hospital. He's a vegetable." It was as though I had been hit with a blow to the stomach. I didn't think there was any point in visiting his hospital bed. Shortly after that I learned that Donald Groves, who, though suffering frustrations particularly as a black man, nonetheless maintained a lively step through the alleys, and, I imagine, the rest of his life, had died.

✓ In my high school and early college days I also sold religious pictures door-to-door—pictures with gold-plated frames of Jesus Christ that lit up. It was an unlikely part-time occupation for a Jewish kid, but it was a way to earn a few bucks. Among the intriguing people I met along the way was a woman named Elma who ran a brothel on Wabash Avenue on the South Side.

I first drove to Elma's as a customer. In a short time, unbeknownst to either of us, she would become a customer of mine. One night, when I was around fifteen, I traveled with several friends in a car to Bronzeville, as it was known. The purpose of the trip was not an uncommon one for boys my age. Most girls we dated just didn't go "all the way." Second base, maybe, or even third base. But, in my experience, never home plate. When "The Pill" appeared, after I was an adult, I understand things changed for teenagers. But before that, guys with curiosity and sex urges and the desire to be big boys piled into cars all over the country and went laughing, maybe to cover up their tenseness, to cathouses.

On this trip, my first of such excursions, one of the guys had broken his leg a month earlier and was in a cast and on crutches. He lay across the laps of four other guys in the bustling back seat, all of us, including me, complaining about the crowding.

We pulled up to a house on a dark street. We all got out, went up the few stone steps of the two-story brick apartment building, and one of the others rang the bell. We waited at the edge of a pool of light created by the bulb above the door. Shortly the door opened a crack, and a pair of almond brown eyes peered out. The guy at the door had been there before and was recognized. The door was shut, the chain rattled, and the door swung open. The person who opened it, I soon learned, was Elma, a tawny-skinned, pretty black woman with a sprinkling of freckles on her cheeks and nose. She had high cheek bones, a slight gap between her front teeth, and a long pony tail, and wore a tight, low-cut green dress that looked as though she had been scooped into it. I could picture her in a cigarette ad, or on one of the liquor billboards that dotted the area.

Behind her shone the maroon tint of the foyer, with a staircase to the left and a small balcony above and behind her.

"Good evenin', gentlemen," she said. I later heard that her boy friend was a prominent black heavyweight boxing contender from Chicago named Bob Satterfield, but I never found out whether it was true. Perhaps she started the rumor simply to keep decorum in the house.

We were shown into a room off the main entrance that contained a red couch and two end tables, a couple of easy chairs, and a phonograph. Some of us just stood around. It was kind of dark, with a pair of dimly lit lamps with fringed shades. The smell in there was unfamiliar to me. I found out later it was incense.

We waited our turn, as in a doctor's office, until one or another was taken away by one of the girls. Meanwhile the rest of us listened with a sense of nervous anticipation while the records of Nat King Cole, Miles Davis, Billie Holiday, and others played. Some guys in the room smoked, and the smoke hung around the lamps in rings, like the planet Saturn.

Elma stuck her head in the room and nodded to me. "Follow me, sweetheart," she said. I did, my legs feeling slightly wobbly, my head spinning.

The window shades in her room were pulled down, and there was a bureau with two folded checked towels on it. In the corner were two wash basins, one for soapy water and one for clear water—she had, she told me, filled them up in the bathroom across the hall. I remember the simple bed and the crucifix on the wall above it. I looked at the cross as I undressed, and crawled into bed beside her. Nothing happened. At least, at my end. But there is no accounting for expertise. If Elma had decided to become a magician, instead of a lady of pleasure, she would have been Houdini. Before I knew it, I was a man.

She may not have had the clichéd heart of gold of her age-old profession, but Elma had a heart and was generous with instruction to an eager young man.

I also learned by bits and pieces of conversation that she had come by thorny trial and error to view the world in a way I had yet to appreciate, with a subtle questioning, perhaps, but with the reality of men and the world she discovered behind her closed doors. While she was in fact an innocent bystander, I nonetheless received an unforgettable lesson in just such skepticism.

With my friends, I patronized Elma and some of her other women several times after that. To my surprise, Elma—whom, looking back, I imagine to have been in her early thirties—and some of her women were quite religious. And when I began selling religious pictures, I sold one to Elma. Not exactly sold it, but bartered it for her services. I had a partner, a high school friend whom I shall call Leon. Leon and I split everything we sold.

At Elma's, a "trick," as the women termed it, went for five dollars. The pictures we sold retailed for thirty dollars. Leon and I made a deal with Elma for six trysts, to be shared evenly between us.

One day I visited Elma. She ushered me into her room, sat down on the bed, and, as usual, began to untie my shoe.

"This'll be five dollars, hon," she said.

"Five dollars?" I said. "No, Elma, you're mistaken. I've only been here twice for this religious picture." I nodded toward the image on the wall. "I've only been here twice for it. I've got one more coming."

"Uh-uh," she said. "Look."

She brought out her red accounts book.

It read, "Ira 2, Leon 4."

"Tha's six," she said. "Tha's all."

"What's Leon doing with four?" I asked.

"Came here last week, told me you said it was okay, that you two had made a new arrangement."

"I didn't make any new arrangement," I said. "I don't know what he's talking about."

"Between you and him," she said.

"Elma!"

"Sorry, baby, but business is business."

I couldn't believe it! Betrayed by one of my best friends! I went looking for him—we had driven there together—looking to kill the son of a bitch. He was in the smoke-hazy sitting room with a couple of other clients, talking casually.

"Leon!" I said with quiet vehemence since I didn't want to disturb the activities in my nearby surroundings—Elma, after all, was a stickler for decorum.

Leon turned around, eyes widening behind his dark-rimmed glasses.

"Did you get an extra from Elma?"

"Well," he said.

"'Well' what," I said.

"I got horny," he said, with a shrug. "I couldn't help it."

"Why didn't you tell me? What's wrong with you? How horny could you have gotten?"

"Pretty horny," he said.

I forgave, but it was hard to forget. And I thank Leon for making me aware as I never was before that you can be trusting, but to keep your guard up, and eyes open, is not a foolish undertaking.

When selling the pictures to customers other than these particular working women, we had to verify check stubs from their job. If we sold a picture, and the people were no longer employed there—that is, no wage assignment could be placed against them—the money for that loss would have to come out of the salesman's pocket. So one had to be careful, and attuned to fabrication. What did their voice say beyond the words? What did their eyes truly tell you? You wanted to make the sale, but was it a sale? As one got burned, one got wiser. It was an invaluable lesson for my future profession. "The most essential gift for a good writer," said Ernest Hemingway, "is a built-in, shock-proof, shit detector. This is the writer's radar and all great writers have had it." All writers, good and great, at least *try*, or hope, to have it.

2

~~~~~~~~~~~~~

Look to the Curtain

MY FATHER, an unassuming man with a clear-eyed view of the world through his thick eyeglasses, had been an orphan during the depression. His mother died when he was twelve, and his father when he was seventeen. He said he remembered as a boy going with his parents on weekends to Romanian restaurants where there was dancing and singing, and he would sing and have pennies tossed at him in appreciation. He loved to sing, and even as a child had a good voice, everyone said. Everyone, that is, except one jealous kid. As my father recalled, the kid would mock my father, saying "Edel mitten Feedele." It was a popular Yiddish song of the time—"Yidel mit den Fiedel" (Jew with Violin). It happened that my father's Jewish name was Edel. Though the boy's words stung, my father just picked up the pennies and put them in his knickered pockets. One of those restaurants was owned by my father's uncle, Baruch, who liked a good time—Romanians have that reputation. Baruch was so expansive with his friends and family that he served numerous meals and drinks on the house.

He went bankrupt, and his wife divorced him—the perils of wine and song, if not also of spouses.

My father's father spoke no English, though he tried, in the common pattern among immigrants here, to Americanize himself by having people call him "Joe" (on my father's birth certificate, the father is named "Joseph") when his given name was Israel Hersh. My father, despite being able to speak Yiddish, his father's language, told me ruefully that he never sat down and had "a real conversation" with his father, as my father would seek at times to do with me. His father was either busy with work or preoccupied about how to pay the bills, or mourning his wife and the children, some of whom were married now, going their separate ways. Joe Berkovitz was said to be a skilled cabinetmaker but then found work difficult to find during the depression, going with empty pockets as did millions of other Americans. After my grandmother died, the family dispersed. My dad lived with his father, living, said my father with a gentle wryness, on every street on the West Side—"You name it, from Halsted to Kildare," he said, a distance of more than four miles. They moved every time the rent, either for an apartment or as boarders, came due. My father remembered being at friends' homes around dinnertime, and smelling the food, and being asked if he'd like to stay for dinner and, with pride because he didn't want anyone feeling sorry for the orphan, saying no thank you. And leaving hungry.

My father had dropped out of high school after his first semester, at fourteen, unable to afford new spectacles when his had broken, and he took a job. He lived at various times with one or the other of his eight siblings, four of whom were born in their native Romania, in a town called Focsani (the family name there was Bercovici, pronounced Berkoveetch, but was changed at Ellis Island by a customs official who wrote it out phonetically, given my grandfather's accent). My father was the baby of the family, and was, after his parents died, given an allowance of three dollars a week for food by one of his older brothers, Max. My father told me once that he spent fifty cents a day for meals.

I said, "But Dad, that's only six days." He smiled. "Never on Sunday," he said.

In his teens, he and two other friends hopped railroad cars and made their way across the country to California. One of my father's sisters had moved there. The boys had no money and no direction but thought California sounded good. It was dangerous stuff—some men and boys were crushed between trains, or beaten by authorities—but it wasn't an uncommon thing to do for youths adrift in those days. My dad and his friends would stop off and knock on doors in strange towns seeking food, sleep with hoboes, then hop another freight. I once spoke with one of those two traveling companions, a man nicknamed "Beer," for beer barrel, which is how he was shaped. "We all went our separate ways to hustle up food, and then we were supposed to meet back at a spot and share the food equally," he said. He said the other guy, on the sneak, would eat some of what he got on the way back. "Your dad never did," said Beer. "You could always trust Harold."

Some time after that he joined the Civilian Conservation Corps, a federally financed organization sponsored by President Roosevelt that created jobs for young unemployed men to take them off the nation's streets. My father was assigned to a unit in 1934 that was building roads through the Colorado Rockies. Hammering away at rocks, he built himself up to such a degree that when he returned home for a visit, his sister Rose's husband, Leo Wolff, a burly detective, said to the tanned nineteen-year-old, "You look so good, Harold, you'd better get back there."

My father was one of the few Jews, if not the lone one, in the CCC camp. He recalled to me one of the few fistfights he ever had. It was with someone in the camp who insulted him with "Dirty Jew." My father recalled that the other guys formed a ring, and my dad took off his glasses and shirt, and he and his antagonist went at it. I'm not sure how it ended, but my dad said the guy never again uttered such an oath to him. It was my father's advice when I was bullied in grade school, that if the guy hit you, you just had to hit him back, even if he was bigger and stronger. Punch him in the nose and he won't forget it. A bloodied nose can change a person's attitude. I tried it—it wasn't easy when confronted with a tough guy.

"Give me a nickel," the kid said one time.

"I don't have any," I said.

"All the money I find I keep," he said, and he went into my pocket. I hit him in the nose. He hit me in the nose. It bled. I didn't like it at all. What was my father talking about? Unfortunately this had to be repeated. But then the guy did lay off. Lesson learned, painfully.

My father was as honest a man as I have ever known. But he was arrested once, when he was in his teens. He had taken a job sweeping up cigar butts and other odd jobs in a bookmaking parlor on the West Side. One day his boss came to him and said, "Harold, you're going to have to take a pinch."

"Take a pinch?" he said, understanding that it meant he was going to be arrested, but he didn't know why. The cops, he was told, needed to make a certain number of arrests to report to city officials.

"You don't give your right name," his boss told him, "and after you get out of the paddy wagon and go up to the police station, they'll release you." That's exactly what happened, and this kind of knowledge of the way of the world, Chicago-style, anyway, would later be imparted to me. (When parking your car with an attendant, for example, leave only the ignition key because a copy of your house key can be made by imprinting it on a bar of soap.)

When we lived on the first floor of an apartment building on the North Side of Chicago, my parents were having several friends over one night to play cards. It was winter and the women wore furs, which my parents placed on the bed in their bedroom. At one point the lights went out in the apartment. My father shouted, "All the men, into the bedroom!" That included me, I presumed. The tone was ominous. And swiftly, but, as I recall, with a certain amount of yellow down the spine, I ran with the other men into the bedroom.

My father had imagined the distinct possibility that some thieves had worked together to blow the fuses and crawl through the bedroom window to snatch the fur coats. As it turned out, it was merely a blown fuse. But from his street experience, my father knew that such ploys were plausible.

Despite his hard beginnings, my father rose. Shortly after I was born, he got a job delivering for a dry-cleaning store, and then sought to open a store of his own. He went to his brother, Eddie, some seven years older. My Uncle Eddie had thick black eyebrows, had been an amateur boxer, and carried a toothbrush and toothpaste in his jacket pocket at all times. He also had a good job as a doorman at the swanky Morrison Hotel in the Loop. Only a few years earlier, when my father was a kid in the streets, Eddie had asked him: "You're not a second-story man, are you?" The implication that my father might earn his bread by stealth and burglary was insulting to him, but, respecting Eddie, he demurred. "No," he said, "I'm not." My father now asked Eddie to sign for a bank loan for him for $300, which is what he needed to open the store.

"I don't sign for anybody," said Eddie. My father's heart sank. "But I will give you the money. It's not a loan. It's a gift. You're my brother, and I'll do what I can to help you get on your feet." Eddie understood that money loaned could simply be money never regained–from my father or anyone else–so better not to *lend* it, thus causing bad feelings if never returned.

My father opened the store, had a rocky beginning, but then the business got its legs. A few months later he returned the $300 to Eddie–plus, gratefully, though it was never even hinted at, the 3 percent he would have had to pay a bank for the loan.

My father went on to own three dry-cleaning stores and a plant with several pressing machines. When I graduated grammar school, I asked him to sign my autograph book. He wrote, "To my son, Whoever said that opportunity knocks just once was either lazy or stupid. Good luck, Dad."

That's how he truly saw the world: there are many doors that may bear knocking. But he had broader interests than the dry-cleaning stores. Feeling a sense of need due to a lack of formal education, he wanted to give himself some "polish," which he believed would be advantageous. He signed up for a Dale Carnegie "How to Win Friends and Influence People" course. He learned how to improve his memory, how to speak in public with eloquence, and he did so well in the classes that he was asked to be an instructor. "They didn't pay much, and I could hardly give up my business to do it," he said.

But in 1953, when I was thirteen and he was thirty-six, he sold his cleaning business. "I was tired of people complaining about missing buttons," he said. He now tried the steel business as a salesman. He had learned that steel was a thriving industry, but what he didn't contemplate was that it was a failing industry. "I was tired from the cleaning business—sometimes I'd come home and was so fatigued I couldn't keep my head up. The steel business seemed a good alternative, but I didn't think it out. I was foolish." When the bottom dropped out of that industry, he went into politics, understanding that there could well be security in aligning himself with people with the right connections. And it happened. He eventually became director of health and safety for Cook County employees. Later he became the major adviser to Jerome Huppert, one of the five county commissioners, considered the most powerful positions in local politics outside of the mayor's office.

By his emergence into the Democratic political machine, he was able, through patronage, to get my mother a job as a bailiff in city hall, to get me that summer job on the garbage truck, and to get my brother summer jobs working in the Chicago Park District, spearing loose paper on the grass and sawing off the dead limbs of trees.

In compensation for these jobs, my father worked as an unpaid precinct captain for the first Mayor Richard Daley and helped get out the vote as part of the Democratic party's vaunted machine apparatus. He would go door to door, extolling the virtues of his candidates, and being open to help with any needs of the voter. My father's assigned precinct was two square blocks.

He was like the godfather of the area, assisting with various family problems, receiving phone calls and requests for numerous favors, such as being able to get one's electricity switched on on a Saturday when Commonwealth Edison was supposed to be closed, or getting a bus stop in front of a constituent's house moved farther down the block.

One of the most memorable moments of my father's street smarts, as I recall, occurred in a basement polling place in the 50th Ward on the North Side, where my father was a precinct captain.

I was sitting and talking with him one election day in the basement polling place when a man, whom he had visited several days earlier, came in to cast his ballot. The man greeted my father cordially, waited his turn, and then entered the voting booth and pulled the curtain. My dad and I continued talking. When the curtain opened and the man emerged, he smiled at my father.

"I took care of you, Harold," the man said.

"You sure did," my father said.

Then my dad motioned to take him aside. I was in earshot.

"It's a free country," my father said, "and you can vote for anyone you want. But you asked me for a favor and I did it, and you had offered—you had told me—you were going to vote the straight Democratic ticket."

"And I did," the man said.

"You didn't," my father said evenly. "You know you didn't, and I know you didn't."

"Harold, next time, I promise," the man said, abashed.

When my father returned to the seat opposite me, I said, "Dad, how did you know how he voted? You were talking to me and not watching him." I also knew that there were no hidden cameras and no one perched over the voting booth giving signals to my father.

"I saw how he voted out of the corner of my eye," my father said.

"Oh?"

"You see the curtain? It drops only to the ankles. If you vote the straight ticket, you stand in one place and pull the lever. If you split your ticket, you have to step over to the right. He stepped over to the right."

It was such observation of nuance that I would seek in daily life, and make an even greater effort to achieve when I became a writer, or began to aspire to being a writer. In the small details, often overlooked by many, a person or setting in a story comes alive.

(Early in my writing career, I was impressed by Red Smith's description of a racehorse owner: "Now he stood behind an expensive cigar in the morning sunshine outside barn 19 at Churchill Downs, hands jammed into the pockets of a hound's-tooth jacket, and talked about his first Derby horse. . . ." Shortly after that, I ran across the following description of an entirely different kind of person and situation, by Sholom Aleichem, in his book *Inside Kasrilevke*: "After him a basket of apples staggered in, and hard behind it a Jewess wrapped in three shawls, all of them in shreds." The exaggerated but felicitous bigness of the cigar and the basket of apples each draw a complete word picture, in a virtual brushstroke, of the grandiose owner and the impoverished Jewess.)

⌒ My mother's mother, Molly Halperin, owned a chicken store on Maxwell Street in the early part of the century. My mother and her three brothers helped in the store, one of the brothers, Jerry, recalled where, in the crowded ghetto, he would go for privacy when he needed a trysting place. He'd sneak into his mother's chicken store at night and hop onto a chicken crate. The downside was that the beaks of chickens pecked through the slats at the buttocks of his beloved. Another of her brothers, Julius, got into trouble with the police. At age sixteen, he was arrested after having robbed a man at gunpoint at a most unlikely place, within four doors of the Maxwell Street police station. That item made the

Chicago Tribune in 1924: "ROBS IN SHADOW OF 'HOOSEGOW'; CAUGHT ON ROOF / Boy Bandit Dodges Cops For Four Blocks." As an adult, my Uncle Julius was pictured being herded with a handful of others into a paddy wagon, after a raid on Al Capone's headquarters. Julius, good in math, was one of those who looked after Scarface Al's financial books. When I knew him, he was a mellow, even gentle middle-aged bachelor who smoked heavily, suffered from epilepsy, and earned a living by playing cards in the several backroom gambling establishments on Roosevelt Road. He lived about a block away from us, and my mother cooked most of his meals for him. He never talked about his past. But when he grew angry about something, such as when I might argue with my mother, there was a look in his eyes that said I'd better knock it off. And I did.

When I wrote my book on Maxwell Street, my mother, who had dropped out of high school after her freshman year to work in the chicken store, urged me to tell the truth and spare nothing. "Write about my brothers," she said, "write about my father being a *shicker*"—the Yiddish word for alcoholic—"and don't forget, Ira, write about the bedbugs where we lived on Maxwell Street. And how we'd flush the bugs out of the coils with a candle, and then kill them with a hammer."

"But Ma," I said, "won't bringing up stuff like that embarrass you?"

"If it's the truth," she said, "you live with it. Doesn't matter what people think." Her tenacity to face the truth, regardless of circumstances, made an impression on me from as far back as I can remember.

My mother was invariably forthright and had few of the nuances that my father possessed. She could also be funny, whether she meant to be or not. Once, I showed her a small stain on my tan pants. I asked her if she had a spot remover. She said yes. Then she sprayed the small stain with an aerosol can. Soon there was a big stain. I looked at it. She looked at it. It wasn't going away.

"Ma," I said, looking up at her, "do you ever wonder about yourself?"

"Yes," she said, "I'm wonder woman."

My mother was a brunette with a slim figure when she was young. My cousin, Errol Halperin, discovered in an attic a home movie, incredibly, of the wedding of his parents, Jerry and Lil, in a kosher banquet hall in the summer of 1938. It was a grainy film, black and white, but remarkably well preserved. One of the bride's attendants is my mother, come to life when she was twenty-one–svelte and looking as lovely as the bouquet of flowers she was carrying. "It's like finding a dinosaur egg," my brother Steve remarked, upon seeing the film. Later in the film, which lasts about fifteen minutes, I see my mother and father sharing a joke with a few others. My dad was wearing a nice suit. I wondered where he got it–perhaps borrowed it from one of his brothers, since he had very little money. But, to my eyes, he looked rather dashing. My father and I almost never shared a dirty joke or even a double entendre. But one day, for some reason, he told me a story of when he was driving down a street near our home and saw a woman walking on the sidewalk with her back to him.

"When I looked at her," my father said, "I said to myself, 'She's got a great ass.' When I got closer, I said, 'My God, that's my wife!'"

My parents met at a party during the summer of 1936 that my mother was invited to but my father wasn't. He and a few of his friends crashed the affair. There my father saw a pretty girl named Shirley, who, he remembered, wore a big red belt. She was twenty and he was twenty-one (soon to be twenty-two). She thought he was nice, but not that nice. He called her (her family didn't have a phone, and all of their calls were taken by a neighbor, who called out, "Shirley! For you!"). She brushed him off. She went on a trip to Benton Harbor, Michigan, with a few friends, and guess who she saw come walking down the street toward her? The guy with the glasses who wasn't invited to the party. Soon she wasn't resisting his persistence, or his charms.

He sang to her–among other places, in the vestibule of the apartment building where he was then living with his sister Rose. He liked the acoustics there. One day, one of my aunt's neighbors, a Mrs. Granat, told Rose, "I think your brother's in love. I hear him singing to a girl in the hallway."

He was invited to eat at the Halperins' home. There was always a lot of chicken there, from my grandmother's chicken store. My father, though at 5-foot-8 he never weighed more than 150 pounds, consumed a lot of it. My mother felt sorry for him because he was so poor. Not my grandfather, Max, born and raised in Grodno, Russia. "He's a Romanische *chosser*," he said, meaning in Yiddish, a Romanian pig. But my grandfather, a short man, had his problems. An alleged biblical scholar in the old country, he found adjusting to the New World a trial. He got a job as a broom maker but thought it beneath him and often went to the Russian tavern to drink with friends instead of going to work. My mother, coming home at night with a date, remembered stumbling over his prostrate body at the door of their apartment in the darkened hallway, having collapsed as he tried to turn the key.

The mortification stayed with my mother the rest of her life, and she was unable even to smell liquor without feeling sick to her stomach, let alone drink any of it.

Since my grandfather worked only sporadically, my grandmother, a stout woman who wore her hair in a bun and went about her business with a quiet, intelligent demeanor, kept up the family finances with her store. Max wanted no part of it. He had his attitudes, to be sure. And when one of his sons, as well as his daughter, got married, he said he wasn't going but needed a pack of cigarettes as a bribe to show up. In the black-and-white film that Errol found of his parents' wedding, my grandfather is seen clearly–short, wearing the traditional fedora common to Jewish weddings in America, and pointing to people where they should stand in the procession. The broom maker, for a moment anyway, had become the general.

My parents in Chicago in 1947, when my father, Harold, was thirty-three and my mother, Shirley, thirty-one.

When my father opened his cleaning store, he recalled one of her brothers saying that my father "will never make it." "I laughed," my father recalled. "I said, 'I hope I'll make it.'" When he began to succeed, he bought new furniture for their apartment. He said he was never as proud as when his mother-in-law told him how happy she was that he was making a living for her daughter. In business and personal relations, my mother was as able as her own mother, and was a great help to my father when called upon to work behind the counter, when the regular help didn't show up.

My father had particular problems with pressers, who seemed to drink well into the night and then forget they had work to do the next morning. But one of them, a man named Collins, came to work in sport jacket and tie and brightly shined pointy shoes—"He always looked sharp," my father recalled. "People thought he was the boss. It shamed me into dressing better." Collins would change into strapped T-shirt, shoes with the toes cut out to reveal his white-stockinged feet, and a nylon stocking wrapped around his head—all of which, as a boy of eight or nine, I found exotic. Collins was a black man who also charmed me with his songs and tales of his growing up poor in Alabama as he pressed clothes in the back of my dad's store, the steam hissing and rising from the machine and engulfing the two of us in a make-believe cloud. Once, when my father took ill and was confined to his bed, Collins came to visit. More than visit. He knelt at his bedside and prayed so fervently that I think my father, with an astonished look on his face, was frightened into recuperating more quickly than he might have otherwise.

⌐ I had one sibling, my brother Steve, five years younger than I. Five years apart is a big difference when you're young, and by the time I left home for the army and then to college, he was just coming into his teens. When my parents would insist that I take my brother with me to a baseball game—or, even once, to a party with my friends—I balked.

Steve was an ornery kid, but, in his Dennis the Menace mode, lovable. When he was five years old and going to visit a friend, the friend's father opened the screen door and hit my brother in the face with it. "You dirty rat," my brother said, as the father helped pick him up, apologizing profusely. It became a family legend, and in later years even my brother smiled about it. He wore glasses from the time he was three, suffering eye problems after a bout with measles. I don't know if that affected his personality—I think kids made fun of "four eyes"—but I know it affected his participation in sports. He played some sandlot games, but he was unable, because of his affliction, to throw himself into the games with the intensity I did. And this despite my attempts to instruct him on how to pitch, complete with windup and follow-through. He bridled at most things I told him since he considered it bossiness on my part. And I did irritate and tease him. It is the unconditional responsibility of an older sibling to bother the younger one, and I did not shirk my duties.

But some things one just can't change. So it wasn't until our adulthood that we grew closer. He became a schoolteacher at the Yates Elementary School in the Humboldt Park area on Chicago's Northwest Side, one of the roughest neighborhoods in the city. On a visit there once, Steve showed me bullet holes in one of the doors. Gangs continually shot at each other, even at the kids in school who were from the wrong side of the alleged gang boundary. But Steve cared about the kids and worked with them, and was in contact with their parents. And we encouraged each other in our pursuits and confided our fears and failures to each other.

Then he took ill, diagnosed with chronic leukemia. He was wasting away. I sat with him in the hospital, where I had to wear a mask so that I didn't spread germs. My mother and father sat facing his bed, wearing masks, the look of dread and helplessness in their eyes.

When my brother died on May 21, 1996, at age fifty-one, he left his wife Judy and seventeen-year-old daughter Shayne, two weeks short of her graduation from high school with honors. My brother had talked enthusiastically about being there, sharing that proud moment with all of us. I was a poor stand-in for him at the ceremony.

I had told Bob Greene, a friend and a popular columnist for the *Chicago Tribune*, about my brother, whom he had never met. That fall, at the beginning of the school year, he wrote a touching and insightful column about him. It began:

"When people of great fame die, statues are built and front-page tributes are written. Television broadcasts are interrupted so that the news can be reported; politicians issue statements praising the person's life.

"But that is not the only way to measure the significance of a person's time on Earth. Few people do work that is more important—and few people receive less recognition—than a good, dedicated schoolteacher. All those celebrated men and women who are written about on the front pages when they die? You can bet that one thing they had in common was that, somewhere along the line, each was lucky enough to be in the classroom of at least one schoolteacher who recognized their potential talents, and helped them start those talents in the right direction.

"Steven Berkow was such a schoolteacher."

Some of the students Greene spoke to praised my brother as "a friend" and said they'd "miss his jokes and stories" that "made everybody laugh and feel good, especially when they were sad."

An eighth-grader named Raquel said, "Losing Mr. Berkow is like losing a part of my heart." I know exactly how she felt.

3

~~~~~~~~~~~~~~~

Thunderstruck

I WAS STARTING my senior year at Sullivan High School and taking an art class. As usual in those times and in that venue the classroom was routine chaos. I was considered a culprit—the instructor might not have been completely mistaken—and the authorities thought that it would be best for all concerned if I did not continue among the easels, paints, and brushes. So I was kicked out of the class.

Needing a minor credit to graduate, I was transferred into another class to get it. The class was also considered a kind of punishment for me. It was Introduction to Typing, and the punishment was that the class consisted mostly of girls. But wearing my letter sweater in a sea of girls filled out in other sweaters, turned out, after a brief adjustment, to be anything but a punishment. Although I received my customary F's in the class— F for fair, or next to failing—I did learn to type with ten fingers (as opposed to the hunt-and-peck style that many journalists employ to this day). And, buttressed by the typing class, I graduated on time.

I don't believe in predestination—I don't think I do, anyway. It's too much like superstition, which my mother adhered to: if you put your clothes on backward by accident, it's good luck; be sure to twist a button when a funeral procession passes; when talking about possible good fortune, spit three times to avoid the evil eye. But some things do work out for the best in the oddest ways. Such as my learning to type, which would be crucial for my life's work.

Something else happened that senior year that would change my life. Suddenly, in my last semester of high school, I discovered the beauty and enchantment of words. I was, to be sure, a reluctant bystander to the revelation. It happened after I had torn ligaments in my ankle and was unable to play the latter part of the basketball season. I was home on crutches. My father had urged me to read during my high school years, but I resisted his entreaties. When he saw me sitting home with nothing to do, apparently he saw his chance. He gave me a book, *30 Days to a More Powerful Vocabulary*. I naturally put it aside. But a few days later—I'm not sure why—I picked it up and began at the beginning.

It changed my life. I fell in love with words—"loquacious," "ubiquitous," "obsequious"—their etymologies, their use in sentences. When I returned to school I had the best vocabulary around, which isn't necessarily saying much among high school students. But there it was. I was one grade short of making the honor roll, of all things, in my final semester, which saved me from finishing just about last in my graduation class. One of my friends, Barry Holt, who played on the basketball team with me, made the National Honor Society. Barry lived near me, and I can't ever remember him taking home any books, as I hadn't. But Barry's grades were so good that I accused him of paying attention in class. It also helped that Barry, who became an attorney, had a virtually photographic memory.

After high school, in the summer of 1957, I had a couple of partial scholarship possibilities for basketball. One was from Upper Iowa University (where several of my friends had gone), another was from Albion College, in Michigan. But I decided that the schools, out of town, were not enticing, so I stayed in Chicago. And the scholarships weren't financially workable, since money was also a consideration. At the time my father was trying the steel business, which was taking a nosedive, and he was having a tough time making ends meet, having to support a wife and two kids. I saw him poring over books with steel statistics. He never looked gloomier. And I was still helping to pay the rent. It happened this way:

While selling stockings on Maxwell Street, my father observed across the way from where I worked a belt stand doing a bustling business. Secondhand belts of all kinds—thick black work belts, skinny pink jazz-joint belts, funny buckled belts—were piled high on card tables. Customers buzzed about as the owner, a man named Klein who wore a cap and stood not much taller than the card tables, along with his two assistants doled out the merchandise. Greenbacks flew from hand to Klein's bulging pants pockets. You couldn't help being impressed by such prosperous commerce.

Contemplating this, my father had the idea that I could open my own belt stand at another spot on the street—quitting my stockings job, of course. Which is what transpired. I was rather reluctant to make this switch, given that I had worked my way up to a good spot on the street and was making as much as thirty dollars on a Sunday, but my father was convincing. "You'll do a lot better than what you're making now," he said. My father found an outlet store that sold those secondhand belts, we managed to get a lively spot on the corner of Maxwell and Jefferson Streets, nearly two blocks from Klein's stand, so there would be no real competition in this dense-as-Calcutta marketplace. We paid the market master—the man in charge of the street stands, a city employee—twenty-five dollars under the table, which is the way it worked there, and got a ticket that said we had paid two dollars for the license. The saying on Maxwell Street was, One hand washes the other. Grease a palm and everyone profits. And by virtue of this theory we enjoyed a good location for our new enterprise. The then mayor of Chicago, Richard J. Daley, father of the future Chicago mayor, Richard M., would become widely known as "The Boss" and for his saying that Chicago was "the city that works." And this was one way it worked.

The market masters were famous for corruption. It was legend that one Louis Krakow in the 1920s was deposed by city hall for "violations" unbecoming a city employee. In other words, he was caught red-handed, and the higher-ups had no choice but to can him. The Krakows had run Maxwell Street for several years before this, and they operated a fish stand on the corner of Maxwell and Halsted, in the center of the marketplace. When the new market masters tried to shorten the length of the Krakow's nineteen-foot stand to the required nine feet, a fight ensued, with not just fists but the five Krakow women heaving buckets of fish at the new market master. The police had to be called to restore order.

(The hulking, curious heavyweight contender Kingfish Levinsky–born Harris Krakow and nicknamed for the fish sold by his family–had worked as a herringmonger there. Kingfish fought Joe Louis in August 1935 in Comiskey Park and was knocked out in the first round, complaining afterward that the reason for his quick exit was sore feet. In fact, out of nervousness he had put his left boxing shoe on the right foot and the right shoe on the left foot. I interviewed him many years later. He was selling neckties out of a box around Miami Beach, and was quite persuasive. He wrapped a tie around your throat and pulled tight until you bought it. A breath or two from being strangled, I bought two.)

The first day of my belt business was a huge success. Busy all day long. My father worked alongside me. We closed up shop, put the merchandise in my father's Chevy, and drove home. We sat at the dining-room table as my father counted out the money, mostly in singles. After expenses, we had cleared close to a hundred dollars. I had to admit, this was certainly better for me than the thirty or thirty-five, on a good day, I could expect peddling my hosiery.

Then he peeled off a bunch of bills and gave them to me. It came to ten dollars. I stared at it.

"What's this?" I said.

"For you," he said.

"That's it?" I said incredulously. "But this is my business."

"The rest helps the family," he said.

"Oh," I said, embarrassed. In my greed, I hadn't considered that, hadn't considered the reason behind my father wanting me to go into "my own business."

It took a while, actually, before I came to complete terms with it. I was a hardheaded sixteen-year-old. It wasn't long before my father stopped going down to Maxwell Street with me. On occasion I would employ my brother, who resented taking orders from me, and a variety of friends, as well as my cousin Ian, who was with me one Sunday in early September 1956 when I ran out of gas on the way home after work. Ian accused me of being inconsiderate and careless about the gas gauge when he was eager to get back and watch Elvis Presley's debut on the Ed Sullivan Show. It wasn't true. I liked Elvis as much as he did. "Don't Be Cruel," in fact, was one of my favorite songs, and made me melancholy thinking about a dark-haired girl in high school I was dating, so to speak, and who gave me less than the time of day.

✍ I entered the University of Illinois in Chicago (it was then housed at the Navy Pier, a long, narrow building that extended like a sore thumb into Lake Michigan), nervous about college. For one thing, guys I knew from high school who were now in college had told me that you were required to take notes in class.

"Take notes?" I said. I had never taken notes in a class before. It seemed daunting. "How can you listen to the teacher and write down what he's saying at the same time?" But I would learn. And I would continue to take notes, well beyond the classroom, for the rest of my life, as my professional life would dictate.

I didn't know if I could really learn to study, to sit and underline passages. Ian, a semester ahead of me in school, enrolled at the University of Illinois in Champaign-Urbana and invited me down for a visit one weekend in his first semester there, while I was in my last semester at Sullivan. I thought it would be a lark, going to bars, as I heard college kids did there, and looking for girls. Neither Ian nor I had ever had more than a beer or two, but we were certainly interested in girls. On Friday night in Champaign we went to, of all places, the library. Just for a few minutes, I thought. But that's where we stayed. Everything was deathly quiet, other than the sound of Ian's frenetic highlighter. Ian was so deep into his books, underlining every sentence with such concentration that I thought if bombs went off he wouldn't notice. His father, Lou, a mail carrier, had told Ian that he'd pay to send him to college, but he had to study. (It turned out that Ian not only got straight A's, he set the curve in every class he took for a year and a half before transferring to DePaul University in Chicago. He eventually graduated as valedictorian of his DePaul Law School class.)

Watching Ian study scared me. His grades in high school weren't a great deal better than mine. But now I wondered if book learning would be too highbrow for me. Maybe I should just go into some kind of business, as some of my friends and classmates did. But other friends and classmates did enter college, so I thought I'd try.

Within a few days after I had enrolled in school, in October 1957, the Soviet Union launched Sputnik, the first man-made satellite in space. The United States was, as Lyndon Johnson, then the majority leader of the Senate, said, "shocked." The Russians had jumped way ahead of us in the conquest of space. Some people feared that the Russians, as one commentator put it, "will be dropping bombs on us from space like kids dropping rocks on cars from freeways." In the midst of the cold war, this was the beginning of the space age. How should America combat this awful threat? Well, by getting more scientists and putting a premium on subjects like physics and chemistry and calculus for college students. Physics and chemistry and calculus: not my major suits. This is bad news, I thought. What kind of future will I have when science rules the world?

Still at a loss as to what I wanted to do with my life–or, perhaps, what life wanted to do with me–I entered a curriculum in business, taking accounting, math, and economics. I thought I'd eventually go into some kind of business, what with my background on Maxwell Street and selling religious pictures. The garbage truck, I decided early on, was not a prospect.

After one day each in accounting and math, I realized as though sandbagged that I had chosen the wrong route to education. I hated both subjects and stopped going to both classes. It was my unsuspected good fortune that all incoming students were required to take an English test and write an essay. I remember using some of the words I had learned in *30 Days to a More Powerful Vocabulary*. The essay was about Marilyn Monroe, and I remember using the word "pulchritude." I was placed in an advanced rhetoric class–a fancy word for an English course–and when I walked in I saw Richard Rubinstein sitting there. In grammar school Richard had been considered a "brain." I thought, if he's in the class, I'm definitely in over my head. Soon it happened that Richard and I had coincidentally picked the same book to write a report on, Dwight D. Eisenhower's *Crusade in Europe*. I happened to learn this in conversation with him. In a following class, the teacher, a stocky but kindly woman, said she was going to read two book reports, and both happened to be on the same book, *Crusade in Europe*.

I stiffened. "I won't say who wrote which one," she said, which gave me only slight comfort. She read Richard's first. I slunk down in my seat. I can't compete with this, I thought. And then she read mine. I slunk down farther.

"Now," she said, after reading my worthless report, "I'll tell you why the second one is stronger than the first." She went on to describe how I focused on the heart of the book while the other student didn't. There were a few more points, but I don't think I heard them. I was stunned. I sat up. I have come to think of that moment as the first time I had a sense of a writing ability I hadn't altogether been aware of. I continued to succeed in that class, though it never dawned on me to consider writing as a profession. I just wasn't bad at writing, that's all. I still had never met a writer and had no burning desire to do so. The thought that I would one day earn my living by writing—writing sports or anything else—was as conceivable to me then as if someone had said, "Here's a pair of wax wings, fly to the moon." (Richard Rubinstein, by the way, became a certified public accountant.)

While I did reasonably well in two of my other classes at Navy Pier, Economics in American History, and Speech, I did expectedly miserably in accounting and math, given my virtual zero attendance. I had entered Illinois on probation since I was in the lower quarter of my high school graduating class. Thus by a hair I flunked out.

I felt lost, and embarrassed. I applied to Roosevelt University, a commuter school in downtown Chicago, and was accepted. I would major in English. I expected my savvy father to say something like, "English? What are you going to do with 'English'? Open an English store?" He might have been thinking it, but he didn't say it. All he said was, "What are you going to do with it?" I said, "I don't know, Dad, but I like it."

"Do you think you can take one course in accounting?" he asked.

"I don't think so," I said.

He nodded. "Good luck, son," he said. He was giving me his blessings, smart enough to know that one had to follow one's heart, though he may have wished for a slight change of mine.

At Roosevelt, immediately following my flop at Navy Pier, in my second semester in college, I made the Dean's List. The next semester I received a scholarship.

I also tried out for the school's basketball team, made it, and became a starting guard. Roosevelt, which belonged to no conference, played a Division III independent schedule and was coached by a black man named Edwin Turner. In high school, on the freshman-sophomore team, I had been the high scorer and had very little concept of passing. I was getting a reputation as a ball hog and didn't like it. It scarred me emotionally; at one point I even considered quitting the team. And while in my two high school varsity years I had a few good shooting games, I concentrated instead on passing and defense. Turner, a soft-spoken, dignified man, urged me to shoot more, to capitalize on a strong point. He said it would help the team. Gradually I did, and eventually became the team's leading scorer at fifteen points a game, though we never rose above a .500 season. But Coach Turner restored my confidence. It was more important than simply basketball; I tried to use this experience for the future. If I could come out of a funk in one area, and take advantage of innate abilities, perhaps I could do it in other areas.

When I turned eighteen, I was aware that I was draft-eligible. Not right away, being in school, but down the road. I didn't look forward to being drafted for three years or enlisting for two, which was standard. So I decided, along with a few friends my age, to sign up for the six-month active-duty program with the National Guard before I was eighteen and a half years old. I would have to attend reserve meetings for only three years, after six months on active duty. Before the second semester of my sophomore year at Roosevelt, I was sent to Fort Leonard Wood, Missouri, and then to Fort Gordon, Georgia. I learned to scrub latrines, perform menial duties as a member of the Kitchen Police, fire an M-1 rifle, and eat creamed chipped beef on toast—"shit on a shingle," as the soldiers' felicitous phrase had it, and perhaps the hardest of all to do. I also had a lot of time to read, and carried books around in the inside of my fatigue shirt (with a kind of pregnant bulge that drew periodic chastisements from the first sergeant). The humility one learns as a private in the army is good armor for a writer: rejection slips can be piercing.

When I first entered basic training I kept a diary. It lasted a short while, until I was so fatigued at night that holding a pen was like trying to write with a baseball bat. But some entries tell of my new world. Sunday, April 7, 1959: "I took a haircut, which is an understatement. I had told the 'barber' I just wanted a trim. I laughed at my joke. He didn't. I was on the chair for 30 seconds. 'Next,' he said. I'm almost bald."

Monday, April 8, at the medical center: "I had four shots given by four doctors with needles, two at a time, simultaneously in each arm. They stood in a square formation and the patient enters with arms hanging bare and a blank stare. It was similar to running a gauntlet while trying to feel immune from pain. I felt the pain."

Sunday, April 12: "Yesterday I was on K.P. from 3:30 a.m. until 7:30 p.m. I was back sink man. It was almost continuous work, scrubbing pots and pans. The sergeants were also kind enough to provide time for me to peel potatoes. None of this I had ever done before. My fingers were raw. . . . The sergeants, especially the mess hall cooks, are constantly harassing. No job is done thorough enough for their likes. Even if everything is spotless. They call this shaping up recruits. Some shape! I can't understand how a man can work on a job where he has to be mean and thinking he has to scream to communicate."

Monday, April 13: "Our company commander is 2nd Lt. Kennedy. He's about 23 years old, the age of a lot of the guys here. He is thin, no chest, and thick glasses. He was leading us in marching and then called 'Double time.' The troops carried rifles, gun belts, ponchos and canteens. He had only his swagger stick. He ran for a very long time, and everyone was huffing and puffing. He said, 'C'mon, girls, get with it. I didn't run track for nothing.' It looks to me like he's trying to prove that under that frail physique he is a real man. I think he's a creep."

Tuesday, April 14: "Not too much. We now have a drummer when we march. It reminds me of the Nazi Youth Program. Tomorrow I clean the latrines."

And that is truly where my diary ended. I would later find that wherever I went, anyone with one stripe more than the other guy–in the military, in newspapers, in business, almost anywhere– had visions of acting in the manner of these sergeants. Power, I learned, corrupts.

In the barracks of my company, Company A, 4th Battalion, there was no partition for toilets. When you sat down on one of the eight toilet seats–they were lined up L-shaped–you were knee to knee to the next guy. In the first couple of days this was too embarrassing for most of us to handle, and we began to suffer from constipation. Then necessity reared itself, and soon we were even holding meetings there, knee to knee. It's amazing what one can get used to.

Once, on field maneuvers in a pouring rain, a chow line served soup and a slab of beef into our steel mess kits. We had been marching and playing war games all the long morning, and I was desperately looking forward to lunch. But burdened with unsteady helmet, slung rifle, and the pelting rain, it was difficult to dine comfortably. Because of the rain, the more soup I drank, the more there was. I managed to find the trunk of a leafy tree to sit against. As I awkwardly bent over to cut the beef, my mess kit tilted and the meat, as I tried to unhinge myself from my rifle, slid slowly into the mud. And there it rested. I stared at it. I was starving. I swallowed hard, then reached over with thumb and forefinger and plucked up the hunk of beef, shook off what mud I could, and consumed it.

And so it went, on into Fort Gordon, where I learned to be a cryptographer. In school there we had to learn the Morse Code in order to send and receive coded messages. We became so proficient at it that, waiting in chow line, we'd speak whole sentences in it (most basically, dit-dit-dit / dah-dah-dah / dit-dit-dit–three dots / three dashes / three dots–for S.O.S.).

I also got my first taste of life in the South. I witnessed my first revival meeting in a field outside Augusta in which, under a large tent, I saw people begin to whirl and stagger and "speak in tongues" as the preacher orated about fire and brimstone and the "evil Devil." As in a movie. I was astonished that anyone could believe this stuff on faith.

I saw water fountains that read "White" and "Negro." I saw a white woman in a five-and-ten store in Columbia, South Carolina, grab her small boy as he inadvertently tiptoed up to drink from the "Negro" spigot. "You don't do that!" she shouted, hitting him on the back of the head. "That's for niggers. It's not safe."

I happened to be passing the water fountains at that moment, and stopped, curious about the scene.

"Is that one contaminated?" I asked her, as though truly seeking an answer.

"The ones the niggers drink from is full of disease 'n' such," she replied. "We ain't takin' no chances on gettin' sick."

Considering all of that, I felt sick myself. While there was certainly discrimination in the North, and in Chicago, where blacks were generally unwelcome in predominantly white areas—except to work as maids and the like—I had never experienced anything quite as blatantly racist as this. But I was naive.

I should have recalled, for example, that riveting and terrible time in the summer of 1951, when I was eleven. A black bus driver and his family had tried to move into all-white Cicero, a suburb bordering on Chicago's West Side, and only a mile or so from where I grew up. They had been greeted by an angry mob of some four thousand neighbors. During three nights of violence their apartment was torched and vandalized. The story made all the television newscasts and the front page of the local newspapers. The family had to move out. I remember watching the newscasts with my parents in horror. "This is terrible," my mother said. "Why don't they leave those poor people alone? Who are they bothering?" My father shook his head in anger at the troublemakers. "Savages," he said. Policemen and firefighters were pelted with bricks and bottles. Finally the National Guard had to be summoned to quell the rioting.

While stationed at Fort Gordon I also got my first experience of consummating a relationship with a woman beyond Elma and her business associates (I stopped going to such recreational facilities forever when I was nineteen, and back from the military).

Several of my friends and I journeyed for a weekend to Myrtle Beach, South Carolina, where I met an older woman–she was about twenty-five. I thought she was very attractive despite her age. She was alone, and on vacation too. We hit it off. I told her I was a private in the army–I wasn't in uniform–and I confessed that I had little money (I was being paid about sixty dollars a month) and couldn't take her "fancy." She said that was all right, that she had a job, and she took me to dinner. Afterward she bought a bottle of wine and we sat on the beach at night on a blanket and under the stars. The waves lapped at the shore, a few feet from where we made love, sandy but sweet. Her name was Linda, she said, and she gave me the address and phone number of where she lived in Columbia, South Carolina, which was just some two hours' drive by car (if one of my friends was driving, since I didn't own "wheels") or by bus from Fort Gordon.

I thought this could blossom into a beautiful romance, and rather inexpensive too. I called Linda the following week. Wrong number. Did I take it down incorrectly? Maybe the "4" was a "9"? I must improve my handwriting. I tried again. Same result. I tried another combination. No luck. A few weeks later one of my friends was driving his car to Columbia, and I asked if I could hitch a ride with him. Sure, he said. I went to Linda's address and rang the bell. An elderly woman answered. "Sorry," she said, "there's no one here by that name." And so ended the love affair with my Southern belle. At least I think she was Southern. She had obviously given me a phony phone number and home address, and probably a false name too. Was she married? Did I not please her? I never heard from her again–one of life's frustrating mysteries. But even if she was no longer in that young soldier's life, the memory remained of moonlight and amour with her.

My active military duty behind me, I returned to Roosevelt for one more semester, having decided that being on a campus away from the city would be beneficial. I still had a full, active, laughing life with friends in Chicago; if I were to leave the city, which I loved, I might force myself to get more serious about studies and what I might do with the rest of my life. My father was now on his feet financially, doing well in politics, and so at nineteen I gave up the stand on Maxwell Street. I had heard about Miami of Ohio—I first learned of it when its basketball team, with its star center, the future standout pro Wayne Embry, played at the DePaul gym. Miami of Ohio? It wasn't in Florida? No, the school, as I learned, was started in 1809 in Oxford, and named for the Miami Indian tribe that lived around southwestern Ohio. Miami, Florida, was a latecomer, not being incorporated until 1896, and well before the University of Miami of Ohio and its thug-laden Orange Bowl football teams, as well as Miami Beach and its storybook pastel hotels. I looked into Miami of Ohio and discovered that it had a highly regarded English department and was in a beautiful setting, in a valley, with the buildings constructed in classic Georgian architecture. All of that proved true, though I didn't appreciate the setting immediately.

I arrived in town—a local population of some 5,000, plus about 7,500 students—on a cold late-January evening. Descending from the bus after a jouncing, seven-hour ride from Chicago, I got directions to Brandon Hall, where I was to room. I walked several long blocks in the dark, long because I wasn't sure where I was going, and excruciating because I was hauling two pieces of green Samsonite luggage that were so heavy it felt I was carrying bricks in them. I had to stop every several feet to get the blood back into my hands. I wanted to turn around and go right back to Chicago. But I didn't. And I'm glad I didn't.

I had become serious about reading when I entered college, and at Miami my interest grew more intense. Instinctively I was making up for the lost years of high school. I read books that challenged me and were sometimes well over my head, but I was climbing. In Professor Edgar Branch's class I read all of *Moby Dick*, even the esoteric whaling stuff, and felt the description of that crazy Ahab's chase for the white beast was like being in that wild, swirling ocean. In Professor John Weigel's class I read Joyce's *Ulysses*, which was difficult but considerably more accessible than the impossible *Finnegans Wake.* Thomas Mann was dull, but Dylan Thomas was radiant. Albert Camus and Virginia Woolf and Franz Kafka were by turns impenetrable and exhilarating. Professor Weigel was like no one I'd ever known. This tall, flinty, long-faced man from Ohio had somewhere developed a patrician voice, though he was saltier than one would imagine of someone who had earned two Ph.Ds (one in English, one in psychology).

He was no basketball fan, but he knew my interest in basketball and told me he thought the stationary ten-foot basket was unfair to small players.

"What they should do," he said, "is lower the basket to three feet and have it move up and down and sideways. A moving target would give everyone a fair chance." It was a thought. One time he announced a quiz for the next class session. But quiz day turned out to be the first beautiful day of spring, after a long winter. About half the class didn't show up. Weigel flunked the half of the class that *did* show up. "Anyone who wouldn't cut class on a day like today deserves to be penalized," he said.

One late afternoon, after a Weigel class, I remember that this relatively unlettered kid from the West Side of Chicago was so thunderstruck by new knowledge and new ideas that I had to hold on to the wooden banister as I staggered down the stairs from the third floor of Upham Hall.

I took a course in music appreciation in which I learned, among other things, about the contrapuntal technique, particularly in Mozart and Beethoven, in which aspects of opposing musical strains seem to conflict and yet work in harmony. It was a lesson to be learned in writing, where, as I recall the mystery writer Erle Stanley Gardner advising, great storytelling is all about "conflict, conflict, conflict."

A course in art appreciation broadened my ability to see beyond the surface of a work of art. When I traveled to the Cleveland Art Museum, for example, I observed how Rembrandt used an economy of strokes. When you looked closely he used, for example, an almost casual brushstroke to depict the vein in the hand of an old man. Again it was instructive in writing, where the simple can reveal the profound. Clutter is just that, intrusive.

All of this, as well as zoology and geology and French and politics and economics and the class Biblical and Mythological Backgrounds in Literature, among others, plus the heady new world of being published in the school newspaper, came at me in a great rush. One of the great influences on my religious thought came from Thomas Paine, the pamphleteer of the American Revolution:

"My country is the world and my religion is to do good. . . ."

Paine believed "in the equality of man," he wrote, and that "religious duties" consist in "doing justice" and "loving mercy. . . ."

I read that Einstein believed there must be a Supreme Being because of the balance of nature in the universe. But even he was stumped by some of the quirks regarding quantum mechanics, and to the end of his days he insisted, though he could not prove it, that "God doesn't play dice with the universe." Good: if Einstein didn't know everything, this gave the rest of us–that is, me–hope in our imperfections and intellectual failings.

(As for eternity, a notorious con man I interviewed years later said something in this regard that I believe put his finger squarely on the subject. This was Joe [Yellow Kid] Weil, one of the canniest flimflam artists that ever lived. One of his scams was made into a movie, *The Sting*, starring Robert Redford and Paul Newman. I met Weil when he was exactly one hundred years old, a small, now bony man living in a nursing home in Chicago.

("Are you afraid of dying, Joe?" I asked him at one point.

("No," he said, "I'm not afraid to die. I always said, 'Death will teach me something or nothing.'")

At Miami I also took a class in Shakespeare, and read him with comprehension for the first time–I had been assigned *Romeo and Juliet* in high school but of course had never read it. Now I found Shakespeare's insights into the hearts and minds and souls of people–the greed, the lust, the striving for power–to be no different than it is today, which is why he is eternally pertinent. And his language was so powerful and rhythmic that it seemed composed by a supernatural force. I memorized parts of his plays and sonnets.

Juliet, from *Romeo and Juliet*: "'Tis almost morning. I would have thee gone, / And yet no farther than a wanton's bird, / Who lets it hop a little from her hand. . . . " "Hop a little from her hand." I loved the alliteration that enhanced the image of love's frustration.

And from the Prologue in Act IV of *Henry V*, in which the English and French forces are readying for battle in the dark of early morning, this remarkable word picture: ". . . Fire answers fire, and through their paly flames / Each battle sees the other's umbered face. / Steed threatens steed, in high and boastful neighs / Piercing the night's dull ear. / And from the tents/The armorers, accomplishing the knights, / With busy hammers closing rivets up / Give dreadful note of preparation. . . ."

And *Macbeth*: "[Life] is a tale told by an idiot; / Full of sound and fury, / Signifying nothing." So clean, so dismal, so beautiful.

I was particularly taken by the power and eloquence and logic of the great defense attorney, the late Clarence Darrow, another Chicagoan, who gained fame with his brilliant arguments, particularly in the Scopes "Monkey Trial" and the Loeb-Leopold "Trial of the Century" murder case.

I now planned to attend law school after undergraduate school. But then, as a twenty-year-old college junior at Miami, I discovered writing for publication.

Dave Burgin, a friend who was living across the third-floor dormitory corridor from me in Brandon Hall, was an assistant sports editor on the *Miami Student*, the school's twice-weekly newspaper. He convinced me to try writing for it, and I did. It was in sports.

4

~~~~~~~~~~~~~~~~

Try Again

I KNEW NOTHING about tennis, having neither played nor followed it, but my first assignment for the *Miami Student* was to interview the Miami tennis coach. The tennis team had an upcoming match against Xavier, a college located in Cincinnati, about thirty-five miles south of Oxford. Dave Burgin gave me questions to ask the coach, which I nervously and dutifully did.

I was required to hand in a typed copy of the story. I wrote out the piece in longhand first, then typed it out. Although I had learned to type in high school, the assignments had always been about copying printed material, never thinking originally at the typewriter. This was different and unnatural, but soon I learned to do it.

And so I began writing sports on the Miami school paper, and I loved it. It wasn't long before Burgin became the sports editor, and he gave me a column, called "From the Desk of Ira Berkow."

I wrote whatever I felt like writing. A number of stories were either dramatic or humorous (I thought they were humorous, anyway) and seemed to make an impact. They were rarely about the games but about people. Walking in the corridors of the school buildings I would sometimes hear students and professors talking about a column I had written, or learn that one of the columns was discussed in a literature class. I would lie awake writing the next column in my head, or rewriting the one that had been published that day.

Growing up in Chicago I had read Red Smith, the syndicated sports columnist, in the *Sun-Times*, and admired him greatly. I found that he was also syndicated in the two major papers of the Miami area, the *Dayton Daily News* and the *Cincinnati Enquirer*.

I continued to read Smith, continued to love his ability to make me laugh, or move me, or make me ponder a topic of current interest in the news. I soon learned that indeed, sportswriter or no sportswriter, he was a literary figure in America, his columns taught in universities as exemplary writing. One of his fans was Ernest Hemingway, who praised Smith in one of his novels, *Across the River and into the Trees*. I even ran across a college English textbook with a column by Red Smith nestled between a short story by Dylan Thomas and an essay by Winston Churchill. Having now fallen in love with writing, I decided, as a junior in college, to send Red Smith two of my pieces from the *Miami Student*. I was looking for help in getting better, and I figured Red Smith would understand.

About a month later, I received a letter back from him!

"Dear Ira Berkow,

"When I was a cub in Milwaukee I had a city editor who'd stroll over and read across a guy's shoulder when he was writing a lead. Sometimes he would approve, sometimes he'd say gently, 'Try again,' and walk away.

"My advice is, try again. And then again." He added a few particulars, such as "Don't write 'precocious phalanges.' That's only a pretentious way of saying 'educated toe,' a cliché you were trying to avoid."

In that first letter to me, he wrote sensitively but firmly, "My first impulse was to paste up your columns and write in marginal criticisms, but they wouldn't have made you happy." He advised that I try again, "and then again." "If you're for this racket, and not many really are," he said, "then you've got an eternity of sweat and tears ahead. I don't mean just you; I mean anybody."

It was true for me too. And perhaps, after reading those two columns of mine, Smith could intuit what truly lay ahead for me. Should I be dismayed that I hardly got a rave review from the great man, or should I be flattered that he took the time to respond? I decided to be flattered. I pasted up the columns and sent them to him with a note:

"Dear Mr. Smith, please make me unhappy." He responded with marginal criticisms that remain invaluable to me.

I exchanged several letters with him over time, with him commenting on my work. They were straightforward, with suggestions, and encouraging–by the very fact that he was taking this time with me–without being laudatory.

I had someone "sprawling to the ground." He put a line through "to the ground." "Where else?" he wrote in the margin. I used the word "ineffably," pilfered from a literature class on James Joyce. "Too strong," he wrote. "Look it up."

When the Cincinnati Reds played the New York Yankees in the World Series in 1961, I got a job at the games in Cincinnati. I was a "runner" for a photographer; that is, he'd take a roll of pictures in his perch above the screen in the upper deck, and then I'd run down to the truck behind the stadium to have it transmitted. After the first game in Crosley Field, I met Red Smith. I waited for him to finish writing in the auxiliary, or outdoor, press box along the first base grandstands. He wore a fedora and sport jacket and tie. Grey peeked out from under his hat, and a pair of glasses was perched on his nose. He was a small-boned man, around fifty-five years old, and smoking a cigarette. I introduced myself to him, along with my friend, and he remembered me! He put down his portable typewriter and we chatted for some forty-five minutes as the ballpark grew dark–this was when all World Series games were played in the afternoon.

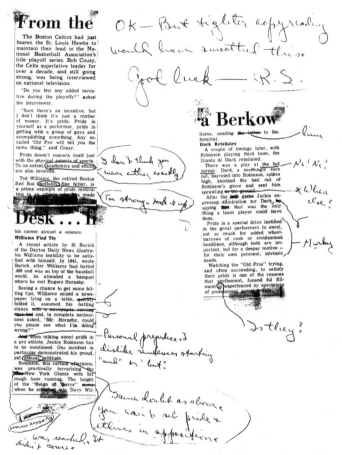

How was it possible that Red Smith would take the time to critique my sports column from the Miami University student newspaper? But he generously did.

Years later, in the foreword to a collection of my columns, Red Smith wrote: "I . . . remember our first meeting at a World Series game that he attended with a classmate while still in college. Didn't writing about games every day grow dreadfully dull, the classmate asked. Only to dull minds, I told him, and I tried to explain that in newspaper work, unlike the wholesale hardware game, today was always different from yesterday and tomorrow refreshingly different from today. . . ."

Smith, however, no longer covered games daily, as he once did, and I had no interest in doing that, either. What I admired particularly about Red's work, beyond his artistry of the written word, was the subject matter. He wrote about people and issues, and created moods, and brought original perspectives, and, at other times, told such wonderful stories that I wished they wouldn't end. He could be emotional, but he was always professionally and deftly restrained. He had also said, on another occasion, that writing was easy: "All you have to do is sit down at a typewriter and open a vein."

Writing, it turned out, wasn't so easy–it could be both a pleasure and a heartache. I had read in a philosophy book a line from Spinoza: "All excellent things are as difficult as they are rare." And so it was, I learned, with the art of writing, or trying to write, well.

At school, one column that drew considerable attention dealt with an incident in my life when I was ten or eleven years old. It was about boys playing baseball in a park, and one of the boys, Billy, overweight and slightly retarded, had struck out. One of the other players on his team–I called him Clyde in the story, but his real name was Donny–said, "Pig, fat slob of a pig. Striking out on my team means the firing squad."

I continued: "One of the fielders called to Clyde: 'Give the goon a break. It ain't his fault he stinks.'"

"'Shut up or I'll give you the same thing,' Clyde huffed. 'Get up there, fat Billy.'"

As the other boys–including me–sat or stood about silently, Clyde proceeded to throw fastballs at Billy: "The ball thumped into Billy's back. He stiffened at the shock and his hands clung tight to the screen." And after several pitches: "Under the blazing sun . . . Billy writhed and fell to his knees. . . ."

Farther down in the piece I wrote: "The other boys waited for the firing squad to be over."

When Clyde was finished, I concluded with: "Head lowered, Billy waddled over the hill toward home. His shoulders shook uncontrollably; tears streamed down his fleshy cheeks. A rip at the seam of his jeans drooped and showed white.

"Then, slowly, like donkeys raising off their haunches, the boys plodded back to where they were before the firing squad had started."

That moment had an indelible impact on me. As I grew older, I was determined to try–at *least* try–to have the courage to stand up to injustice, perpetrated against me or anyone else.

In some ways it became a motivating force for my career as a writer. I did not wish to live with such a sense of helplessness again. I hoped never to sit silently and let the Clydes or Donnys of the world have their way without at least an argument or protest from me.

That column also showed strains of influence from my readings in literature classes. I tried to tell the story with strong visual images–the pathos of Billy, for example, as exemplified by his torn pants–and leave an impression for the reader to understand by feel rather than by hitting him over the head with explanation. That, as I was coming to learn, was the root of storytelling. In years to come I would understand that this technique was better served, in the view of some, in a feature story rather than in an opinion column. But I was convinced that it could work in a column as well. It seemed I wasn't the only one.

I had sent the column of Billy and Donny, along with another column, to Red Smith. And he wrote back:

"Dear Ira,

"You keep getting better. Stay with it, and God bless. Now may I offer suggestions:

"Don't write: '"Shut up or you'll get the same thing," Clyde huffed.' Clyde said it or hollered it or something. I don't know what huffed means.

"Don't say: 'Billy shunted to the wire screen.' I don't know how he got there, but you shunt a freight car onto a siding; I think shunt is a transitive verb requiring an object, but in any case it is a damn poor word to describe how anyone walks.

"Go through these two columns and get tough with yourself about adverbs and adjectives. See for yourself where deleting a word would strengthen the line. And be careful; don't say 'raising' when you mean 'rising.'

"These are good columns, Ira. One big, black pencil would make them fine.

"Yours, Red."

A coincidence was that the sports columnist for the *Cincinnati Enquirer* was also named Smith, first name Lou. Sometimes Red's brilliant syndicated column would be laid out alongside Lou Smith's. The comparison was stark. Lou Smith was as bad as Red Smith was good. If there was a cliché, a banal thought, a sloppy phrase that Lou Smith missed, I wasn't aware of it. He was an object lesson in all the things Red Smith had warned me against. If Red Smith would write, deprecatingly, about himself— "the tenant in this literary flophouse"—Lou Smith would mention "us scribes." Or, Red Smith: "Not even Eddie Arcaro ever rode faster than his mount could run." Lou Smith: "Citation ran like the wind."

Sometime after I had received Red Smith's letter about my column on Billy, I received another letter, less welcome under the circumstances. I was still in the National Guard, but since there were no units in Oxford, and the closest one was thirty miles away in Hamilton, and I had no car, I was placed in a control unit. That is, in a national emergency I could be called up for active duty at any time and placed in another unit that needed my military job classification. In the fall of 1961, this happened to me. With the onset of the Berlin Crisis, when the Soviet Union planned to build a wall around West Berlin, the National Guard was called up, and I was assigned to a guard unit from West Virginia. I wrote a letter to President Kennedy, asking for a reprieve until I could graduate in January. I got back a standard letter, saying no.

In the *Miami Student*, the editor of the paper, a friend named Ted Margolis, wrote an editorial about my situation and me, titled "Bye, Bye, Ira." It appeared on October 17 and began: "Red Smith and Ira Berkow sat in the press box at Crosley Field just two weeks ago and talked sports writing. Smith, the dean of American sports writers, thought the Reds would win the Series, and Berkow, the dean of *Miami Student's* sports columnists, thought he'd graduate this February.

"As it turned out, both Smith and Berkow went zero for two. . . .

"With only four months left before he would have his degree, Ira was rather disturbed when he received his letter from Uncle Sam. But as he so nobly stated to us, 'If the country is in danger I'll go out and defend it and risk my life, but it's polishing my boots and shining my helmet that bothers me.'

"Although we will truly miss the talents of Ira Berkow, we will also feel more secure that he is somewhere, 'over there,' defending our school, our state, and our nation, while he polishes his boots and shines his rifle.

"So long, Ira, we'll miss you!"

I'm not sure whether they did miss me—Ted was more than generous. But I know I missed them, and the campus life. Never more so than when on K.P. Indeed, I didn't go to Berlin and had no need to risk my life. For nearly a year I was stationed at Fort Meade, Maryland, where I became vaguely proficient at Ping-Pong, a task on which my comrades and I spent numerous hours during the day, when I wasn't polishing my boots.

But I had one particularly memorable and harrowing experience in the army. Most of my unit was from the Kanawha Valley of West Virginia, men who had signed up for the National Guard primarily for the extra income it provided. Also, when they rose in rank, especially as noncommissioned officers, they could boss people around in a way they couldn't in civilian life, where they were, to a large extent, truck drivers, mechanics, and construction workers. While some of the men in this unit, the 150th Armored Cavalry, had sophistication and schooling, most didn't. They liked to call themselves "ridge runners" and "twig suckers," exemplifying a rural existence in the mountains. They even taught me to

Private Ira Berkow (left), of the 150th Armored Cavalry, on bivouac at Camp A. P. Hill, Virginia, in March 1962, with friends in the platoon, Lou Burke and Dick Boyd.

smoke cigars and inhale. After a few coughing bouts, I settled into liking it. I was becoming one of them, almost.

One of the West Virginia boys, Brucie Jones, who obviously did not have the highest intelligence and was protected and humored by most of us, sometimes came to me for a loan. I'd give it to him—rarely more than five dollars, which seemed considerable to him since we were paid such paltry salaries. Sometimes he'd even remember to pay me back. We had a gentle acquaintance-ship. One day, when I was about to make a trip back to Oxford to visit friends at Miami during a short leave, Brucie appeared at my locker as I was packing. "Got something for you," he said. And he reached into his wallet and pulled out a small, old, wrinkled packet. It was a condom. I don't know how long it had been in his wallet, but it looked like something uncovered in an archaeo-logical dig. "You might need this," he said earnestly.

I took the flaking wrapping and thanked him. I didn't need it, as it turned out, and, though touched by the gesture, I tossed it away shortly after I left the base.

One day Brucie came to me with a questioning look. "Ah-ra," he said, calling me by name, "Mack Rollins"—another guy in the unit—"Mack Rollins said you was a Jew. Is that so?"

"Yeah, it's so, Bruce. Why so surprised?"

"I thought Jews has horns in their heads."

"Do I look like I've got horns in my head?"

"No." He was looking, too.

"And I'm a Jew from head to foot."

"Oh," he said, and walked away, perhaps as confused as ever. I think he, along with some of the others, still had doubts about my Jewishness because I was a starting and contributing player on the company's baseball and basketball teams, when the common wisdom was that Jews weren't athletic.

And I'd periodically hear a remark about Jews—there were three or four of us in a unit of some two hundred—but it was nothing to get exercised about. Until one night when we were on bivouac in the hills of Virginia. It had snowed heavily, and we'd had difficulty putting up our tents—huge white canvases that covered some twenty cots, ten to a side. After maneuvers, a number of the men gathered in the "beer tent." This was the recreation area. I had nothing better to do—the lights in the tent were too dim for reading—and went for a beer. Some of the sergeants and specialists were getting drunk and some of them began to make disparaging remarks about Jews. I was the only Jew in the tent. Rather than sit there and defend myself and my historic race, and perhaps get into a fight where I was significantly outnumbered, I decided to leave. I trudged through the dark night and deep drifts to my bunk. Once there, I thought: I won't remove my fatigues, and I won't crawl into the sleeping bag on the cot, and I'll keep my boots on, and I'll lie there with my rifle at my side, even though I have no bullets. If those sergeants and specialists had the notion to come after me—I truly thought it might happen, since they were drinking heavily and in a foul mood—I would take one or two of them with me by virtue of a swinging rifle butt. I was angry, and I was scared. I slept little and unevenly that night. And when the dawn seeped through an opening in the tent, I felt a flow of relief. That was the end of it.

I later read a remark by Benjamin Disraeli, when he was in the British Parliament, in which he responded to a taunt by a fellow member who had slandered him about being a Jew. I wish I'd had the presence of mind to say something along the lines of his retort. "Yes, I am a Jew, and when the ancestors of the right honorable gentleman were brutal savages in an unknown island, mine were priests in the temple of Solomon." I'm sure that would have gone over big with those mountain boys.

In August 1962 I was discharged from the army in time to return for my last semester at Miami—and in time to meet Willee Eskew. One afternoon in December of that year, in the Miami library, I passed the carrel in which a very pretty blonde was seated, reading a book. I backtracked, as though reversing a film, and struck up a conversation. Willee (born Wilda) was an English major, like me, and from a small town in southern Indiana. She was the daughter of a circuit court judge there. She was smart, she was curious, and she had even read my column in the school paper. We began to date, seeing each other more or less exclusively in the month-plus from the time we met until the time I graduated. In a school that was notably Greek—that is, with an abundance of fraternities and sororities—I was not in a fraternity. Although I played on the sports teams of one fraternity and was often invited to parties by another, I had no interest in joining anything. I had my own small apartment off campus and was happy with that, preferring it to living in a frat house. I also had been to the army and to another school, and the very thought of "belonging" to an organization was outside my interests. I think Willee liked the idea of this seeming independence—a semi-bohemian writer in her eyes, perhaps—and I liked the fact that she liked it. (Willee in fact was in a popular sorority on campus, but she had grown less and less active in it.)

Willee stayed at school with me during the semester break before my graduation, our romance heating up, and attended the graduation. My parents came to the graduation on a snowy day and a rocky flight from Chicago. I introduced them to Willee, and my mother particularly looked warily at her. Was this serious? Was this attractive young lady after her son's money, or whatever it was my mother may have considered was worthwhile about me? On second thought, it couldn't have been money. And, it was apparent by her blonde looks and her name that she wasn't Jewish. She was a *shiksa*, the Yiddish word for a Gentile female. My father, on the other hand, seemed to take meeting Willee in stride and, after talking with her—we all went to lunch—came away liking her. So, eventually, did my mother. My parents were always impressed with people who didn't try to be something they weren't. And Willee was just that despite, as I knew, her nervousness in hoping they'd like her.

Willee also didn't seem to mind that I was one of the few college guys—perhaps the only one—to walk around campus smoking a cigar, a legacy from my military days with the mountain boys.

I had been applying myself as diligently in college as I hadn't done in high school, and was a Dean's List student. When I graduated, finally, that January, I returned home to Chicago. Willee was still on my mind, and we were regularly in touch. I applied for a newspaper job on one of the four city dailies. Insufficient experience, I was told.

Then an ad in my neighborhood newspaper, the *Nortown News*, caught my eye. The *Nortown News* covered some hard news but also a lot of frilly stuff regarding the far North Side of Chicago, where I lived. One of its headliners was the gossip columnist Ann Gerber. She was advertising for an assistant, or "leg man," in the newspaper vernacular. At the end of each of her columns was a paragraph that stated in bold: "Annie's Catty Comment." A catty comment followed. If there was a less prestigious element in American journalism, I wasn't aware of it.

I applied for the job.

I got Annie herself on the phone. I explained that I was seeking a job in journalism and saw her ad.

"Do you have any experience in the business?" she asked.

"I wrote a sports column for my college newspaper," I replied, not certain how much weight this carried.

"That's it?"

"That's it."

"Why do you want to be in journalism?" she asked.

"I like it. I think it's exciting, and I think I might be good at it," I said.

"If you get into newspapers," she said, and I'll never forget her exact words that followed, "you'll rue the day."

Maybe Annie was just having a bad day. Or maybe—and I tend to believe this—she was giving me very good advice, along the lines of Red Smith telling me, "if you're for this racket, and not many really are." And if I wasn't for this racket, I'd better find some other work in order to eat.

Annie didn't hire me and, for better or worse, her advice fell on deaf ears.

But I had an in of sorts at *Chicago American*. A family friend, Sam Rogovoi, had a friend (who had a friend, if memory serves) who was an important editor there, Harry Romanoff. Although I was several degrees removed from knowing his close friend, I was able to arrange an interview with Romanoff. I got all dressed up and ventured forth. "Go to graduate school," Romanoff told me, from beneath his green eyeshade. "It should open doors." And then he shut his door. Red Smith had said something similar to me—if I couldn't get a job on a newspaper, go to graduate school. And so I did.

I later learned that another young man from the city streets in Chicago had been recommended to see Romanoff, in much the same way I had, but some twenty-five years earlier. In James Atlas's biography of Saul Bellow, he writes that Romanoff gave Bellow the brush-off too.

It was 1938, Bellow had a bachelor's degree—his was in anthropology—and was married and unemployed. He had notions of being a writer but was having little success. "One solution was to get a job," Atlas wrote, "but they were in short supply. Bellow put on a suit and went downtown for an interview with a Hearst executive by the name of Harry Romanoff, who"—and Atlas quotes an observation by Bellow—"had a nose 'like a double Alaskan strawberry.' Romanoff looked him over and told him he would never make a newspaperman; in fact, he might as well forget about writing altogether. He had no aptitude for it."

Romanoff's instincts were partly right. Bellow didn't become a newspaperman. Instead he had to settle for developing into one of the world's greatest novelists.

I, on the other hand, applied and was admitted on scholarship to Northwestern University's Medill Graduate School of Journalism in Evanston, a few miles from my home. In May 1963, Willee graduated from Miami and, as we had arranged through our letters and visits, moved to Evanston. We set up housekeeping, sharing the finances. She got a job as an English teacher in a suburban junior high school, and I had my savings, my scholarship, and, still, my occasional foray into selling religious pictures.

One of my professors at Medill, a man who favored suspenders perhaps because a belt to circumvent his girth was a rare find, and with the unlikely name of Neil McNeil, gave me a taste of the gruffness and skepticism of editors and writers I'd not infrequently encounter in the years to come.

One of my assignments for a course in news writing was to cover the women's court in downtown Chicago. In the small but tumultuous courtroom I saw a parade of ladies of the night, dressed in a great array of low-cut blouses and spike heels, get light or suspended sentences. I approached one of them as she was leaving the courtroom, and she consented to a cup of coffee and an interview. Her name was Simone, a twenty-one-year-old black woman. She had large gold earrings and a stiff, straw-colored wig that fit haphazardly on her slight but sweet face. When she scratched her head, her wig tilted. She'd been charged with prostitution after a police officer caught her in a gangway on

Wells Street in a compromising situation with a young man who had agreed to pay her $15. She was fined $25 and given a suspended sentence. She'd been in jail "'bout 10 or 15 times," she told me, and she was "gettin' bored with hustlin'." She said she averaged $200 to $250 a week. She charged $10 and up. "Whatever I can get," she said, "long's it's reasonable."

She was a far cry from Elma, the woman I had once done business with on the South Side, but she was in the same profession—a kind of minor leaguer to Elma's major league status, as I saw it. I asked Simone if she did all her transactions in gangways. "Oh no," she said. "Most of the time it's in hotels or the tricks' apartments. Sometimes we have parties like the one last week. Six girls and six tricks in an apartment. I like those best."

The story I wrote was about eight hundred words. A simple check from the professor was a passing grade for the paper, a check plus was an excellent grade. I received a check minus. He wrote at the top of the first page: "I'm not sure how much of this is fiction or not—but it's a pretty good story—which, with some toning down, could make a newspaper."

Whether it would make a newspaper or not, I didn't know, but it was all true. It reminded me of a line from Churchill. When he was asked if he believed whether the legend of Camelot was true, he replied, "It was all true, or ought to have been, and more and better besides."

Neil was encouraging at times in his raw way—as in "could make a newspaper." In that story about Simone, he added, "Do not use dialect—you will find this a rule almost anywhere you may go."

This was so, but there had to be exceptions, otherwise who would ever have heard of "Stengelese," for example, the unusual speech used by Casey Stengel? When, for example, Mickey Mantle kicked a water cooler in the dugout after striking out, Stengel said to him, "It wasn't the water cooler which got you out." In his telling me of this, I noted that the "which" was essential in capturing Casey. But you could hardly capture his voice on paper. If, as someone once remarked, the old senator Everett Dirksen had a stained-glass voice, then Casey had one that was cracked stained glass. And though his syntax was cloudy, it was as compelling as rubbings on churchyard tombstones.

(Years later, when I was a sportswriter in New York, I asked Stengel to compare the two greatest home-run hitters of his lifetime, Babe Ruth and Henry Aaron, who was on the verge of breaking Ruth's record for career home runs. "Now this fellow in Atlanta is amazin'," Casey began. "He hits the ball the best for a man of his size. But I can't say he hits the ball better than Ruth. Ruth could hit the ball so far nobody could field it. And that's even with the medicinal improvements today. They come along now with the aluminum cup and it improves players who only used to wear a belt and it's better for catching ground balls.")

But one had to be careful and sparing in the use not only of dialect but of every word in every sentence. I took early notice, along these lines, that even in Mark Twain's use of dialect he invariably put a "g" at the end of "ing" words. Too much "nothin'" and "everythin'" grows tiresome to the reader (though, to my ear, "amazin'" works). In one of the most beautiful phrases in the English language, in my view, Twain had Huck Finn saying, as he and Jim got to the edge of a hilltop at night, that "the stars over us was sparkling ever so fine."

I learned to live with McNeil and appreciate him. But, evidently, not everyone did. A few years after I had graduated Northwestern, Neil came to an unfortunate end. His wife shot him in the head as he was sleeping in their connubial bed.

I received my degree from Northwestern in the spring of 1964, and that summer Willee and I were married. Willee's parents, who were always considerate to me, were not exactly thrilled about her marrying a Jew. Then too, I wanted to be a writer, and what kind of money can a writer make? Along the lines of what my parents wondered, and most other people I knew. As my father said to me, it's just as easy to marry a Jew as anyone else (also, it's just as easy to marry a rich girl as a poor one), and, in regard to religion, you wouldn't have any problems down the line in raising kids. He may have been right, but we never had kids, and so that never became an issue.

But Willee's parents were observant Methodists, and while I accompanied them to their white-steepled church on the Sundays I stayed at their home in Corydon, I always felt uncomfortable and an outsider in church, to be sure. I read the prayer book and softly sang "Rock of Ages," in case the Judge and Mrs. Eskew, as well as Willee's stern Aunt Mary, who taught high school algebra and gave even Willee no slack in her class, had their ears cocked in my direction.

I didn't go to synagogue myself, and my interest in religion, other than the purely tribal, was not a priority. My parents were casual about religion—we just never got around to talking about it at home. As was customary, my parents dressed in their finest clothes and went to temple with their friends on the High Holidays. Growing up I went with them, but after I had my Bar Mitzvah, which I studied for under virtual coercion, I rarely went again. I did, however, feel deeply about who I was in relation to the culture and history of the Jews. And I often thought about the partisans, half starved and with limited arms, who fought off the powerful Nazi army for thirty incredible days in the Warsaw Ghetto uprising. I always wondered how I would react under such circumstances—what kind of courage it took to smuggle in weapons, to scrounge for food, to face such a deadly fighting force head-on. I hoped I would be up to it if ever put in a situation that demanded fortitude, whether it was life and death, or one involving jobs or personalities. I had only the briefest taste of such a plight that night in the snowy hills of Virginia when my rifle and I were on bivouac and, I imagined, life alert.

Willee had no special worry about marrying a Jew. At Miami she had dated and found Jewish guys "appealing," she said. Like me, she was going to do what was in her heart to do, regardless of consequences. And despite some concerns about religion, my parents totally embraced Willee, whom they considered "a lady" and thoughtful in helping my mother around the house. She was at ease with our family and their friends. I think both our parents were relieved—at least outwardly accepting—that we were married in a civil ceremony instead of choosing a religious one.

Willee and I had planned to travel to Europe, and so we both worked for a few months to save money for the trip. While she taught English, I got a job as a caseworker for the Cook County Department of Public Aid. I had the impression that if I got a job in journalism, then quit after a few months, I would be somehow stigmatized as a flight risk. With the caseworker job I felt comfortable in quitting in a short time. This was also a remarkable learning experience in which I developed an intimate relationship with the poorest people in the country, some of whom had no idea how to take care of themselves and depended on the goodwill—and competence—of others in the bureaucratic system. One couple didn't know how to run the bath so never took one. Another kept cold water running from the faucet on the milk carton for her small child because she didn't know how to reach me to get her refrigerator fixed. I know there are welfare cheats, but in my experience most of the people were not. These unfortunate people needed help, and sometimes desperately.

Periodically I received letters from my constituents asking for help (not all were literate enough to write, so they called):

"Dear Mr. Berkow:

"I am writing you this note because I would like to know about some clothe for my brother he need a coat, shoes and pamts. Shirts and undercloth for he need the clothes for the winter.

"Thank you, Margaret Lugo."

And:

"Dear Sir: I did go to one of the store like you told me to same day he tright to talk to you. But he did get no answer from you that what he told me. So that is why I am writing this aost card. Sir to let you know whate he told me to let you know what he say to me.

Sir. But I did not get the madress yet account that Because he want talk to you first. Thank you very much. Mrs. Lottie Posen."

It happened that I had been out in the field when the man who owned the mattress store tried to call me. I saw to it that Lottie got her mattress and Margaret got the clothes for her brother.

In February 1965, Willee and I left our jobs and traveled as planned to Europe. For half a year we saw the continent by train on a Eurail Pass. It was amazing to learn, for example, that Crete had a vast sewage system seven thousand years ago, that the "horns" on the head of Michelangelo's "Moses" in Rome were supposed to symbolize a halo and not the embodiment of the Jewish Devil. In a bed-and-breakfast in Chipping Norton, in the fairyland-like English Cotswolds, I slept in a room with a slanted floor that was so old Shakespeare might have slept there. The ancient became the moment, and it boggled the brain. Old in America, often, was twenty years ago.

Our conversations with people we encountered on the trip, on trains or in restaurants or on the streets, were often mind-expanding. In Communist Krakow, Poland, our young woman guide informed us that the Polish people were not yet "sophisticated" enough to have democracy. In Paris we discovered that America and Americans were still "too young" to be world powers–never mind that we helped save the French from Nazi occupation.

When Willee and I returned to the states to seek my fame and fortune in journalism, I wrote to about twenty-five newspapers, from the *New York Times* to the *Los Angeles Times* to the *Cedar Rapids Gazette*, asking for a job as a general-assignment reporter.

I received several polite responses, saying that I was of interest but there were no openings now. They'd keep me on file. An editor at the *Los Angeles Times* even suggested, "if you're in the neighborhood, stop by." I didn't know if the neighborhood extended two thousand miles to Chicago, but I was tempted anyway. Then in June 1965 I received a call from an editor at the

Minneapolis Tribune, one of the dozens of papers that had originally turned me down. Some people had died or moved on, and there was a slot open in sports. Would I be interested? "Yes," I said. "Yes definitely."

I packed my socks and underwear, my portable Olivetti typewriter, my books, and, at my side, my wife of ten months, and we took off in our blue Plymouth for the eight-hour drive to the Northlands, excited and apprehensive, but understandably unaware of the mysteries and adventures and romance, the "sweat and tears," that surely lay ahead.

5

~~~~~~~~~~~

Who Moved the Spike?

THE CITY—the Twin Cities, that is, Minneapolis and St. Paul—were as clean as a declarative sentence, as easy to move around in as one of those great old houses on Lake of the Isles in Minneapolis or on Summit Avenue in St. Paul. I've never again seen the changing of the leaves in fall as gorgeous in all their hues of yellow and brown and purple and red as they were along the banks of the Mississippi, or in the well-tended parks in which you saw their reflections in the area's many lakes. Willee and I liked it from the beginning.

But it does get cold there—the snow comes as though left over from the Ice Age. Signs on some of the larger streets informed drivers that these were "Snow Emergency Routes." The signs drew a glance from visitors and were not taken down even in summer. Not having seen such signs even in Chicago, I asked someone about this. "Remove them?" she said. "For three days?"

I was once invited to go ice fishing. I was told about this quaint local custom, in which people either sit outside, mufflered like mummies, and peer down a hole, or they erect wood and tin shacks as soon as the lakes freeze over. People in those houses bring in furniture and heaters and television sets and schnapps, carve holes in the ice of the living-room floor, and dangle lures down those holes.

I thought I'd try it. "We'll go to White Bear Lake," my host said. "It's pretty safe there."

"Safe?" I said. "You mean some aren't safe?"

"Well," he said, "some guys rush the season, or there's a weak spot in the ice. And sometimes people driving their cars or trucks on the lake go down in it. Houses float away sometimes, too."

"In other words," I said, "people drown while ice fishing?"

"Happens all the time," he said.

I didn't make it ice fishing that weekend, and it is still something I have yet to try. It's an acquired taste, I'm sure, perhaps like powdered snake, a Japanese delicacy that I have also been offered and turned down.

I had been at the *Minneapolis Tribune* for nearly two years when I was assigned to cover the Kentucky Derby, little knowing that I'd be covering a drama that went beyond the stables and the twin spires of Churchill Downs, and the mint juleps.

Dr. Martin Luther King, Jr., who had organized boycotts of buses and shops and restaurants in seeking to bring equality to blacks, now lent his support to a movement in Louisville that threatened the orderly running of an American sports institution, the Derby.

It was early May 1967 when I went to Louisville to cover the 93rd running of the legendary race. At the *Tribune* I had been covering everything from high school and college sports to the professional teams, the baseball Twins and the football Vikings, as well as auto racing, golf, tennis, ice skating, and anything else that, in many cases, no one else wanted to write. Being low man on the totem pole as well as in the scheduling, I offered my services wherever there was an opening. I also wrote book reviews and did my required—and anguished—stint on the copy desk when

I wasn't out reporting. The routine of the copy desk was stifling to me—writing headlines, editing other people's copy, answering phone calls from readers irate or otherwise—especially since I wanted to write. But the experience was helpful in dealing with the great difficulties of getting the facts right, a problem that plagues all writers. Every time you think you remember something and don't have to look it up, your memory will (in too many cases for me) play a trick on you. And the copy came in droves. You had to be on your toes. More than once, in March 1966, I wrote a headline using the team that lost instead of the team that won. Sometimes the mistake was caught.

To add a little zest to my life on the copy desk, I would try to write amusing headlines or cutlines (captions) to photographs. Once, I was assigned the cutline for a picture of the Vass Loppet, the biggest ski race in the world, in Mora, Sweden. In the photo, taken presumably from a mountain overlooking the start of the race, it appeared that the figures of all 6,597 competing skiers from 13 nations (I noted those statistics) were in view, though no face was discernible. "Sweden's Janne Stefansson won the 50-mile race in just under six hours," I added. "In the photo, Stefansson, very unofficially, is 322nd from the left." Of course, it was impossible to tell from the picture just which one Stefansson was.

The executive editor, a man named Bower Hawthorne, who received the first edition of the paper at home, phoned the sports desk, howling that this cutline had to be changed. "Not funny," he said. I was admonished never to put anything false in the paper again. I thought it *was* funny, but I also thought, upon reflection, that Hawthorne was right. You had to trust what you were reading if the paper were to retain legitimacy, even in a cutline about a madcap ski race.

The Kentucky Derby, however, was a plum assignment. Maybe it was a reward for never having called in sick—hard to say, as I look back on it, since I never considered myself in the favored-nation category at the newspaper. The paper didn't normally cover horse racing since pari-mutuel betting was illegal in the state. But an influential local businessman had a float in the Derby parade, and the editors thought this might be a good time to cover that as well as, if it had to be, the Derby itself. It would the first time in twenty-five years that the *Tribune* had a live body at the event.

I would, of course, report on the Derby hopefuls, such as Damascus and Ruken and Successor, the favorites, and give less attention to a long shot named Proud Clarion. And I'd report on the history and color and geniality of the Derby, and sniff around for other stories, like "Is the blue grass really blue?" (it's not—it's not even turquoise but green, like mundane grass).

From the very start of my arrival, though, I began writing two stories a day, one for the sports page from the racetrack, and one for the front page from the streets, at the request of the city desk.

Demonstrators had been marching for several weeks in Louisville, with the slogan, "No Housing, No Derby." On the Monday I flew into the city, May 1, several demonstrators, including the Reverend A. D. Williams King, brother of Dr. King, were jailed in sit-ins around the track after efforts to dramatize demands for an open-housing ordinance.

On Tuesday of that week, the day of the Derby Trial, a terrifying scene took place. I was seated in the press box, a perch above the stands, with a clear view of the handsome track, the neon lights of the scoreboard, the infield that was already filling up, the trees that shaded the barns on the backside, the clear, wide blue sky above on this sunny day. During the running of the first race, a race I had decided not to wager my two or four dollars on, I was looking over the form chart when someone nearby let out a gasp. Someone else shrieked, "Oh my God!"

Startled, I looked up to see five teenage black males in street clothes suddenly and inexplicably appear at the head of the home stretch. They sauntered down the muddy track toward the finish line, as if meandering down a city boulevard to an ice cream parlor, their backs to the horses that would soon be bearing down on them.

As the charging horses, weighing some twenty tons combined, made the turn for the stretch drive, the youths began to trot. The horses neared. I sat stunned and horrified as I watched this scene, fearing the worst. The kids ran. At almost the last possible moment before being trampled they leaped over the inside rail as the horses pounded past. Many in the crowd let out a sigh of relief; there was even a patter of applause, in appreciation that no one had been killed.

The teenagers were chased by policemen on the infield and caught and arrested, along with twelve others in the grandstands who were suspected conspirators, for disturbing the peace and trespassing. It was obviously another protest action by open-housing supporters. Although Dr. King disavowed a direct connection with this group, the incident only heightened the atmosphere of uncertainty and peril.

The annual Pegasus Parade was scheduled for Thursday, two days before the Derby, but was canceled by the Festival Committee for fear of disruption.

The civil rights group threatened a demonstration at Churchill Downs on the day of the big race. I remember attending a rally led by the civil rights leaders, including Dr. King, at a West End church in Louisville, and feeling the passion and determination that was thick in the air.

On the Friday night just before Derby Day, a group of about forty open-housing advocates, black and white, sat in a light rain in front of the main entrance to the empty, dark Churchill Downs tracks. They burned candles, and their faces were partially in shadow. They sang freedom songs and, while they did, policemen in helmets and riot gear arrived and hauled them off to jail, charging them with disorderly conduct, as I watched and as I would report.

Early the next morning, Dr. King spoke at a news conference, with, among others of his entourage, a young minister named Jesse Jackson, with whom, in his forays into sports, I would occasionally cross paths again in years to come.

Dr. King said there would be no protest march on Churchill Downs. "The action would prove," he said, "that we did not want to disrupt the Derby for the sake of disruption. We hope that we are proving good faith, and that it will influence the people and the city fathers to improve their flexibility."

Derby Day dawned grey and rainy. At Churchill Downs, despite Dr. King's assurances, there was an air of tension. A security force of about 2,500 was spread around the track.

The umbrella-dotted crowd was believed to be about 15,000 fewer than the 100,000 annually reported for the Derby. Whether the smaller crowd was due to civil rights concerns or the wet day was hard to say.

The Derby was run without incident, other than that the 30-to-1 shot, Proud Clarion, with Bobby Ussery in the irons, came from well back in the pack to win.

Dr. King did not attend the race. He boarded a plane to Atlanta at eleven that morning. One year later, in Memphis to organize a protest against the all-white hiring practices of the sanitation workers, he was assassinated.

While my reporting from Louisville was as objective as I could make it, the writer invariably has his human emotions and predilections. "All writing slants the way a writer leans," wrote E. B. White, "and no man is perpendicular, although many men are born upright." Whether my leanings seeped into my reporting or not, I'm not sure. I would hope not, for, as the saying goes in sportswriting, there should be no cheering in the press box. No booing, for that matter, either.

But my sympathies lay unequivocally with Dr. King and his intentions. I had grown up on the West Side of Chicago, a neighborhood that, by the time I was nine or ten years old, had become racially mixed. My first black friend, neighbor, and classmate was Willie Rockett, a soft-spoken but genial kid with a warm smile. He lived a block away from my apartment house, in what I recall was a wooden structure beside an alley. Willie's father did janitorial work, and I distinctly had the impression that Willie's family was poor. Years afterward, I ran into Willie in a restaurant in Chicago, and we recalled some of the times we had together. I remembered in my mind an afternoon when some of us were playing baseball, and the mother of one of the white kids came by and grabbed her son. "You're not going to play with *him*," and hauled him off. "Willie, I never asked you this," I said, while we stood talking, "but when did you realize you were black?" "When I was about nine or ten," he said, "and a mother took her son away when we were playing ball." Although I remained silent in the face of an adult's action, I remember feeling sick when that happened. I can scarcely imagine how Willie felt.

My mother worked with my father in the dry-cleaning store, which was on the corner across the street from where we lived on Springfield Avenue and Roosevelt Road. When I was a small boy, the man who came around to wash the store windows with a long-handled squeegee was a black man named Calvin, who wore glasses and an ever-present cap as he appeared carrying his water bucket. I never knew his last name. He was a good golfer, I learned, playing in "Negro tournaments," as they were called, and sometimes spoke to my father about wishing he had had a chance to play in the Professional Golf Association tournaments. He was prohibited from doing so by a "Caucasians Only" clause in the association's rules.

It seemed unfair, even to my adolescent sensibilities, that Calvin should be excluded because of how he was born. I didn't dwell on it, though, until years later when, as was the case with the King-led protest in Louisville for open and fair housing practices, I came in direct contact again with prejudice and discrimination.

Was I more sensitive to it because I was Jewish? I don't know. But growing up, the words of my father would resonate with me in this matter, as they have for all of my life. He had said, regarding the blacks, "Their freedom is our freedom." And: "If you're in a room with some people, and the black man walks out, and the others start talking negatively about him, rest assured that when you walk out they'll be saying similar things about you."

When he was the director of health and safety for Cook County employees, my father was once asked to take a few visiting Japanese politicians to lunch. On the way, the visitors mentioned that they had been told that black people in America were lazy, that they didn't like to work.

"Let's take a ride before lunch," my father said.

He drove to Forty-seventh Street on the South Side of Chicago.

"See that postman there delivering mail?" he asked. The mailman was black.

"See that beauty shop there?" he asked again. The beauty operators, the Japanese politicians could plainly see, were black.

"And the bus driver," he said, nodding toward the bus that had stopped at the corner to pick up passengers.

The visitors got the picture.

And so had I. Stereotype people at your own risk, and ignorance.

As for stereotypes, in 1965, my first year at the *Tribune*, there were no black professional coaches or managers or even quarterbacks: it was a rule of thumb among the white football establishment that (a) they were too dumb to remember the plays (this includes colleges) and (b) white players wouldn't take orders from them. All that has changed. When I began at the *Tribune*, women athletes were considered virtually nonexistent; ballplayers were happy to have you take them to lunch because they weren't earning much more than you (I began at $120 a week); and people were flying in machines to outer space only in science fiction.

In some ways it seems like an eternity ago. In other ways it's only yesterday. Stories from the press box today are sent by computer, but stories when I first began at the *Minneapolis Tribune* were sent to the paper by Western Union telegrapher. A far cry, however, from the days when carrier pigeons were used to transmit stories from press boxes. Ben Wright, who was then a CBS-TV golf commentator and a weekly columnist for the *Financial Times* of London, told me this story:

In a stadium in Glasgow around the turn of the last century occurred an exciting soccer match between archrivals the Celtic, who were Catholic, and the Rangers, who were Protestant. The press box was near the roof. On the roof were the pigeon coops. With them was the dispatcher who took the running play-by-play of the reporters. The dispatcher quickly folded the copy, slipped it into a capsule on the pigeon's foot, and with a slap of the hand and an "Off! Off!" sent the pigeon fluttering away to the home office and the anxious editor. As the match continued and tension mounted, the number of pigeons on the roof dwindled.

Finally, just one pigeon remained. The game ended in a great flurry. A winning goal was scored! Frenzy on the field, and in the stands, and on the roof!

A reporter named Frank Moran dashed off the final score and thrust the paper at the dispatcher. The dispatcher, who was also caught up in the moment, grabbed the note, snatched the last pigeon, slapped the winged courier, and shouted, "Off!"

The word had barely escaped his lips when the dispatcher looked down in his hand. He stared at the piece of copy paper he was still holding with the score on it.

Above the tumult, the dispatcher screamed at the soaring pigeon: "CELTIC 2, RANGERS I!"

Wright said that Moran insisted the story was true. As for Ben Wright, he said he never did ask Frank whether, for the next match, they used parrots.

When I began my professional journalism career my newspaper refused to cover television. I once proposed a story about the local television announcers for the Minnesota Twins' baseball games, who were "homers," as the vernacular has it, that is, essentially cheerleaders instead of objective reporters, offering one-sided views of a contest in favor of the locals. "We're in competition with television," said the managing editor. "We don't write about our competition." How that has changed! The hiring of broadcast "homers" by ball clubs, however, is still in obvious evidence.

At the *Tribune* I ran into difficulties early. On the sports desk was an old, gruff, bald-headed man named Lou Greene, whose very stare could wither even a veteran reporter. He was often the slot man, with his paste pot handy for tearing a story apart, the last man to check the copy. At night he saw the paper to bed. Lou Greene was such a tough egg that stories abounded about him. One night he was taking copy from the copy boy and looking at each of several stories and then spiking the ones he didn't want to use on the long-needled spike to his right. As was his custom, he slammed the stories down without even looking at the spike, knowing exactly where the steel needle was. But once it happened that he clapped a piece of copy down, and another, without looking at it. Then he glared straight ahead at the several copy editors around the desk.

"Who moved the spike?" he growled.

His hand was bleeding because somehow the spike was not in the expected spot on the desk.

"Boy!" he called to the copy boy, "get me a wrap." He still had not looked at his hand.

No one took credit for having moved the spike. I assume it was just an error, though sometimes I still wonder.

One night shortly after I arrived at the paper, I was working the desk. The paper was on deadline, and Lou Greene was downstairs in the composing room. I marked the last of the hockey copy—some of which was supposed to be agate (that is, small type, about 6-point)—and sent it down to him through the pneumatic tube. Within moments I heard a tremendous bellow that shook the building.

"Who set the agate in 9-point type!" It was Lou Greene, rather enraged. I had mistakenly done that.

One pictured the type overflowing the composing table, and Lou Greene's thumbs twitching to get at the neck of the young deskman who had marked the copy incorrectly. Greene obviously restrained himself, for there was nothing in the news afterward about his having committed homicide.

Another of my tasks was answering telephone calls to the sports department from local sports fans who, surely, had only left their ice-fishing shacks to gather more fortifications against the bone-chilling cold.

Once, a fairly inebriated voice, with more inebriated voices in the background, said, "My buddy and I got a five-dollar bet. I say Billy Conn went the distance against Louis in their first fight. He says he didn't. Which is it?" I looked it up and came back to the phone.

"Louis knocked him out in both fights," I told the man.

"You see," he hollered away from the receiver, "I was right. Conn went the distance."

You were supposed to jump up and grab the phones, but I was not eager to do this since I was unhappy on the desk and wanted more of a chance to write. Lou Greene and the sports editor, Sid Hartman, were often less than pleased with my desk performance. Hartman, the legendary, widely read columnist, has been the butt of jokes, good-natured and otherwise, for years in the Minnesota area for his sometimes dubious persistence in chasing stories (he once followed an athlete into the shower) as well as cozying up to sports figures.

He was narrowly focused: I remember him getting into an accident as he drove his car while reading the sports section with which he had covered the steering wheel.

One of the legends concerning Hartman dealt with Zoilo Versalles, the Twins' star shortstop. He had come to America from Cuba, just before Castro came to power. But now his wife and children were in Cuba and having problems getting visas out of the country to join Versalles here. Hartman repeatedly went by Versalles's locker to ask when his wife was coming to Minneapolis.

One day Versalles looked at Hartman before answering yet another of Sid's questions. "Seed," Versalles said in his Cuban accent, "how come you always asking about my wife? You want to fook her?"

When I wrote one of my first stories, a piece of about five paragraphs on a local high school football player, Hartman came by the desk the next day and slapped me on the back. "Good story," he said. "Keep 'em short."

When I was off the desk and on assignment, such as doing a sidebar on the Twins, I was enthusiastic. One time I told Hartman, who was at the ballpark, that I had two stories. I soon reported what I had to the sports desk. I was told, "Just do one story."

I had been hired over Sid Hartman's head, it turned out, and he hadn't been thrilled with it. He was told he was getting another writer. He was skeptical. "Everyone wants to be Damon Runyon," he had told someone on the desk.

At one point Greene and Hartman seemed so antagonistic toward me that I had the feeling they wanted to fire me. One day, perhaps two months after I had joined the paper, Hartman called me into his office. I had no idea what it was about. Hartman was not about circumspection. "You're a smart young man, but I think you picked the wrong profession," he said. There wasn't much more. I staggered out of his office. It was dinner-break time– I started at four to get the first edition out at seven, and worked until one in the morning–and Willee was picking me up to go out for a meal together.

"What's wrong?" she said, seeing my expression as I got into the car.

I was near tears.

And I told her.

She was encouraging, but I wondered: How do I go back to Chicago a total failure? What would I do next? Go back to Maxwell Street?

The managing editor, the top person in the news department at the *Tribune*, called me into his office. I wasn't being fired, but he explained to me that I had to do better, particularly on the desk. "But," he said, "I think you have a bright future." He had also given me a few suggestions about my stories–I was trying too hard, I was sometimes too wordy. He supported me. There were very few Jews on the *Minneapolis Tribune* in those days—I really didn't ascribe my situation to anti-Semitism—and only two, Greene and Hartman, in the sports department. But the two of them gave me some of my most difficult moments. The managing editor's name was Daryle Feldmeir; he was of German descent.

This was just twenty years after the end of the Holocaust in Germany, a moment in history that seemed close to me. Not only had I read a lot about it, and knew survivors—some of them relatives—but just a year earlier I had traveled to Europe with Willee and we had visited Auschwitz, the death camp in Poland. The barracks into which the Jews had been herded, the chimneys where Jews had become smoke, the glass cases to the ceiling that contained the canes and crutches of the slaughtered, and their eyeglasses, and the saved hair that was to be used for lampshades, was all there. I walked around the premises for perhaps two hours, the whole time with a choking feeling. When I went to Germany, every German in uniform, from a trolley-car conductor to a hotel doorman to a policeman directing traffic, made me feel uneasy.

And now here was Feldmeir giving me a needed boost, with never a mention by either of us of any of that. I was grateful to him, of course, as a young man just starting shakily in his dreamed-of profession. And it also dispelled what stereotypes of Germans I might still have harbored.

In July 1966, a year after I joined the *Tribune,* I was assigned to cover a golf tournament, the Trans-Mississippi Amateur Golf Championship, held in the Edina Country Club in suburban Minneapolis. I knew virtually nothing about golf, having played only a few times as a boy when my father and his friend took me to a public course in Chicago. And my father, whose work consumed much of his time, had tried it a few times in those days only because his friend was an avid player. So I was apprehensive but delighted to get a writing assignment. I spent four days following the golfers around, and I latched onto Mike Lamey, who was covering the event for the *St. Paul Pioneer Press*. Mike knew golf and was generous with insights. What's that? And Mike explained.

Why are they doing this? And Mike was free with information. Mike and I became friends. The four-day match-play tournament turned out to be more interesting than I had imagined—especially the semifinals, in which future pros Bob Smith beat Bob Dickson, and Jim Wiechers, the eventual winner of the tournament, defeated Bob Murphy.

The heat, however, was stifling, the matches long and grueling, the golfers weary and sweat-stained as both semifinal matches went into extra holes, beyond the scheduled thirty-six. Smith and Dickson went forty-two holes and the other match thirty-seven. My lead was: "It was a simple tale, really. Nothing more spectacular than four guys playing exciting pressure golf until they nearly dropped." My pieces on the tournament were well received.

A few months later, at the annual Newspaper Guild of the Twin Cities' "Page One" Awards ceremony, I found myself being handed the first-place plaque for "best spot-news story of the year" for my account of the semifinals of the Trans-Mississippi golf tournament. Mike Lamey came in third with his story on that same tournament. For a while after that, Mike Lamey gave me the cold shoulder. It was deserved.

My situation improved at the *Tribune*, but there were still glitches. Pat Reusse, then a copy boy at the paper and now its fine sports columnist, told a story relating to Hartman and me. In the book *Sid!*, written "by Sid Hartman with Patrick Reusse" (the only writer's autobiography I know of that was ghostwritten by someone else), Reusse writes the following in his preface:

"Berkow had occasion to cover a game in which a team kept making comeback after comeback, only to fall short. Berkow's story compared the losing team's effort to Sisyphus's attempt to push a heavy stone up a slope. Sid saw that lead and bellowed across the newsroom: 'Sisyphus? Who is he writing about now? I never heard of Sisyphus. What team does he play for?'

"Berkow kept going to Sid and complaining about the lack of opportunity he was being given to write truly inspiring sports stories. Finally, Sid decided to give the kid a break. He stretched the *Tribune*'s sports travel budget and sent Berkow to Louisville for the Kentucky Derby.

"This was the mid-sixties, when out-of-town copy was transmitted directly to the sports desk by Western Union machines. The transmitting operator would bang the key that sounded the bell jangling a few times to let the people in the newsroom know that a story was starting. Sid had been waiting nervously to see what young Berkow was going to transmit on the first day in Louisville–spending all that *Tribune* money, twenty-five bucks for a hotel, six bucks for dinner, a few bucks for cabs.

"The Western Union machine jangled and Sid raced across the room. As it turned out, Berkow had gone to see the famous racehorse Citation, retired at a thoroughbred farm in the rolling hills of Kentucky. Not only did Berkow see Citation, he engaged in a mythical conversation with the great, four-legged champion.

"Sid watched as the story came in, line by line. First, he looked puzzled. Then, he turned ashen, as the realization of what Berkow had done with this first great opportunity to write, struck him.

"'I knew this was a terrible mistake,' Sid said. 'The son of a bitch interviewed a horse.'"

Quite a story, I must admit, though only some of it is true. I interviewed Citation's trainer, down to the colorful Kentucky accent that I tried my best to capture. I imagine it sounded like a horse to Sid, or whatever he believed a horse speaks like, since I don't think Sid was ever near an actual live horse.

But maybe Pat was remembering an auto racing story I did, where there was an old car and a new car on exhibit, and I had the cars in a dialogue and comparing their experiences and valve distributors. The piece worked well enough that the organizers of the exhibit sent me a case of a dozen bottles of wine, each bottle from a different country. It was terrific, and troublesome. I knew there was a policy against accepting gifts–or, as the paper saw it, bribes. But this was harmless, wasn't it? And the wines looked so good! I circled the box that sat in our living room for a couple days, then called one of the editors and explained the situation. Sorry, but you'll have to return the wine. And I did, painful as it was. It had, though, a cleansing feeling of the incorruptible reporter.

I was now getting more and more assignments. In fact I had become the auto racing editor of the paper. There was little auto racing, and no one on the staff wanted the job anyway, so I jumped at it as another chance to write. Which is how I came by the nickname "Wheels." The assignment was short-lived. I hated it. I never got excited about seeing cars run around and around an oval. (I never got very excited about cars, period, and never learned even to fix a flat tire.) And when you figure in the pit stops, you never know who's ahead and who's lapped whom. Besides, what kind of sport is it, anyway, when your garage mechanic is paramount to your success?

I also thought that auto races like the Indy 500 were for people who had either lost their minds or were just indifferent to life in general. At the Minnesota State Fairgrounds I interviewed Johnny Rutherford, who would go on to win the Indianapolis 500, about a crash he had had that year at Indianapolis, in which the driver Eddie Sachs was killed. We stood in the infield the day before the race, as the practicing cars made such loud noise with their vroom, vroom that I nearly had to read Rutherford's lips to understand him.

"Sure, you feel bad when something like that happens, and you get cold chills thinking about it," he said, as I put my ear right up to his mouth, "but I felt no fear before or after about racing. If I did, I'd quit."

I asked Mario Andretti, "After all these years, do you still get nervous before a race?"

"It hasn't changed in twenty-five years," he replied. "You still get butterflies because you never know how it's going to come out. I can't wait till it's over." That made two of us.

I also covered some of the smaller tracks around the state. I did a story on one of them in which I thought the owner of the track was engaging in financial shenanigans.

The aggrieved track owner wrote me a letter, addressed to "Mr. Dum Dum Berkow." He left out the "b's" in Dum Dum, which gave me satisfaction.

I was trying hard to impress, and thought I had to make every story a prizewinner, and break news, and, most important, give the reader the most truthful portrayal I could. Once I went too far.

I had covered a basketball game between two private high schools. The teams weren't of the highest caliber, but one of the schools had a tall freshman center.

After the game the coach of the team with the freshman center, the team that lost, said to me in the cramped locker room after the game that his center was awkward and had a lot to learn.

I wrote the story, quoting the coach the way he told this to me. The next day I got a call from the coach. I thought he was going to compliment me on a factually accurate story.

"It was a factually accurate story," he told me, "and you had my quotes right. But I'm sorry you had to repeat my remarks about the kid. He's only a freshman, and I didn't mean for you to write that. Thousands of people are going to read this. He's just a young amateur player. It hurt him. I hope it doesn't impact on his future."

I hoped it wouldn't either. And I apologized to the coach. A reporter has to use judgment and taste, and, in this instance I didn't use either. I was mortified and hoped the kid would recover—I believe he did—and that I would learn from this knock in the head.

Covering a University of Minnesota football game at Memorial Stadium in Minneapolis in early October 1966, I learned that Vice President Hubert Humphrey, class of '39 and once the mayor of Minneapolis and a senator from the state, was in the stands. He was with the governor, Karl Rolvaag, and was wearing a "Yea, Yea Gophers" button on his suit jacket lapel. I went up to get an impression of the game from Humphrey. In the closing minutes, the Gophers were losing to Kansas by an insurmountable margin. Rolvaag rose to go. Humphrey put his hand on the governor's arm to keep him in his seat. "If the ship goes down," said Humphrey, "we go with her." Two years later, nearly to the month, Humphrey was narrowly defeated by Richard Nixon in his bid to become President of the United States. It was widely believed that his insistence on his loyalty to President Johnson's ill-fated backing of the Vietnam War, and his refusal to come out against the war until it was too late, influenced the margin of difference. As with the Minnesota football game, it seemed to me that Humphrey "went down with the ship."

At the *Tribune* I continued my periodic correspondence with Red Smith.

Now I was a professional writer, but I was still learning the craft, to put it kindly. I wrote a book review, the first piece with my byline at the *Tribune*, about a Chicago lawyer I admired named Elmer Gertz. The book was called *A Handful of Clients*, one of the clients being Nathan Leopold, for whom Gertz had secured parole, after thirty-three and a half years in jail. Leopold, of course, along with Richard Loeb, made up the infamous pair of brilliant teenagers who in 1924 murdered Leopold's cousin, a boy named Bobby Franks, in what had been called the "Crime of the Century." The boys were, as I wrote in the review, "saved from the gallows by the oratory of their attorney," Clarence Darrow. The review appeared about a month after my arrival, and I sent it to Smith. He replied, August 25, 1965:

Dear Ira:

It was good to hear from you and I think that was a good review. I don't have it at hand now, but may I quibble with a single word?

If I remember, in the second column of the wrap-around (strange how clear visual memory can be) you referred to "self-styled censors" or maybe to "self-appointed" something else. I can't remember the exact context, but I do remember thinking that you really meant the other word, whichever way it went.

This is, admittedly, lint-picking. I wouldn't raise an objection of the error (if it was an error) if it appeared in a news story written on deadline, because as my old professor of journalism used to hammer into us, "Newspaper work is knowing, not writing." In other words, the essential thing is to report the facts; if there's time for good writing as well, that's frosting on the cake. But in a book review where there's time for it, we should grope for the exact word.

I apologize for quibbling.

Best, Red.

Yes, I'd go for the essentials. But I was also seeking that "frosting on the cake." It was, after all, what set Red Smith apart. Did I say "seeking"? I guess it was more like "lurching" toward it.

In a typed memo to me, with carbons to the assistant managing editor, Wally Allen, as well as to the sports editors Sid Hartman and Merrill Swanson, managing editor Daryle Feldmeir wrote the following, dated September 26, 1966, regarding my coverage of a football game between two prominent local high school teams:

"Ira . . . I attended the Edina-Richfield football game Friday night and when I read your story in the barber shop on Saturday, I thought it was an excellent account of the game.

"The story had a major defect, and I want you to know what it is because I believe it will improve your future stories. It was the same defect which was present in your Saturday story of September 17.

"Quite simply, your first three paragraphs were overwritten. Once you are beyond the lead paragraphs, the story flows smoothly. But the lead paragraphs are so artificial and contrived, they affect the reader adversely. I believe you simply are trying too hard to draw the reader into the story. Believe me, you do not have to worry whether the readers will read the account of this game. A straightforward news lead is all you need.

"I know that sportswriting tends to be more colorful than straight news reporting, but the tendency too frequently is to overdo it. Much of the color can be present in the construction of the story. It is not necessary to garnish the story with overly dramatic opening paragraphs.

"Once I was beyond your lead, the story was an excellent account of what happened."

Not only was I learning how to develop my prose, as it were, but I was gaining other lessons, sometimes equally embarrassing but instructive. To use a common vernacular, I was getting my consciousness raised.

It got raised in another area as well. Growing up in my days, girls never had much to do with athletics, apart from cheerleading. A women's softball league operated in the Chicago area, with the best team being named the "Bloomer Girls," the stars a pair of sisters, Freda and Olympia Savona. But they seemed aberrations and quite a bit more muscular than most women or girls of my acquaintance. And so, on July 31, 1966, I published a story about young women playing softball, which bore the headline: "Yup, 'Diamonds' are a Girl's Best Friend," with the subhead: "Let's Get 'Em, Guys."

I didn't write the headlines, happily, but now wish I hadn't written the story, either. The story began: "In a game with a hair-raising—if not hair-pulling—denouement, the little softball ladies from Ron-D-Voo beer parlor clawed and scratched (figuratively) their way to a 4-1 win Saturday over les femmes from Addison tippling house. . . . This was for all the cookies. . . . It was—grip your seat—for the championship of the Women's Park Board Slow Pitch Tournament." It may be hard to believe, but it got worse.

In a day or so I received a tear sheet in my mailbox at the *Tribune* (our companion paper, the *Minneapolis Star*, shared those boxes with us) with my story and a note appended to it:

"This is what I call exploitive journalism & inaccurate reporting. Your brand of humor we, the female jocks of Minneapolis, don't need." Signed, "Sarah Jones, shortstop, Star and Tribune Newsettes."

It was mortifying. I thought I was simply having fun. But it was the line from E. B. White that struck at the heart of the matter. "He was full of fun," White once wrote, "but he wasn't funny." The note made an impact on me. How stupid not to comprehend it before—that the women were as serious and taking as much pleasure in their sports as guys do.

How I hadn't comprehended the feelings of women before that was stunning to me. It was one more lesson I learned, or hoped to, in my growth as a sportswriter, and a man.

⌒ Over a Christmas vacation, Willee and I drove to her parents' home in Corydon, in southern Indiana. I was driving our blue Plymouth down a dark country road that was newly paved, with our headlights the lone lights on the road. The road shimmered in its blackness like a pitch of ebony sky illuminated only with the yellowness of the moon. I had just rounded a bend, one of several on this road, and I stepped on the gas pedal to proceed when Willee shouted, "A cow! A cow!" I slammed on the brakes and simultaneously swerved slightly, which probably saved our lives, but we crashed into the animal, knocking it to the side of the road. If we had caught it straight-on and it had rolled up the hood and onto our windshield, we would have been crushed to death. Our headlights were shattered, and I heard the fan belt groan to a halt. I pumped the gas pedal. It was dead. I tried the light knob; nothing. Willee and I got out of the car, shaken. She said she was okay, other than a scratch on her face when she bumped against the windshield upon impact. It was cold. I put my arm around her and felt her trembling. Everything was darkness, save for the chirp of crickets and our uneven breathing. But by the light of the moon and stars we were able to see the dead cow, lying in a ditch. At some point a pair of illuminated tentacles glided toward us. A rumble came into earshot. A car slowed and pulled off to the opposite side of the road. A young man emerged.

"Hey," he called from his driver's seat, "you all right?" We assured him we were. He said he'd call the police, and left. Soon a squad car appeared, along with a wrecking truck, to haul away our car.

The cow had crossed the road, it turned out, because the electricity on the fence where she was kept had gone off. But as I looked at the bloody corpse, I noticed standing near her another cow. Her companion. The red light that flashed from the police car shone on her, and she had the widest, saddest eyes I'd ever seen.

I've thought of that over the years. For, in another way, certainly less disastrous, Willee and I, were growing apart. We had had some good times in Minneapolis, making friends, enjoying the theater and the cultural activities of the Twin Cities. Willee was particularly active and had a talent for theatrical activities at the junior high school where she taught English. But there were problems. My hours at the paper generally called for me to work at night, sitting at the copy desk when I wasn't out reporting. I was off during the day, and only a few weekends. And she, teaching, went to school in the daytime and was off weekends. It was an untenable situation. She also wanted children. I didn't, not at this time, anyway. I told her that, as I was trying to make my way as a writer, I needed the freedom to move to another part of the country if the opportunity presented itself. A family with children, I thought, would greatly inhibit me.

And, as not infrequently happens in such situations, the parties look for other interests, other people.

One man of our acquaintance, who wasn't married, became a particularly good friend of hers, I learned. He was available when I wasn't, and he was a good companion to her, gentle, well-educated, a good guy. And even when Willee and I were together, I know I was often distracted, given the pressures—some self-imposed, to be sure—of trying to make my mark in the world of journalism, Minneapolis style. A young, attractive woman, with a broad intellectual curiosity, can find this lifestyle not only boring, but stifling. And I know Willee did.

In the passing days and weeks, however, there was increasing pain for Willee and me in the marriage, and confusion. It was a time when I searched my background for answers. I wondered if my not having a lot of women close to me in my life—that is, no sisters, no female cousins with whom I had close associations, no real understanding of women—was responsible for some of the problems Willee and I had. I tried to look inside myself, and get a handle on all this. I had had girl friends, I'd had relationships with girls and women, but was I lacking maturity? Was I lacking insight? Was I lacking sensitivity? Or all of the above.

Willee and I saw a marriage counselor. That was of little help. Perhaps Willee and I, with differing personalities, were simply not suited for each other. Maybe there was no one answer. Maybe there never is. As it was, the marriage unwound.

In the summer of 1967 I got a phone call from my old college friend and sports editor of the *Miami Student*, Dave Burgin, who had first introduced me to journalism by having me write for him.

"Murray Olderman is going to call you. He wants to hire you," said Burgin. Olderman was the sports editor of Newspaper Enterprise Association, the Scripps-Howard feature syndicate that had some 750 newspaper subscribers, from the *Chicago Daily News* to the *Lompoc* (California) *Gazette*. Burgin was on the staff of NEA. I had met Olderman, who was a nationally respected sportswriter and sports cartoonist, when I visited Burgin in the NEA office in New York City. And I had talked with Olderman again in Louisville when we were both covering the Derby earlier that spring.

"He's going to offer you $180 a week," said Burgin, "but hold out for $190. You can get it."

Hold out? Was he kidding? I was making $130 a week. Besides, why risk an opportunity to go to New York, which for most journalists was the mecca of the profession, where the greats like, well, Red Smith, plied their trade? I was 27 years old. I might never get a shot like this again.

"Okay," I told Burgin. But I still wasn't sure—not about the job, since I was dying to take it, but about haggling, even with my Maxwell Street experience.

Shortly after, the phone rang again. I thought I should let it ring twice, which is cool. I picked it up after the first ring. So much for cool when you're anxious. It had to be Olderman. It was. Sandy Padwe, one of the members of his staff, was leaving to become a sports columnist with the *Philadelphia Inquirer*, he told me. So there was an opening. "I'd like you to fill it," he said.

"Well, Murray," I said, losing my mind, "I'm kinda happy in Minneapolis."

"Well," he countered, "this is a great opportunity. You'll be expected to cover the big events and the biggest names in sports."

"That sounds enticing," I said.

"We can offer you $180 a week."

"Gee, New York's an expensive place to live, as I understand." At this point I should have been committed to a mental institution. Or maybe it was just my Maxwell Street genes in overdrive.

"How's $190?" Olderman asked.

"Sounds great," I said, returning to my senses. "When do I start?"

6

~~~~~~~~~~~~~~

You Can't Write That

I ARRIVED IN NEW YORK ALONE. Willee and I had separated after a four-year marriage. She decided to remain in Minneapolis, where she eventually married a man who was a news writer for the *Minneapolis Tribune.*

Not even Chicago could prepare one for life in Manhattan. I first lived for about a month in a hotel on Times Square before getting an apartment in Greenwich Village. My cousin Ian visited me once and, walking down the streets with the lights and sirens and people and cars, he remarked, "This is an assault on the senses." Another friend of mine, Herb Sirott, also from Chicago, noted the jostling crowds. We had breakfast the day after he had arrived in town. "You don't realize it until later," he said, "but after walking around the city all afternoon you've got black and blue marks all over your body." In Chicago, on an afternoon, an elevated train might be two or three cars long. In New York, at all hours, there'd be ten or twelve for a subway train.

And there was competition. I happened one morning to get a copy of *Newsday*, the Long Island daily, and read a terrific feature story about Willie Mays by Steve Jacobson, which gave me a sinking feeling. I thought, Can I ever match a piece like this?

In the first few days at Newspaper Enterprise Association, doing copyediting, I made a mistake that embarrassed me. And I worried that my boss, Murray Olderman, would think he'd made a mistake in hiring me. That night I remember lying in bed in my hotel room, the lights from Broadway flashing through my window blinds, and thinking, "Can't I do anything right?"

Just two weeks after I had begun work at NEA, at the beginning of October 1967, Muhammad Ali came to town. He had been exiled from boxing by disgraceful and cowardly officials just a few months earlier for his refusal to be drafted into the army during the Vietnam War. He was seeking ways to support himself and his family.

"Have you ever met Ali?" Olderman asked me.

"No," I said.

"Good. Call his hotel—it's the Americana on Seventh Avenue—and ask to see him," Murray said. "He'll be open to it. He does like to talk. And write what's there, what you see and what you feel."

So I did, and Ali was, not surprisingly, open to talk.

I knocked on his hotel-room door. "Come in," I heard a voice call. The door had been left slightly ajar. And there, in bed, covers to his neck, was The Champ.

He had a sheaf of lined notepad paper in his hand.

"This is what I gotta be restudying all the time," he said, his eyes widening, as I took a seat. "It's from the teachings of Elijah Muhammad, Allah's messenger. It's so pretty, and true. I been going all over the country preaching—San Diego, San Francisco, Chicago, Phoenix, and Newark."

Then he began to read slowly, about America—"the most sinfulest country in history"—and about whites—"the most evilest men on earth."

"Since the government took my title away," he said, "I been converting people to the Muslims. About seventeen hundred put X's on their names in five months. Boxing's child's play to this.

"I'm bigger now than I ever been. Peoples all over the world feel sorry for me. I got letters just yesterday from Athens, Greece, Germany, Asia, people wanting to know who this America is to take the world's title from me. It's not America's championship, they say, it's theirs and the world's."

Ali was then twenty-five years old, two years younger than I, but he seemed, even with his youthful demeanor and, as he admitted, "pretty face," to be carrying a great weight on his shoulders. I liked him—you had to like him, had to like his strength of character, his boyishness, his charm, even if you didn't agree with a lot of what he said, especially the business about "the white devil," since that would have included me. But in some areas he unquestionably made sense. He was a conscientious objector to the Vietnam War, and I too held a belief that the war was wrong. I didn't find America or white people as bad as he said they were, but there were things wrong with our society and with some of our people, without doubt.

I wrote what I felt. As I wrote other pieces about Ali, and the wrong perpetrated upon him by the pusillanimous boxing mainstream, I drew hate mail, all of it from whites who despised Ali. Some of the mail was marked with swastikas and "Jew liberal bastard" and lamented that Hitler had "missed" me. And some came from newspaper clients of NEA, particularly in the South, threatening to cancel their subscriptions to the feature service.

But others were taking notice and seeing it from a different standpoint.

In the 1972 book *Rip Off the Big Game: The Exploitation of Sports by the Power Elite*, by Paul Hoch, advertised as a "hard-hitting, radical, controversial analysis of the Sports Establishment," Jack Scott, a sports firebrand who would gain notoriety with his befriending of Patricia Hearst when she was on the lam from authorities, wrote the following in his introduction to Hoch's book:

"The various ills of American sports have been aptly described during the past few years by journalists such as Leonard

Shecter, Bob Lipsyte, Sandy Padwe, Ira Berkow, and a number of other courageous sportswriters who saw their work as something more than shilling for the sports establishment. . . ."

By then I was sports editor as well as a sports columnist for NEA. Olderman had moved up to managing editor, and he supported my stance toward the so-called sports establishment, even when some newspaper clients made good on their threatened cancellations.

I've saved a comment sent to Murray Olderman by a man named Jack Hairston, who was sports editor of the *Florida Times-Union* in Jacksonville.

"Dear Murray:

"The other day my managing editor asked if I would go along with canceling NEA. My first thought was of your superior work over the years and I asked that we be permitted to continue NEA. His reaction was such that I considered it an okay.

"Since then, the only things that have caught my eyes are a continuous campaign to make Cassius Clay the national hero and a batch of crap which I consider un-American." He then mentioned his distaste for a writer named Leonard Shecter. "Evidently," Hairston continued, "Berkow and others on your staff have leanings similar to his.

"I have advised my managing editor that I would like to have NEA cancelled and that if it is not cancelled, we will not be running any of it anyway, unless it is positively prize-winning material. . . .

"P.S. This is not a case of one or two articles displeasing me. It seems as though it's been months since Berkow wrote anything that we had use for whatsoever."

Now, NEA was in business to sell its product and not to lead crusades. But what was the business if you couldn't write with integrity and conviction, even if others disagreed? Olderman felt the same way. And I'm indebted to him for standing up for what he believed to be one man's honest opinions arrived at in a reasonable manner. Which is what he told me.

In that early interview, Ali had said, "I'd like to have a movie made of my life. Just one, for all these people to see. It would be a true-life story of me. Oh, I'd like that. It would start off on Monday morning, January 17, 1942, in Louisville General Hospital."

Ali's hands circled his left eye.

"The camera focuses down on this little ole baby boy who's crying. The music goes dum-de-dum-dum." His voice grew deeper. "This is the actual story of the man who shook up the world, who came from a little country town and was destined to sit with kings and monarchs, who turned down millions for a principle. . . . That would be a helluva movie, wouldn't it?"

It would, and several decades later such a movie along those lines was made called *When We Were Kings*, and won an Academy Award.

When Ali, who had retired as heavyweight champion, made his comeback in 1970, he was matched against Jerry Quarry in Atlanta, in a week-long scene that was reminiscent of Carnaval. Arriving from all over the country were more big, black cars, more ermines and pearls, more spiked heels and alligator shoes, more Borsalino hats than are seen in a year—a decade—anywhere else. I covered that event, which Ali won with a technical knockout in the fourth round, opening a gash so deep over Quarry's right eye that the ringside doctor said he could look down it and see the eyeball.

Ali's next major fight was against Joe Frazier, who had assumed the heavyweight title after Ali had been stripped of the belt. The fight essentially matched two undefeated world heavyweight champions—a first. I was there as well, in Madison Square Garden. It was the single most electric sports event I have ever covered. Every sportswriter I've ever spoken to who attended the fight has said the same thing. The hype, the hullabaloo, the anticipation of a stupendous event was sensational. In the pressroom before the fight, Bill Cosby was talking with reporters. "This is so exciting," he said, "I wish it could last forever." And for one of the few times in my memory, the event itself actually—and improbably—exceeded expectation.

Ali, the master showman, was the other side of the coin from Frazier, who was dogged and direct, unadorned with artifice or nuance, and packed a left hook that struck like a wrecking ball. A month earlier, when Frazier was training for his bout in a Catskills resort hotel, I thought it might be interesting to spar a round with him, just to see what it was like to be in the ring with such a menacing combatant. There is a small history of participatory journalism like this, and being thirty-one years old I thought I still had some of that left in me.

"Spar with him?" asked Yank Durham, Frazier's white-haired manager.

"Uh, yeah," I said. "Just to get a flavor? Give me greater insight into the sense of who he is and what he does."

"Did you ever box?"

"Some," I said. "There was a boxing ring in the third floor of the Fillmore police station where I lived on the West Side of Chicago. And I boxed a bit there. And I took a course in boxing in college."

"I see," said Durham. "Are you in shape?"

"Well, I play some basketball and I ride my bicycle around where I live, in Greenwich Village."

"Hmm," said Durham thoughtfully. "Then you'll get only two or three of your ribs broken. My man, he don't know how to play."

"Hmm," I replied. "Yank, I think I'll take a rain check on that sparring thing."

For the fight, I sat in the second row at ringside in the Garden, beside Olderman. I saw Frank Sinatra at the ring apron taking pictures for *Life* magazine—he cadged the credentials for the best seat he could get in the house—and nearby was Burt Lancaster, assigned to do radio commentary. The place was loaded with notables.

Then Frazier came through the ropes. The working man's boxer. Few frills. The crowd took quiet notice. And then here came Ali, in a striking crimson robe and white boxing shoes with tassels. The crowd erupted. The star of the show had come on stage. Under the hot, bright lights, Ali bounced around in his corner and then began a little journey around the ring—and suddenly brushed up against Frazier in the far corner! It appeared Ali threw a light, almost playful jab at the back of Frazier's head. Frazier turned nastily, and it appeared the fight might break out right there. But the combatants did wait for the opening bell in order to try to pummel each other.

Ali was so charismatic I couldn't take my eyes off him. As the fight went on, and he did his shuffle and his various crowd-pleasing maneuvers—he was the graceful toreador to Frazier's grim bull—my focus was virtually on Ali alone. After about the end of the fifth round, I said to Olderman, "I've got Ali on my scorecard winning all five rounds."

Olderman said, "I've got Frazier winning four rounds." I was stunned. What fight was Olderman watching? Then I realized I had been watching only half the fight because I was so mesmerized by Ali.

At the end—a brutal brawl that Frazier won by a clear decision, knocking Ali down twice—the other judges concurred with Olderman's observation. I had been fooled by Ali's show. I vowed never again to watch half a fight—or half of anything—and judge it on such evidence.

While I drew insights into the character of Ali and into boxing in general, I had meanwhile drawn another perspective on sports from what seemed a most unlikely source, an elderly woman who, it happened, also had once met Ali and been charmed by him ("Admittedly the classiest and the brassiest," she had said, taking a page from Ali's rhyming dictionary). She also happened to be one of America's most admired poets, Marianne Moore. She lived in Greenwich Village and was distinctive in her dress with the tricorne hats she favored, which looked like the kind of hats worn by men like Ben Franklin in colonial times.

But beyond her curious but engaging fashion statement, Miss Moore was no ordinary woman, or poet. I knew of her interest, however eclectic, in sports, and about her poems dealing with a racehorse named Tom Fool, the Brooklyn Dodgers, and baseball. In "Baseball and Writing," she wrote: "Writing is exciting / and baseball is like writing / you can never tell with either / how it will go / or what you will do."

I interviewed her in her fifth-floor apartment on East Ninth Street. She was eighty years old, a slight, grey-haired woman who still did exercise by hanging from a bar put up in the doorway to her bedroom.

She also had taught typing and shorthand at the Carlisle, Pennsylvania, Indian School in 1912 and 1913. One of her students was Jim Thorpe. "He was so limber and could perform wonderful feats with the grace of a leopard, and took no credit for his achievements," she said, in a thin but precise voice. "A very unaffected person. And, you know, he wrote in an old-fashioned Spencerian hand, very deliberate and elegant."

Only a few times in my four decades of writing professionally have I given a story to an interviewee to read before publication. This was no controversial piece, and I was relatively young and wanted to get the great poet's words right. I had taken notes, not tape-recorded her.

She made a few comments, all relatively minor, in the margins of my four typewritten pages. But one suggested change in particular struck me. In the original interview, when I asked if she looked forward to the coming baseball season, she said, "I look forward to it with much élan." She changed it, with a soft pencil, to read: "I have a lot of appetite for it." "Appetite" is much earthier, and considerably more baseball-like than "élan." She caught—and edited positively—the spirit of it.

And she told me something that has stayed with me through the years, giving me a greater appreciation of what athletes do, and another way to relate to them through my craft. "Sport," she said, "should be viewed as a legitimate triumph, a feat of skill, like writing."

⌒ Within two months after I arrived in New York, a remarkable thing happened to elevate a good portion of the city's population, and no one in the mayor's office had anything to do with it. It was the first step toward the era of what is still referred to by New York basketball fans as Camelot—the hiring of Red Holzman, who in December 1967 reluctantly took the job as head coach of the last-place Knicks. He had been the Knicks' chief scout for ten years, had seen six coaches fired by the Knicks in that time, and liked what he was doing.

Scouting gave Holzman enough time to challenge his creativity by analyzing and projecting the abilities of the players he observed; gave him time to spend with his wife, Selma, in their house in Cedarhurst, on Long Island, which was not much larger than a postage stamp; time to enjoy his glass or two of Scotch and a glass or two of wine with a steak dinner; time to watch the old movies at home while resisting a color television set ("What's wrong with black and white?"); time to read mystery novels and not have to shop for suits (he had nine, all the same color, navy blue: "Who's looking?" he wanted to know—so he ordered his clothes by mail: "They know my size"); all without the pressure of coaching. He had already coached professional teams in Milwaukee and St. Louis, had had some success, had been dismissed, and knew that coaches were hired to be fired.

At forty-seven, his once-red hair was turning grey and receding. It wasn't a time to switch horses. Unless . . .

"I had the strong feeling," Holzman later said about taking over the Knicks, "that if I didn't accept the job, I'd be fired."

No one ever accused Red Holzman of being stupid. His insights were even then the stuff of nods and smiles:

"Never trust a bald barber."

"Never accidentally raise your hand to make a point when the check is coming."

"Never talk money with your wife at night—otherwise you'll get no sleep."

"The best feeling in the world is to wake up early in the morning when you don't have to go anywhere."

When he coached the St. Louis Hawks, and the Hawks were suffering a beating, Holzman gathered his team at halftime. He pulled a picture of his baby daughter from his wallet and held it up for the players to see.

"Isn't she pretty?" he said. "Well, you guys are going to kill her if you keep playing this way. I'll get fired and I won't be able to feed her."

And later with the Knicks, when he was named general manager as well as coach, he had height notches cut on the side of the door to his office. When a new player and his agent came into his office, and the agent said, "Well, my man here is 6-foot-8," Holzman would reply, "No, he's 6-6." Holzman had measured the player by sight as he walked through the door.

The two of us went to dinner one night in a private restaurant in Madison Square Garden. The waiter, who was friendly with Holzman, came over and greeted him. He prepared to take the order. Holzman said, "James, is your soup hot tonight?" The waiter's eyes widened at the strange question. "Oh, certainly, Mr. Holzman." Red ordered the soup. Turned out, Holzman had had the soup the last time he was in the restaurant and found it lukewarm. So as not to insult the waiter now, but seeking to make certain the soup was hot, Red asked that unorthodox question. When the soup came, it was piping hot. The waiter had made certain it was. It was this kind of "backdoor" slant, the subtleties, that Holzman used with his players to great effectiveness.

So, using the uncommon common sense that he became widely known for, and which, as time went on, I cherished as we developed a close relationship, he became William (Red) Holzman, Knicks coach. As we all watched, he began to perform seeming miracles, and he did so with the kinds of players who were as accomplished after basketball as they were on the court, which is saying a great deal.

One was elected three times to the United States Senate and was a candidate for the Democratic presidential nomination (Bill Bradley); one graduated Phi Beta Kappa and could memorize the first five hundred pages of the Manhattan telephone book (Jerry Lucas); another became one of professional basketball's greatest coaches (Phil Jackson); one became a professional basketball coach and general manager (Willis Reed); another was a former player-coach who became a general manager and head of a new professional league (Dave DeBusschere); another became a professional and college coach (Cazzie Russell); another was a long-time basketball television analyst (Walt Frazier); one earned a doctor's degree in finance (Dick Barnett); and another was as brainy, talented, and funny—he had once aspired to be a stand-up comedian—as any of them (Earl Monroe).

They were bright, they were witty, they were insightful, they were hugely talented, they were generally forthcoming, they were adult. They became sure of themselves and one another, gained confidence in their coach, and played with such grace and intelligence and skill that Madison Square Garden began to rock like never before.

"You make a few steals or work for a few good plays, and you have the feeling that it's going to be one of those nights," Frazier once said. "The whole team gets into it, and then the crowd picks it up, and you come to the sidelines for a time-out and listen to the standing ovation, and it makes you jingle inside."

After one game I remember Joe Caldwell, then with the Atlanta Hawks, shaking his head in the locker room after being run through by Holzman's team. "Way it looks to me," he said, "is that the Knicks have gone and sold their soul."

Running that spectacular show was the team's understated but brilliant coach. The team won the National Basketball Association championship in 1970 and 1973—the only championships in the team's history—and, if not for injuries to its center and captain, Willis Reed, would conceivably have won again in 1971 and

1972. It catapulted several of its players to the Pro Basketball Hall of Fame: Bradley, Reed, DeBusschere, Frazier, Monroe, and one day surely Jackson—and one William (Red) Holzman.

It was a team that I spent considerable time around, and wrote about, and studied, from virtually my first days in Gotham. With Walt (Clyde) Frazier, I wrote *Rockin' Steady: A Guide to Basketball and Cool*, published in 1974. It was an idiosyncratic instructional book, coffee-table size, with great photographs by Walter Iooss, the *Sports Illustrated* photographer, and illustrations by John Lane, whom I worked with at NEA and had a lot of respect for. Among the instructions were these: "How to Shoot a Hook Shot." Frazier: "I never could shoot a hook shot." End of hook-shot section. Frazier was noted for quick hands—so quick, it was said, he could catch a fly. So we had illustrations of how to catch a fly in midair and when the fly was in a sitting position.

The book was divided into five chapters and was modeled on the classic writing manual, *The Elements of Style*, by William Strunk and E. B. White. I wanted to write a basketball book that was as entertaining, as lucid, as filled with love for the subject, as instructive, as *The Elements of Style*. And with the nation's most stylish basketball player.

The Elements of Style is also divided into five chapters and has been a kind of Bible of writing for me and thousands of other writers (including Red Smith, who said he tried to read it once a year). White's essays generally have also been a great influence on my writing. William Zinsser, in his fine book on the craft, *On Writing Well*, captured a quality I was striving for: "The writing that we most admire over the years—the King James Bible, Abraham Lincoln, E. B. White, Red Smith—is writing that has the strength of simplicity."

When it was published, I decided to send a copy of *Rockin' Steady* to White, not knowing if he had any interest in basketball. But I did want to thank him for his unwitting contribution to the book.

He wrote back, from North Brooklin, Maine:

At a Sports and Society class I taught at New York University in 1976, one of my guests was Walt Frazier, then a star guard for the New York Knicks.

"Thank you for 'Rockin' Steady.' It has kept me steady for several days and I have been enjoying it, particularly since I had never heard of Clyde. (I live a sheltered life.)

"My friend, John McNulty, now dead, would have liked this book, because of sentences like, 'Sometimes they'll come in and stand real quiet, to listen if I'm still breathing.' He would have liked that.

"I shall pass the book on to my youngest grandson to whom basketball is the key to life and who will understand the diagrams. . . . Sincerely, E. B. White."

It happened that one morning Dorothy Lamour, the movie actress who had attained her greatest popularity in the late 1930s and 1940s, came into the NEA office to be interviewed by our entertainment editor, Joan Crosby. Miss Lamour was still attractive but had, inevitably, lost some of her luster. She was about fifty-five, still had luminous black hair, and her eye shadow was also dark and looked even darker set against her very pale complexion. She was wearing not a sarong, for which she became famous in such roles as that in *The Jungle Princess*, but a fashionable fur coat, more practical in the New York winter.

On my desk, by sheer coincidence, was a copy of White's brilliant collection of essays, *One Man's Meat*, in which, in the essay titled "Bond Rally," he writes about the sultry Dorothy Lamour coming to Maine in October 1942, where he lived, to drum up donations for the war effort.

"Miss Lamour's train pulled in cautiously, stopped, and she stepped out," White wrote. "There was no pool, no waterfall, no long dark hair falling across incomparable shoulders, no shadow cast by the moon. Dorothy the saleswoman strode forward in red duvetyn, with a brown fuzzy bow in her upswept hair."

I took the book and walked out to where Dorothy Lamour and the entertainment editor had sat down. I was introduced to her and asked if she'd ever seen the essay–which had first appeared in *Harper's* magazine–or the book. She said she hadn't, which surprised me. And so I gave her the book. "Thank you," she said. I also took the liberty of inscribing it: "To Dorothy Lamour–with love–Ira."

I thought E. B. White just might be interested in this *ménage à trois*, and decided to write him of the encounter.

White replied: "I was glad to get news of Lamour. It's a small world. I had to visit a Bangor dermatologist the other day, and when I remarked at the elegance of his home he said, 'This used to be Cratty's house.' (It was from Cratty's room at the hotel, if you recall, that the furniture was removed so that Dottie could have all the comforts.)

"Sorry to hear she has walked out of your life but glad she had a book of mine in her hand. Thanks for giving it to her."

He added a postscript: "Dottie Lamour doesn't write letters–I have discovered that."

Obviously, even White's resplendent prose couldn't elicit a response from the Hollywood goddess. It was a lesson in unrequited allure that would sustain me in certain moments of my life that had such echoes.

I don't know if I made a Knicks fan out of E. B. White—I surely didn't with Dottie Lamour—but I think White would have appreciated Red Holzman, sometimes himself as cool as Clyde Frazier, other times furiously racing along the sidelines to inform the referees about a mistake they'd just made that cost the Knicks, his tie and the tail of his sport jacket flapping madly in the breeze he created.

Of the numerous reviews of *Rockin' Steady*, one of the most pleasing to me was from the *Cincinnati Enquirer*, written by a reviewer for the paper who generally wrote about much more literary subjects than hoops. It was John A. Weigel, my English professor from Miami, who mentioned in the lead that I had been a student of his, a disclaimer of sorts in that he praised the book. One paragraph in particular, however, which related to Frazier the man, was reminiscent for me of the thought-provoking Weigel of the classroom:

"I have always been pleased with the confident bearing of successful performers of any kind, from teachers to wrestlers. To know that one is a star, that one can do something better than practically anyone else in the world gives a man or woman a stable center of gravity and a dignity which is apprehended as conceit only by dullards and defeated competitors."

⌐ Anyone fortunate enough to cover those peerless Knicks of the Frazier era was unfortunate in another way: it spoiled you for covering any other team—forever.

Of the qualities that endeared the coach, Red Holzman, to his players, beyond his evident savvy, was his shunning of the spotlight (he was happy to let those like Clyde, for example, bask in it). Unlike many other coaches or managers, he wanted the players to be the focus of attention.

Holzman was an average-sized man (5 feet 10½) in an oversized world. He had an ego, to be sure, but it was cleverly concealed. If one is to succeed in anything, there will be obstacles, and a firm belief in one's self is essential for the chance to succeed. Ergo, ego.

A good example was my first interview with Holzman. It was shortly after he took over as coach of the Knicks, and the team began winning almost immediately. We met in his small office in Madison Square Garden. I had hoped to engage him in a discussion about how he worked his magic.

"What have you done to help your team's success?" I asked.

"Some stuff I've done has evidently appealed to them," he said.

"What do you mean 'stuff'?"

"Offensive and defensive stuff," he explained.

The conversation continued in this fashion, and as it did, Holzman began slowly to disappear in a cloud of his own modesty. As if now he were not King Arthur of the Round Ball but Merlin.

I would have to go elsewhere to learn in detail his great dependence on defense, his mastery of matchups, his arduous repetitions (during one twenty-five-day stretch in the earliest days, the Knicks played eight games and had twenty-one two-hour practice sessions), his ability to communicate and motivate. Perhaps most important, he'd always be hollering–"See the ball!" on defense, and "Hit the open man!" on offense.

"The real genius of Holzman," Bill Bradley said, "lies in his handling of players. Most men would have failed as coach of the New York Knickerbockers. Great college coaches often cannot make the adjustment from coaching boys to controlling men. Holzman does not beg players to do good deeds, nor does he set up elaborate codes of conduct. He expects everyone to act as a responsible adult, and he treats players accordingly."

One of the most significant moves Holzman made was to trade Walt Bellamy for DeBusschere. Bellamy, at 7 feet, was someone Holzman was unable to reach. He did things in his own time on the court, which did not usually fit the time of the rest of the players. DeBusschere, it would be said, was the "last piece of the puzzle" to make the Knicks a championship team.

With former Knicks coach Red Holzman in 1997. When I introduced Holzman to the comedian Jackie Mason by saying, "This was the brilliant coach of the Knicks," Mason looked him up and down. "Doesn't look so smart to me," said Mason. Holzman, a fan of Mason's, was tickled by the remark. (Photo by George Kalinsky)

Holzman told me: "After we made that trade, I was so happy I went out and got drunk for three nights."

I never saw Holzman inebriated–and neither had anyone else I knew–but I understood his joy. "And," he said, "you can't write that." And I didn't, in his lifetime.

To be sure, Red wasn't perfect. In an early scrimmage in the Knicks' training camp in the mid-sixties, the chief scout watched one of the rookies he had scouted–the team had followed his enthusiastic advice to draft the player high–and now anticipated that he would be a productive member of the team.

On the sideline, Scout Holzman noticed a flaw in the player that he hadn't noticed before: he had trouble getting through screens on his left. During a break in the action, Holzman went onto the court to demonstrate to the player how it's done.

"You have to look out of the corner of your eye and then fight through the screen," Holzman told the player.

"I can't look out of the corner of my eye," the player said.

"You can't?" said Holzman, skeptically. "What's so hard?"

"I'm blind in my left eye," the player said.

Holzman looked around to see if anyone was in earshot. No one was.

"C'mere," said Holzman, and led the player to a corner of the gym. Holzman whispered, "Don't ever tell anyone you can't see, okay?"

"Okay," said the player.

Holzman, born in New York City, was an all-American guard for the City College of New York in the early 1940s. And he played in the NBA with the Rochester Royals, one of a trio of outstanding guards—along with Bobby Wanzer and Bob Davies—on a championship team. His greatest influence, however, was his college coach, Nat Holman, one of the most celebrated players of the 1920s, in the formative years of professional basketball.

It was from Holman that Holzman learned the importance of defense and team ball. When he applied it as a coach, he influenced another generation of coaches, most particularly Phil Jackson, who won nine championships with the Michael Jordan Chicago Bulls and the Shaquille O'Neal–Kobe Bryant Los Angeles Lakers.

When Phil Jackson won the award for coach of the year with the Bulls, he said, "I know the official title of this is the Red Auerbach Award"—Auerbach, of course, had been the outstanding coach of the Boston Celtics—"but for me, it's the Red Holzman Award. It was Red who taught me what coaching basketball was all about."

To this point I had spent a considerable part of my youth and young manhood absorbed in basketball, playing it as a boy in the cold and snow, by the light of nearby streetlamps, shooting alone with gloves on at a park near my home in Chicago, and playing in summertime, sweating so much in the heat that I'd wring out my shirt and it would be a waterfall. It would be the same in the park leagues, and playing for my high school, and for Roosevelt University in Chicago, and for years afterward in pickup and league games.

For me, one of the aspects of staying active in competitive sports, and basketball in particular, was to keep trying to improve. And one of the added pleasures as a sportswriter was being around the best players and coaches in the game, picking up bits and pieces of advice that I would try to use to my advantage in my own game. On rare occasions it worked. I'd learn from Frazier that, on a drive, you want to have the first step longer than a normal step. But I found I had trouble maintaining the dribble this way, and went back to my normal, bum drive. (But I concentrated on keeping the elbow near my chest on the shot, as Clyde said.)

Sometimes, in pickup games, my knowing the rules–since I saw them applied regularly in professional games–caused arguments. For example: the top of the backboard is in play if the ball bounces back in fair territory. If it bounces behind the backboard, it's out of play. An argument ensued one time with a player named Whitey. Next time I came to the gym, I brought the rule book to show him. "You can stick the rule book up your ass," he said, cordially. I thanked him for his consideration and told him how much I admired his intellectual curiosity, in pretty much the same terms he had used. But the next time it happened, he said that the ball, when it bounced on the top of the backboard and fell fair, was indeed in play. Of course, in this instance Whitey was playing on my side and the ball had come down to our team.

Being on such an intimate level with the professional players– in the locker room, going to lunch or dinner with them, peppering them with questions–gave me greater insights in writing about what I and the interested public were observing. For all sports, not just hoops.

⌇ NEA had some of the best comic strips in the country, including "Peanuts" and "Garfield." It had a Washington bureau for politics as well as writers on film, fashion, food, and, of course, sports. When I was hired, Murray Olderman was the sports editor of a three-man staff, including himself. The job required that we interview and write about many of the best-known people in sports. But we also wrote about issues and trends. Olderman was creative, innovative, and daring in his approach to sports and sports themes. And I was thrilled to be out of what had become for me a stifling atmosphere at the *Minneapolis Tribune.*

Olderman was unusual—no, unique—in being not only a standout sportswriter but also a superb cartoonist (he combined both for NEA, and won awards for both). He was also the only Phi Beta Kappa I know of in sports, having graduated from Stanford and having also earned a bachelor's degree from Missouri as well as a graduate degree from the Medill School of Journalism at Northwestern.

He was a linguist too, fluent in German and French. As a second lieutenant in France at the end of World War II, he interrogated German prisoners in German (he would return to Germany years later and conduct an interview with Albert Speer, Hitler's architect, when he was released from prison), and, because of his knowledge of French, was assigned to close the brothels in Metz at night and make sure the GIs got safely back to the barracks. Dark-haired, six feet tall, handsome in a craggy way, Olderman was a kind of Renaissance man in that he was also a very good athlete, particularly a tennis player. In tournaments for writers, he invariably won the trophy. I had learned to play some tennis since my days at Miami of Ohio and enjoyed sweating and racing around to return shots. I had never really studied the fundamentals of the game, and anyone who grew up taking lessons or played regularly and was moderately adept at the game could beat me. (I did have my moments, however, and once beat the Olympic pole-vault champion Bob Seagren, who was a worse tennis player than I. He wouldn't speak to me afterward because, I assume, he thought he should have won since he was an Olympic athlete and I was a mere scribe.) But when I played with Olderman he showed no mercy. And all I could show for my effort was a sweat-blotched shirt.

Olderman made many friends in the sports world–athletes, in particular, trusted and were flattered by someone drawing them as opposed to the rest of us who only reported on them (no one likes to be judged, which is one of the jobs of the honest writer). One of them was the Reverend Bob Richards, the great pole-vaulter of the 1950s.

Richards, retired, came up to the NEA office on Forty-third Street in Manhattan to visit Olderman shortly after I had come to work there. Murray introduced me.

Richards seemed genuinely delighted to see Olderman, whom he hadn't seen in a number of years.

"Murray, you look great," said Richards. "How do you do it?"

Olderman smiled. "Clean living, Reverend," he said.

One day, before leaving the office, Olderman was at his drawing board. We began to chat, and he said, "I think it's a good idea to get a specialty, so people look to you as an expert in a particular field." Olderman had done this with football. He was, along with Tex Maule of *Sports Illustrated*, considered the preeminent authority on professional football and the author of several widely respected books. He had started the Jim Thorpe Trophy for the Most Valuable Player in the National Football League. And for years it was exclusively an NEA promotion.

I considered what Olderman said, but what I wanted as my specialty was simply to be a good writer–or the best writer I could possibly be. Somewhere along the line I did gravitate to basketball perhaps more than any other sport. But I never wanted to be known as strictly a basketball writer. I found that limiting. And I hoped to expand my outlook and to write about people in all sports–and in time in the world beyond sports.

From the beginning, Olderman and I struck a common chord, and he treated me the way I'd imagine he'd have treated his son, if Mark Olderman were a journalist. Murray showed me how to get around town, in a variety of ways–that is, where to go (cocktail parties were great for meeting people and creating relationships, he told me), who might be good sources, and how to get a story.

But I had to learn a lot on my own. Like the time I approached Willie Mays behind the batting cage at Shea Stadium, when the wondrous center fielder was a little less wondrous, in one of his last seasons in the big leagues. It was 1970, Mays was still with the San Francisco Giants, and he was thirty-nine years old (he would play four more seasons).

His body, powerful chest and arm muscles, and bowlegs seemed to hold him up admirably. But his eyes appeared to say he was in the twilight of his career. They were large, brown, and knowing (in a "country-slick" way, as someone once described them), and at the corners were creeping crow's feet.

Mays walked in a cloak of applause. As soon as fans in the stands saw him they began to cheer and call his name. But that, apparently, was hardly enough.

"Willie," I said, rather innocently, "is the safe off your back after getting your three thousandth hit and six hundredth home run?" There was a lot of footage in the press and sportscasts about Mays closing in and then reaching those career milestones.

"What safe?" He said sharply. I was slightly taken aback at his curtness.

"What's wrong?" I asked.

"Because, man," he said, "you start askin' me these questions and you don't even say, 'Hey, congratulations on three thousand hits, on six hundred homers.' I mean, not many people ever hit that many."

He was right!—on two scores: the home runs *and* the fact that even Willie Mays wants to hear something positive. "Willie," I said, "you're absolutely right. It's an amazing achievement, all those home runs." But eventually and before the conversation ended—when I felt the timing was right—I was able gently to steer Willie around to my angle, that is, how long "some" players can play. And he was cooperative. He eased into talking about those milestones: "The three thousand hits was easier because the homers are harder to hit."

Mays opened my eyes in another way. In fact, I really thought my eyes were playing tricks on me. Later I thought maybe it was my mind, too. Virtually everyone who played with Mays says he was perhaps the smartest player they'd ever played with or against. It was beyond pure baseball instinct, which Mays had plenty of. It was baseball brains. He made what I consider the most astounding play I've ever seen in baseball. It was also the greatest play that the opposing catcher–turns out it was Johnny Oates–had ever seen. But all three of us–Mays, Oates, and me–seemed to remember, or see, slightly different things.

It wasn't the famous, stupendous, back-to-the-plate catch in center field off the Vic Wertz drive in the 1954 World Series, or any other of Mays's acclaimed swats or snares. In my mind's eye, this is the situation I saw from my seat in the press box:

Shea Stadium. An afternoon game in July 1973. The great "Say Hey Kid" was no longer a kid, and no longer even greeting people with his trademark, "Say hey." Mays was then forty-two, and in the twenty-second and last season of his brilliant, Hall of Fame career.

Close game against the Braves. Late innings. Mays is on second base. The batter–don't remember who–drives a hit to right field. Normally the runner would score from second fairly easily, but this is no ordinary runner. Mays seems to trudge around third, like, well, an old man, and heads home, cap still on head–remember, in his speedy heyday the cap used to fly off as if he were in a wind tunnel. The right fielder winds up to fire the ball to the plate, certain to nail Methuselah Mays. But incredibly, Mays picks up steam and there he is racing to the plate like, well, the Say Hey Kid!

He beats the throw and is safe at home. Not only that, but because he drew the throw to the plate, the batter is able to go to second, sitting there now in scoring position.

In an instant, Mays had craftily set the whole thing up in his marvelous baseball mind. He obviously had run slowly at first to draw the throw, knowing all along he could make it home.

For me, there is nothing quite as exciting in sports as watching a player—particularly an aging veteran—use his experience, his intelligence, and his considerable if waning skills to accomplish something remarkable under pressure. One hesitates to use the word "genius" in such endeavors, especially with such folks as Einstein, Picasso, Freud, and Frost looking from the proverbial stands. But in my view certain athletes performing certain feats may indeed possess a kind of genius.

Some three decades later I recalled the play to Mays, describing it as I remembered it. Did he remember it?

"Absolutely," he said. "It was against the Braves. But there's more to it. See, I was on second base and Felix Millan was a runner at first. Ralph Garr was in right field. But not only did I score, I slid into the catcher—it was Johnny Oates—and I pinned him to the ground so Millan could score too."

I didn't remember the pinning business, so I later called Oates, at his home in Virginia. "I always tell that story at banquets," Oates said. "It was the smartest play I've ever seen, and an embarrassing one for me."

I told Oates what Willie had told me.

"I was under the impression that it was a sacrifice fly," said Oates. "And I don't remember him on top of me. He made a perfect slide and took my legs out from under me. My recollection is that I wound up on top of him. But definitely we were lying on the plate, and somehow Willie wouldn't let me get up. The throw went over my head, and the runner behind him did indeed score—how he found the plate with us lying on it I don't know."

To check further for details, I called the Elias Sports Bureau, located in Manhattan, the record keeper for Major League Baseball. Elias confirmed the play essentially the way Mays remembered it, with him and Millan scoring on a hit by Wayne Garrett.

(Those runs gave the Mets a 7-6 lead in the eighth, but they lost the game, 9-8.)

I like Johnny's version of the play; I like Willie's; and I still like mine.

In the spring of 1968, Olderman assigned me to cover the Preakness, the second of the Triple Crown thoroughbred races, held at Pimlico Race Course in Baltimore. I was staying at the Lord Baltimore Hotel, the headquarters for the sportswriters. One night I was in the hotel dining room eating alone when I saw a smallish man, grey-haired, in suit and tie and glasses, enter and take a table, also alone. It was Red Smith.

I was finishing my meal, and while I had run into Smith a few times in the year I had been in New York, I was still, in my view, for him just another guy on the beat. And I certainly wasn't about to impose myself on him. I wasn't sure whether I should even pass his table and say hello. But then I thought that would only be polite.

He greeted me in his raspy voice and, to my surprise, asked me to join him. I sat down. He was drinking a glass of Scotch and offered me a drink. I politely accepted. He asked what I'd been doing at the track, and then I asked about him. That morning he had been to the barns and mentioned an interesting anecdote about a trainer.

"Red, that's great," I said. "Would you mind if I spoke to him tomorrow?"

"No, of course not," he said. And he told me the trainer's name and which barn he worked out of.

"I'd better write this down," I said.

I went into the inside pocket of my sport jacket to get a pen. No pen. I tried the other inside pocket. Nothing. I went to my pants pockets. Same result. I was mortified. Me, ace sports reporter, without a writing utensil, and in front of Red Smith, of all people.

"Uh, Red," I said, "I don't, uh, have a pen."

"No problem," he said. "Use my pen."

And he went into his inside jacket pocket. Nothing. The other. Same. His pants. No pen.

"I don't have one, either," he said, with the shake of his head. "The waiter will have a pen," and he hailed the man.

What a relief, I thought. Even Red Smith can come up empty!

Yet I've never known whether Red Smith—so smart, so prepared, so gracious—did, or did not, have a pen.

7

~~~~~~~~~~~~~~~~~~~

Steamy

IT WAS MAY 1976, my ninth year at NEA, and I had been riding high there. I was used in a high percentage of the 750 client newspapers (despite the *Florida Times-Union*s of the nation), had my pieces chosen several times for the prestigious Best Sports Stories annual, and recently had a collection of them published as *Beyond the Dream*. Not only did I have this collection published—unusual for a sportswriter in daily journalism—but Red Smith, generally considered the leading sportswriter in America, when asked by the editor to contribute a blurb for the dust jacket, offered instead to write a foreword to the book.

At NEA I had been working under a two-year contract which was due to expire soon. I asked the executive editor, Bob Metz, when we could talk about the new contract. He delayed. I asked again. "Soon," he said. No problem. Then one morning he called me into his office with the managing editor, Bob Cochnar. We all had become social friends, and I expected a nice chat and a healthy raise.

"You tell him," Metz said to Cochnar, as we sat down.

"No, you're the executive editor," said Cochnar, "you tell him."
My head swiveled from one to the other.

"Well, will someone tell me," I said, with a waning smile.

"Ira," said Metz, "you've gotten so good we can't afford you anymore."

"Oh," I said. And of course I understood immediately. They weren't going to renew my contract.

"How long do I have?" I asked, adding nothing else.

"As long as you want," said Metz.

NEA had been bought by another organization and faced a cost-cutting move. Even though I was considered one of their prized "talents," or so they advertised me, I was expendable when they looked at the profit line. I was hardly making a king's ransom, even for those days, maybe $30,000 a year. But NEA proceeded to divest itself of virtually all its writers, including Murray Olderman and Tom Tiede, who had won the prestigious Ernie Pyle Award for his coverage of the Vietnam War.

The decision by NEA not to renew my contract came as an absolute shock, to say the least. I felt as though I had been dropped down an elevator shaft. But business is business, I learned. I also learned something else: you could be traveling in style, but you could ride right off a cliff if you were not careful—or even if you *were* careful. The other lesson was: nobody is indispensable—well, at least, *I* was not indispensable.

I was on the street, just like that. And at a loss. I had no job, no income, no immediate possibilities. I had been doing well for several years in New York, gaining national recognition, being promoted—I went from sportswriter to sports columnist to sports editor to general columnist (and still writing sports columns) and senior editor—winning awards, my self-esteem rising, the notion wafting through my brain probably that I was essential to the company and maybe even to the whole craft of journalism, for God's sake.

In June, shortly after it was announced that NEA was dispatching me, the head of sales for the organization, Mike Poynter, a man I had known only casually, wrote a memo to Cochnar: "I have contacted several salesmen in regard to our discussion about Ira and they all feel their client editors will have a legitimate gripe if Ira is no longer a part of the service. . . .

"During a period of change and rate increases I think the value of the service will suffer considerably by dropping Ira Berkow. Actually, I wish I could sell Ira's column separately because I know his work could hold its own in the competitive syndicated market. . . .

"I think his name is going to be among the tops in the literary field in the near future and that can only help to enhance the image of NEA.

"The salesmen I have contacted have agreed to send the tear sheets and client editor's responses [to Ira] to me. Then, we will present the evidence in hopes that Ira's contract will be continued."

In the surveys, while I did well, I hardly got 100 percent approval, and not only at the reaction to my support of Ali. In a survey sheet I happened to have saved, dated March 16, 1975, from the *Malden* (Massachusetts) *Evening News*, a comment in the entry marked "Sports" reads: "Would like to have a sports cartoon. Why was Olderman discontinued? Berkow is too 'high brow' for sports fans."

Regardless of friend or foe, I was history at NEA. At one point after I left the organization, I went into debt. I recall going to my bank to cash a small check and looking through the barred windows at the teller, thinking, "How lucky she is, getting a weekly check." But that sentiment was short-lived since I knew I'd be clutching those bars to be let out if I was in her position.

At this point I recalled what my father had written in my autograph book when I was graduating grammar school. "Whoever said opportunity knocks just once was either lazy or stupid." And while I'd had a good job—a good opportunity at NEA—I thought I'd knock some more, seeking another. I had no choice if I wanted to eat. My father's advice was reminiscent of the beginning of

Bellow's *Adventures of Augie March* (my father, I know, never read *Augie March*, which was published coincidentally around the time of my graduation):

"I am an American, Chicago born—Chicago, that somber city—and go at things as I have taught myself, free-style, and will make the record in my own way: first to knock, first admitted; sometimes an innocent knock, sometimes a not so innocent. But a man's character is his fate, says Heraclitus. . . ."

I called *Time* magazine and made an appointment with a "personnel assistant." I don't know why, maybe it was just after I returned from the bank. I knew people at *Time* but was too embarrassed to call them for advice or a recommendation. So I went in cold to see a young woman who had never heard of me. The building on Sixth Avenue seemed so corporate and so distant when I stood in its cavernous lobby, echoing with voices and footsteps. I had been a columnist syndicated in some 750 newspapers for nearly 10 years and still thought I had a certain standing in the journalistic community. Not to this woman, it turned out. She was a small woman seated behind a large desk, wore glasses, and almost never glanced up at me. She asked me some cursory questions, as though I were a college applicant. Very depressing. I left the Time-Life building thinking, "Now what?" Was my life, at 36, a thing of the past?

I dug in. What was I to do? I began a novel about a baseball player (I received a small advance from a publisher) but lost enthusiasm for the idea when I had to meet my bills, and never completed it (I even offered to return the advance, which, gratefully, wasn't accepted). I wrote several freelance magazine stories, including a cover story for *People* magazine on Pete Rose and one for, of all publications, *Chic* magazine, Larry Flynt's then-notorious periodical. The *Chic* piece explored heavyweight boxing's "Great White Hopes"—the subtitle on the story read, "Is There a Real-life Rocky? Here's the Best of the Honky Heavyweights." It was published between the soft-porn photo layouts of a young woman named Julia and another named Marie-Claire, both white hopes of a different sort. Neither of those magazine stories could be classified as haute literature, but both paid well, the stories were honest–and the bylines were mercifully small.

I made a few inquiries about newspaper jobs but with only half a heart. At the moment I really didn't want one. I wanted to be a writer. Maybe journalism, the daily grind of the transitory, was no longer my bliss. Besides, no one was beating my door down. The phone stopped ringing. I wrote proposals for screenplays, wrote the book for a musical, sent out an assortment of other ideas, and my mailbox filled up with rejection slips.

There were, however, glimmers of light. *Harper's* magazine and the *New Yorker*, among other quality magazines, were encouraging about short stories I had submitted, saying I was close and to try again. I eventually published a short piece of fiction in *Seventeen*, about a betrayal of young love involving college students. The editors said it was "steamy."

I received a book contract. In 1974 I had written a column for NEA on the occasion of the twentieth anniversary of the 1954 DuSable High School basketball team in Chicago, a team that had meant a lot to me when I was fourteen, and after. I had followed up that story with a two-part series on the team in *Chicago* magazine, and now I followed *that* with a book, published in 1978, *The DuSable Panthers: The Greatest, Blackest, Saddest Team from the Meanest Street in Chicago*. It was about a high school team from the inner city of Chicago that captured the imagination of many of us living there with such future college and pro stars as the seniors Paxton Lumpkin (who later played for Indiana University and the Harlem Globetrotters), Sweet Charlie Brown (later a starting forward along with Elgin Baylor on the 1958 Seattle University team that lost in the NCAA finals to Kentucky), and Shellie McMillon (later a star for Bradley University and a center for the Detroit Pistons). They played with the flair of the Globetrotters–pressing opponents on defense, running and gunning in an era when slow-down basketball was the rule—and went undefeated, winning by impressive margins through the city and state tournaments. But they lost in a controversial Illinois state final to Mt. Vernon, a small-town, southern Illinois team with only one black player. DuSable was an historic team, being the first all-black team with a black coach to succeed at the highest level of integrated sports. The team and its sociological significance are represented today in a separate section of the Basketball Hall of Fame in Springfield, Mass.

To this day many DuSable followers believe that two white downstate referees called the championship game against the black team from Chicago. I saw the game on television and cried, I was rooting so hard for DuSable. I wasn't aware that they might have been jobbed—even though their stars were in foul trouble early, and three of them eventually fouled out of the game. But in later years, as I researched it, it grew in my mind as a distinct possibility. It wasn't exactly the Black Sox scandal, but it was a dramatic story, and it had resonance. In May 1954, just two months after DuSable lost to Mt. Vernon in the last minute, 76-70, the United States Supreme Court ruled 9-0 in *Brown v. Topeka (Kansas) Board of Education*, ending school segregation. The DuSable players broke racial barriers and continued to break racial barriers, and seemed to be in tune with the times, as manifested surely by the Supreme Court's nation-changing decision.

The book was swiftly optioned to a Hollywood producer, but no movie came of it. It has since been optioned many more times—that is, a producer pays a certain amount of money for an agreed-upon time, say a year or two or three, for the exclusive rights to try to interest studios or networks in making the film. It has been more than a quarter-century since the book was published, and as I write this it has been optioned again. As a friend of mine has said, regarding options that have lapsed for his several books, "You know Hollywood, they never make any movies." But they sometimes do help pay the rent.

After publishing *Rockin' Steady* in 1974, I had thought I'd like to do a similar kind of off-center instructional book for baseball. And who better for this assignment than Casey Stengel. I had arranged a meeting with Stengel in his hotel room when he was in New York for a Baseball Writers Dinner in late January 1974. He was eighty-three years old, white-haired but still spry. When he explained the art of catching a ground ball, he leaped from the couch to demonstrate, bowlegged, the cuffs of his black pants pulled up and his black socks curled below his ankles to reveal lumpy calves, and he fielded the imaginary ball that bounded under the coffee table.

I already had the title for the book: "Casey Stengel's Inimitable, Historical, Instructional Baseball Book." When I showed him the Frazier book, he thumbed through it with his gnarled fingers. "It's a perfection thing," he said. I was delighted with the response. It meant he liked the book, I thought. Would he then do it?

"Let me think about it," he said. "I'll let you know."

And he did. He wrote a letter to me that arrived some two weeks later at my office at NEA. It was written in a firm but uneven hand on lined notebook paper. The letter was in blue ink, though the envelope was written in green ink. The envelope, which was personal stationery, announced at the top left:

Casey Stengel
1663 Grandview
Glendale, California 91201

The letter read exactly as follows, with Casey's unadulterated punctuation, grammar, and spelling:

Dear Ira:

Your conversations; and the fact you were the working Writer were inthused with the Ideas was Great but frankly do not care for the great amount of work for myself.

; Sorry but am not interested. Have to many propositions otherwise for the coming season.

Fact cannot disclose my Future affairs.
Good luck.
(signed) Casey Stengel
N.Y. Mets & Hall of Famer

Stengel, still one of the most quoted sports figures in history, essentially created his own language, called by sportswriters "Stengelese," and proved that to be able to communicate, to get your points across, you don't have to speak the King's—or Queen's—English. But you do have to be (a) knowledgeable and (b) entertaining, not necessarily in that order.

Casey told me: "Today I make speeches all over. People ask me, 'Casey, how can you speak so much when you don't talk English too good?' Well, I've been invited to Europe and I say, they don't speak English over there too good, either."

Two years later, out of work and looking for projects, I thought again of the Casey idea. But he had died in September 1975, leaving a huge hole in the sports world—and, from my view, a somewhat smaller one in the literary world.

(I eventually published such a book in 1992, with Jim Kaplan, the onetime *Sports Illustrated* baseball writer. The idea was: though Casey was no longer around in the flesh, his words and aura survived. So Jim and I researched Casey's remarks and interviewed players, coaches, and writers who were part of Casey's long life. The title was *The Gospel According to Casey*, and I added the subtitle from years before: *Casey Stengel's Inimitable, Instructional, Historical Baseball Book*.)

✍ A few months after I had arrived in New York, a friend had introduced me to Nancy Pratt, an artist and teacher. We dated, and fell in love. After a four-year courtship, I married her, in 1971. She had two boys, then ten and twelve. That would seem to contradict my desire about not wanting to be tied down with children, but I thought now I could handle it. We rented a three-story, three-bedroom house on a leafy street in Kew Gardens, Queens. But it turned out that, as much as I cared for the kids–and I did–and as deeply as I cared for Nancy, it still didn't work for me. After a four-year marriage, Nancy and I divorced. We stayed friends and confidants, as odd as that seemed to some people. But we were truly friends, as I was with her younger son especially–Tim Pratt, now an outstanding reporter for the *Las Vegas Sun*. For several years prior to this, there had been a lack of communication. Tim had gone to live in Colombia, became fluent in Spanish and was a successful freelance writer, married, when he decided to return to America. We got back in touch and have remained close ever since.

Several years after Nancy and I parted, she came down with multiple sclerosis. I stayed close and did what I could for her, whenever I could. Through it all, Nancy maintained her quirky sense of humor, which attracted me to her in the first place. One aspect of the terrible disease resulted in a great loss of weight–she had already had trouble walking and was confined mostly to a wheelchair. Somehow, in one conversation, she recalled some guy "grabbing" her ass (it might have been me, I don't remember the full context). "I no longer have the ass I did–that's when I had an ass worth grabbing," she said to me one day by telephone. "I could cry. Imagine, here I am mourning the loss of an ass."

My father had his thoughts on my marital proclivities.

"You're like a movie star, with your marriages and divorces," he said, not necessarily approving. "It wasn't easy, Dad," I said, "but if something isn't working out, I want to have the courage not to stick in a situation. It's not good for anyone. I want to be honest with myself about my feelings, and honest with the other people involved."

I had made my choices, and when things weren't working out, all parties knew it. There were no huge arguments, no throwing of dishes, just a sense of distance. Whatever possessions both Willee and Nancy wanted, they got, including cars and furniture. I got the bookcases. When there was money needed, or help with family, I remained there for both of them. Nancy wanted to write, and, while we no longer lived together, I introduced her to publishers. She wrote several newspaper and magazine stories and published two books about antiques, a passion of hers.

After I had been divorced from Nancy, on a February night around nine o'clock I was walking up Second Avenue from my apartment on East Thirtieth Street in Manhattan. I was headed for a store on the corner of Thirty-fifth Street and Second Avenue to get the Bulldog, the early edition, of the next day's *New York Daily News*. It was dark, but I could clearly see in the light from the streetlamps a beautiful woman in a tan leather jacket with dark, shoulder-length hair walking toward me. As we passed, and I was about to enter the store, I said to her, "Hello." She said, "Hello," without losing a stride. And for some reason, I said, "I'm going in to buy a *Daily News*. May I buy you one?"

She smiled politely. "No, thanks," she said.

I went into the store, made my purchase, came back out, and walked to Thirty-fourth Street where, waiting for the light, was the beautiful dark-haired woman in the tan leather jacket. I, on the other hand, was wearing a dark ski jacket and navy blue knit cap and hadn't shaved in a day. If someone was looking for a suspect as the Boston Strangler, I might have been hauled into a police station immediately. But I wasn't thinking about that.

"Hello," I said.

"Oh, it's you again," she said.

"Well," I said, "I know you said you didn't want the newspaper, but as long as we're standing here, would you mind if I read you the news?"

She shrugged and looked up at the red light. "Well, I guess I'm a captive audience," she said. "Go ahead."

I read a few quick items, and then the light changed. It turned out she lived across the street. I walked her to her apartment building; we chatted. I got her name and where she worked. Her name was Dolly Case. She was a manager in a computerized telephone company, and her exotic looks came from the fact that her father was Filipino and Spanish, and her mother German.

Dolly Berkow, who at long last succumbed to my offer of marriage.

I called her at work a few days later.

"Hi," I said, "this is Ira."

There was a slight pause. "Who?" she said.

"The guy you met on the street corner on Friday. You know, who read you the news?"

"Oh, you," she said.

"Look," I said, "I'm not busy for dinner tonight. And I know this is short notice, but you seem like a person who doesn't stand on ceremony. If you aren't busy, I'd love for you to join me for dinner."

There was a pause. "Okay," she said.

Dolly, like Willee, had graduated with a degree in English and had been a pom-pom girl at the University of Arizona, which I found out several years after we were married when accidentally thumbing through an old yearbook of hers. Unlike me, she often left long-ago parts of her life to the long ago. Dolly was funny, well read, straightforward, totally without affectation, as unpretentious as—well, as my mother, and one of the finest people I've ever known. Dolly would have agreed with an assessment of my mother's about a woman she knew who liked herself very much. "Self-praise stinks," my mother said.

Dolly was a divorced mother of a boy, Allen, who lived with his father in a New York suburb and whom we would see regularly. He became an integral part of our life together.

In our early courtship I told Dolly that I had lost my job and had very little money in the bank. She had a roommate at the time, and the roommate said to her about me, "You go out with rich guys, prominent guys. Don't you think you should be dating someone more glamorous than—*him*?"

In time, when asked why she took an interest in me, especially when it became known that I had limited prospects, Dolly has laughed and said, "Because poverty is sexy." She has a way with words. Some thirty years later, we are still together.

When we married, Willee came up from Washington (she was now remarried and living in D.C.) and took Dolly and me for a celebratory dinner in a French restaurant. Nancy sent us a dozen roses. I maintain that both women did it because they couldn't believe their luck that they had gotten rid of me.

⤸ Now, backtrack a few years to a moment that would have an impact on my life: In the cold, early-morning hours of January 2, 1972, five men carrying suitcases and wearing masks and tuxedos entered the lobby of Manhattan's prestigious Pierre Hotel and handcuffed nineteen startled guests and employees, including five security guards. No one could enter the gilded doors of the hotel without being apprehended by one of the bandits, and you couldn't call in or out without unwittingly speaking to one of them at the front desk. In less than two and a half hours they took an estimated $10 million in precious gems and cash from the hotel's safe deposit boxes, then disappeared into thin air. They left no clues, no fingerprints, and no physical harm was done to any of the hostages.

Steamy

I heard about this sensationally brazen—and seemingly perfect—heist that night and read about it the next morning on the front pages of all the New York papers. The following year it would be listed in the *Guinness Book of World Records* as the greatest hotel robbery in history. The thieves also did the same at several other tony midtown Manhattan hotels, including the Regency and the Sherry Netherland. Little did I know that those robberies—and one of their two masterminds, Bobby Comfort—would bear directly on my life.

One day, while still unemployed, Sayre Ross, the book designer for *Rockin' Steady*, called me about a matter beyond basketball.

It happened that Ross had published a boxing book with Rocky Graziano, the former world middleweight boxing champion, and Rocky, liking Sayre as most of us did, sent two alleged literary agents over to his office. Rocky knew a great many people, some of whom had crooked noses. The agents in question were named Johnny (Peanuts) Manfredonia and Yonkers Joe Celestino. They were representing, as it were, a jewel thief named Bobby Comfort. Comfort's crimes were front-page material, but he had served a prison sentence in which he had paid his debt to society, according to the government, and was now retired and willing to tell his tale. Sayre said to me, "Would you be interested?"

I was. It looked not only like a good story and a good book, but a surefire movie. This could be my retirement fund. It also would provide me with an intriguing insight into a netherworld that few, besides the crooks and assorted miscreants, ever experience. Such knowledge, I knew, would hardly be a detriment if ever I returned to the business of sports.

So it was that on a sunny May morning in 1978 I took a plane from La Guardia Airport to Rochester, New York, landing about an hour later on the gleaming tarmac, on schedule. I had been told that the man I was to see and discuss doing a book about—the notorious jewel thief Bobby Comfort—would be waiting for me in the

151

terminal. He was a dark-haired, middle-aged man and would be wearing a red sweater so that I could readily identify him.

When I came off the plane I walked through the small terminal and in and out of the coffee shop and candy store looking for a dark-haired, middle-aged man in a red sweater, but no one I saw fit that description.

Did he forget? Was he just late? Was there bad traffic? There had been no message for me on the public-address system. But, then, maybe this was a case of a prima donna with little sense of time or consideration for others. I was getting increasingly heated, remembering some of the prima donna athletes I had known. Once, for example, I approached Richie Allen, a star slugger with the White Sox, when he was sitting in front of his locker well before a game and smoking a cigarette. I introduced myself to his back. "Do you have a moment?" I asked. "No," he said, without turning to me. He then casually blew a perfect smoke ring into the air. End of interview. I wasn't interested in getting involved with another such type. I had convinced myself that I would board the next plane back to New York when I looked up to see a dark-haired, middle-aged man in a red sweater hurrying toward me. It was Bobby Comfort. He apologized for being tardy; as we walked out of the terminal and climbed into his blue Buick, where his wife Millie sat behind the wheel, Comfort explained why he was late.

It seemed that one of the first men off the plane fit my general description, as given to him by Sayre Ross. This man had approached Comfort and asked, "Are you the one I'm supposed to meet?" Comfort replied that he was. They walked to the car, settled in, and Millie drove off.

Comfort observed how tightly the man held his valise, and thought it strange. Then he was surprised when the man referred to "going to the store" instead of to Comfort's house for the arranged talk. At this point Comfort and his wife exchanged glances, both wondering about the so-called writer in the back seat.

After a few polite questions, the confusion was cleared up. Comfort learned that his passenger was not a writer at all, but a salesman.

The three laughed at the peculiar mix-up, and Millie turned the car around and headed back to the airport.

"By the way," Comfort said, as they pulled up to the curbside of the terminal, "who were you supposed to be meeting?"

"Someone from Hershberg's," the salesman said.

"Hershberg's!" Comfort said. "Is that right?"

Comfort got out of the car to say goodbye to the departing salesman. He jokingly advised him to be more careful about getting into cars with strangers. The man grinned sheepishly. They shook hands and the salesman disappeared into the terminal.

When Comfort finished the story, I said, "I've never heard of Hershberg's. What is it?"

"Hershberg's," Comfort said with a smile, "is the largest jewelry store in Rochester."

"Oh?"

"And just before he left, the man said, 'Lucky for me you're an honest citizen, because I'm a jewelry salesman'—he tapped his sample case—'and I'm carrying over half a million dollars in diamonds in this thing.'"

I spent more than three years off and on with Comfort, with his family, his friends, with many of his associates. I interviewed scores of people in law enforcement and lawyers who had come into contact with Comfort.

Bobby had a ready, masculine charm—along the lines of Jack Nicholson, as many perceived him, including me—and he had a quick sense of humor, even about the twenty years, overall, he'd spent in a variety of prisons, though not about guards or wardens. He plea-bargained his way to just two and a half years in Attica for the Pierre robbery. He was caught when the fence he had used for years was caught by the FBI and turned informant. Comfort was smart about a lot of things, and I felt that if he did not possess a legitimately criminal mind he could have been CEO of a large corporation. As things have turned out, his crooked predilections might well have qualified him to be CEO of a large corporation anyway.

Some people marveled at Comfort's "guts." In fact, he told me, a lot of people would be thieves if they had the courage to do it. He might be right, but there are also a lot of people who would rather not point a gun at someone and demand their wristwatch or earrings. One of Comfort's lawyers suggested to me that Comfort was a sociopath, without remorse or morals–that he was more nature than nurture. That fits Comfort to a degree. After all, when he robbed one rich woman, Janet Annenberg Neff, of her black onyx pendant, she said it was a sentimental piece and wasn't worth much. Comfort told her that if she were right about the price of it, he'd return it. And he did, by way of a messenger: a note about the return was published in the *New York Daily News* shortly after she had reported the robbery. People can be complicated. That's no revelation, but it's startling sometimes to come in direct contact with such an unusual and intriguing case.

Comfort was good on details, as he had been when casing the Pierre as Dr. James Wilson, the name on the credit cards he had stolen. Up every morning for a week at 4 a.m., he scrutinized the entire routine of the hotel staff, including who came and went, and when, at the walk-in vault off the main desk. This adherence to technical points reminded me of football coaches going over plays in the film room, winding and rewinding the tape.

Comfort was also one of the laziest people I've ever known. He was content–when I came to know the retired Comfort, in his early fifties–to lie on his couch in daytime and watch talk shows, often arguing back to on-air personalities like Phil Donahue. He'd play with Queenie, his cocker spaniel, go to the afternoon PTA meetings for his two young daughters–usually the lone father in attendance–or do some shopping for Millie. And he turned down jobs such as the Lufthansa robbery at Kennedy Airport that became a critical element in the movie *Goodfellas*. Comfort, after all, was no longer in "the business." Before, he'd plan a robbery,

The notorious jewel thief Bobby Comfort, the subject of my book The Man Who Robbed the Pierre, *in retirement in 1977 (after having served a three-year-plus sentence in the Attica penitentiary) with his wife Millie and daughters Stacy and Nicole, outside their Fairport, New York, home.*

pull it off, and then cool it for about six months. Then, having run through his bankroll, he'd return for another heist. Now, though, following the Pierre, he obviously had enough stashed away to live comfortably.

He no longer even played cards for any real cash, as he once had with his brother-in-law, Yonkers Joe, during some between-robbery intervals. He and Joe were also card mechanics. In the parlance of the society in which they traveled, a card mechanic is a card cheat. Comfort was a professional, though not quite as good as Joe. Joe was so good at manipulating cards that even when he was allowed to play in a card game with friends, they insisted he wear gloves. Members of organized crime often hired him to play in card games they had set up.

Comfort and Joe were adept at dealing "seconds"–that is, knowing the top card and dealing from the bottom of the deck until they needed the top ace. They were also slick at manipulating "coolers," the duplicate set of cards they had previously and meticulously arranged. They wore sport jackets with pockets sewn inside to hold the cooler. The sucker in the game shuffled the first deck and handed it over to Comfort or Joe to cut, whereupon one of them switched the decks and returned the cards to the sucker, who dealt his own losing hand.

They did have some close calls with card players who cast a suspicious eye, but both Bobby and Joe lived to tell their tales, and both died of natural causes.

They taught me how to perform those tricks, and I practiced. But I had neither the inclination nor the dexterity, let alone the fortitude, to try it in mixed company. My job was to try to write the book. I was content with that.

Comfort and I would visit each other or speak regularly on the phone. One day he told me it was hunting season in Rochester, and it was disturbing his rest.

"I know they're hunting something because I hear the guns going off all day," he said, referring to the area behind his house. "They're not supposed to be shooting back there. It's posted, but they don't care. Maybe it's pheasant they're after. I'm pretty sure it's not deer because I haven't seen any guys coming around here with trees on their heads.

"Some of my relatives drop by for coffee before they go out to try to kill the deer, and they wear the trees on their heads. Not actually trees, but branches. They can't get through the door.

"Now, my watchdog Queenie, she attacks them when they come in. Oh, a walking tree! Trees are the only thing she's not afraid of. She's the biggest coward in the world. And she doesn't like hunters at all. When she hears the hunters shooting, she falls on the floor and lays there.

"July Fourth is a terrible time for her, with all the firecrackers. She thinks it's the middle of the hunting season. She tries to run into the vacuum cleaner to get safe."

We laughed. We often laughed. Despite being fully aware of his dark side, I still had a soft spot for Bobby. Maybe that was my failing, but I saw him as a fallible human being, perhaps more fallible than most. He died on June 6, 1986, of a heart attack. He was fifty-three years old. And while hotel managers and jewelry store owners in New York City probably breathed a sigh of relief, I felt a distinct loss.

⌒ In 1980, while still working on the Bobby Comfort book, Murray Olderman and I wrote a story together for *Inside Sports* magazine, a creative, groundbreaking magazine which was relatively new but already highly regarded. The editor was John Walsh, whom both Murray and I had known in our journalistic travels. I had told Murray about a remarkable story that had come to my attention, but that I couldn't work on because I was busy with Bobby Comfort. Murray pitched the idea to Walsh, who gave Murray the green light. I hadn't known this. I kept thinking about the story, and called Walsh, pitching the idea to him. He told me he had already talked with Murray and given him the go-ahead. So I called Murray and told him of my interest. "Since it was your idea to begin with," he said, "let's do it together." And we did, sharing the byline.

The story was about Bruce Gardner, an All-American pitcher for the University of Southern California in the late 1950s, a handsome, smart, musically talented man who never realized his dream of making the major leagues. One night, when Gardner was thirty-two years old, he went to the mound at the USC field, the scene of some of his greatest triumphs, and put a gun to his head. He was found dead there the next morning. Gardner had left a diary written throughout his life. That diary plus the research and interviewing that Olderman and I did turned out to make a compelling story, one that was widely discussed around the country and anthologized in several publications.

I identified in some ways with Bruce Gardner—there but for the grace of God go I. It had a lure for me that few stories have had. Gardner was just a year older than I when he killed himself. He was a pitcher, as I was in high school, Jewish, and a good student in college. But while he lost his way, I happened to find mine. Although I've been low at times in my life, I've never contemplated ending it.

Using many diary entries, our story read almost as though Gardner were talking to us from the grave. His father had died when he was two; his mother and grandfather became dominant—he thought overbearing—influences on his life; and when he didn't realize his dream of pitching in the major leagues (he got as far as Triple A ball in the Los Angeles Dodgers organization), he drifted into the stock market, which turned bad in 1971.

As a college junior, Gardner had been offered a big contract with the White Sox. He had been named College Player of the Year and fervently wished to turn pro. His mother insisted, however, that he stay in school and get his college diploma. He hurt his arm after that, which ultimately led to the disappointing end of his baseball career.

And then, on the last night of his life, he wrote a suicide note in his apartment in Los Angeles: ". . . I saw no value in my college education. I saw life going downhill every day and it shaped my attitude toward everything and everybody. Everything and every feeling that I visualized with my earned and rightful start in baseball was the focal point of my continuous failure. No pride of accomplishment, no money, no home, no sense of fulfillment, no leverage, no attraction. A bitter past, blocking any accomplishment of a future except age.

"I brought it to a halt tonight at thirty-two."

On the mound at USC that night, he shot himself with his framed college diploma, an All-American plaque, and the suicide note on the ground beside his prostrate, bloodied body.

How could someone give it all up like that? How could someone be that depressed? I didn't understand that lack of hope. Especially someone of Gardner's relative youth and talents. But I did understand that without hope life becomes a cul-de-sac. It chilled me. Everyone's brain works so differently. Each has his wires crossed in inscrutable ways, and all the answers to these workings seem to leave only more questions.

I've tried in my reporting to fathom the motivational roots of people like Bobby Comfort and Bruce Gardner, so different from each other but somehow their similarities are striking in their aberration. Oddly enough, the story of Bruce Gardner would be instrumental in changing my own life in a decidedly positive fashion.

8

~~~~~~~~~~~~~~

Good News and Bad News

ON NEW YEAR'S EVE, 1980, as Dolly and I were about to leave our apartment on Thirtieth Street in Manhattan for dinner with friends and an early party—we had actually opened the door to leave—the phone rang in our apartment.

"I'm not going to answer it," I said. "Whoever's calling now—it can't be that important."

"Oh, answer it," Dolly said. "You never know."

So I answered it.

It was Sandy Padwe, the deputy sports editor of the *New York Times*. While I had known Sandy for years, since shortly after I had come to New York to work for NEA, I was surprised to hear from him. He had never before called me.

"Red's been pretty much under the weather in the past year," Sandy told me, referring to Red Smith, then a columnist with the *Times*. "And he's up in age. We don't know how much longer he can write for us. So we're looking for a possible replacement for him one day. Would you be interested in talking with us?"

"First, I hope Red writes forever," I said. "You know, I've had a long relationship with him."

"I understand," said Sandy. "We love Red, and we hope he writes forever, too. But that's not realistic. Joe Vecchione and I would like very much to discuss this with you."

"Sure," I said.

And we did. I wasn't sure about returning to journalism since I had started another book and had worked on writing a musical with a stage director who had done Broadway shows, Bob Livingston. But I thought that working for the *New York Times*, even for one year, would look good on my resumé, regardless of what I wanted to do after that.

The *New York Times* was a dream, to be sure. Whatever complaints people may have of it, it is unquestionably the top of the line in journalism by virtue of its history, its standing as an institution in the country—if not in the world—and its immersion in coverage. So I talked with Joe Vecchione and Sandy. And I agreed to come on board. My first day on my new job was March 1, 1981, two months past my forty-first birthday.

It was Sandy's place at NEA that I had taken when he left to become a sports columnist for the *Philadelphia Inquirer*. Dave Burgin, with NEA at the time, had recommended me to Murray Olderman when Sandy left. Burgin had introduced me to Sandy, and Sandy and I had an acquaintance, nothing more. But I knew he read my stuff and on occasion would comment favorably on it.

I had been freelancing for four years when the *Times* called. Sandy Padwe had read the Gardner story and showed it to the sports editor, Joe Vecchione. Padwe, as I understand it, also brought in a copy of my book *Beyond the Dream*, with the foreword by Red Smith. At one point in his foreword, Smith, to my great surprise and satisfaction, wrote:

"I am proud of Ira Berkow. We became friends by mail when he was an undergraduate writing sports for his college newspaper. He sent samples of his work for criticism, and I am pretty sure I responded with free advice, yet in spite of this he became sports editor of Newspaper Enterprise Association.

"It can be stated as a law that the sportswriter whose horizons are no wider than the outfield fences is a bad sportswriter, because he has no sense of proportion and no awareness of the real world around him. Ira Berkow knows that what is important about a game is not the score but the people who play it. . . ."

I have a hunch that those remarks from Red Smith did not hurt my chances for a position at the *New York Times*.

In my two years at the *Minneapolis Tribune* and nearly ten years at NEA, I had learned something about how office politics may infect the workplace even in the world of journalism. At the *Times* I was determined to stay as far out of politicking as I could. Turns out, that was impossible. The *Times*, in certain ways, works as intricately as the Kremlin. And try as one may, one eventually and inevitably gets caught up in at least some of it.

Meanwhile I was sometimes substituting as a columnist for Smith, who was having health problems—particularly with his kidneys—and was in and out of hospitals. Then, nine months after I joined the *Times*, Red died. Vecchione called to ask me to write Red's obituary. I did, even noting that Smith was "generous" with advice to college students, and I quoted his advice to an anonymous kid, who, my friends knew, was me. I was deeply saddened at Red's passing. I was happy doing what I was doing at the *Times* and didn't need a regular column, but it came to me following Red's death. How curious that my relationship with him, starting from when I was a junior in college more than twenty years earlier, should come full circle. Red Smith's kindness, his instruction, his sensitivity changed my life. I am forever grateful. I miss him—and his column—to this day.

When I picked up the *Times* on my doorstep the next morning, January 20, 1982, I was at once surprised and ambivalent to see my obituary of Red on page one. As a writer I was pleased by my first page one story in the *New York Times*. My reaction was bittersweet because the story related to the death of my mentor, friend, and model, perhaps the single most important reason for my entering the world of my life's work. It was Red Smith's inspiring prose, and his encouragement, that were a driving force for me.

About a year later Jack Dempsey, the great heavyweight boxing champion of the 1920s, died. As it is in the newspaper business, writers are often asked to write advance obituaries on celebrated people who are growing old. Red Smith had written the Dempsey obit.

Smith died before Dempsey did, but when Dempsey's obit ran, it had Red Smith's byline in the *Times*'s first edition. The macabre notion of someone composing from the crypt was quickly caught, and Red's byline was removed in following editions.

In the office the next morning, Vecchione had the first edition. Several of the staff were around.

"You see," said Vecchione, "Red writes better dead than you guys do alive."

⌒ One of my first stories for the *Times* appeared in April 1981, a little over a month after I had joined the paper. It was about Isiah Thomas, then a sophomore guard for the Indiana University basketball team that had recently won the NCAA championship. Isiah, at 6-1, was the star of the team, and there was speculation that he would already turn pro. I went to Bloomington to see him. He was in hiding, virtually, from Bob Knight, the iron-fisted and iron-minded head coach. I tried to interview Knight about Thomas's situation, but he refused to see me or anyone else from the media about it. Knight didn't want Thomas to leave, saying he would get more experience and be worth more to the pros if he played out his career at Indiana. It was a selfish attitude on Knight's part, hoping for two more championships with Isiah, though Knight in later years would rewrite history and say he encouraged Thomas to take the money. It was a blatant lie.

The difference between Knight and Al McGuire, who had been the head coach at Marquette, was, well, the difference between night and day. Some ten years earlier, when McGuire's star

6-11 center, a junior named Jim Chones, was offered $1 million—few other players got that kind of money then—McGuire said, "I looked in my refrigerator, and I looked in Jim Chones's refrigerator, and I said, 'Jim, take the money.'" Chones, like Thomas, had come from a poor family.

I searched the campus for Thomas and found him in an apartment. I knocked on the door. He answered it and was surprised to see a reporter, realizing that somehow his cover had been blown.

But he did invite me in.

"Where are you from, Isiah?" I asked.

"From Chicago," he said.

"I know that," I said. "But where in Chicago?"

"West Side."

"Where on the West Side."

"Congress Street," he said.

"Isiah, Congress and what? Lawndale, St. Louis, Central Park, Millard, Homan, Kedzie? Exactly where?"

"My God," he said, "you really did a lot of research."

"No, Isiah," I said, "I grew up in the neighborhood."

Nineteen-year-old Isiah Thomas was soon selected by the Detroit Pistons second overall in the next NBA draft and received $1 million for signing. He made the All-Star game in that first year and was named rookie of the year.

Thomas could hardly have done better even with two more years of college experience.

I have had a solid relationship with Isiah from the first time I met him in Bloomington through his playing and coaching and NBA front-office careers, to the time he took over as general manager of the New York Knicks in 2003.

In 1987, after the Pistons had lost to the Celtics in a riveting playoff game in Boston Garden, and eventually lost the chance to meet the Lakers in the finals, Thomas was deeply disappointed. And angry—angry at losing, angry at himself for having thrown the errant in-bounds pass that Larry Bird stole and swiftly passed to the cutting Dennis Johnson for the winning basket, a one-point difference, with five seconds left in the game. Afterward Dennis Rodman, a Pistons rookie, remarked that Bird was overrated. It was repeated in the locker room to Thomas, the captain of the team.

"I think Larry is a very, very good basketball player," said Thomas, "an exceptional talent, but I'd have to agree with Rodman. If Bird was black, he'd be just another good guy."

This caused a great stir around the country. Bird was a most valuable player, one of the superstars of the game. Were Thomas and Rodman correct, or was there an element of racism in their remarks?

A day later I called Thomas and asked him about it.

"What I was referring to," he told me, and which I wrote in my column, "was not so much Larry Bird but the perpetuation of stereotypes about blacks. When Bird makes a great play, it's due to his thinking and his work habits. It's all planned out by him. It's not the case for blacks. All we do is run and jump. We never practice or give a thought to how we play. It's like I came dribbling out of my mother's womb.

"You hear it on television, you see it in the papers. I remember watching the NCAA finals between Syracuse and Indiana. I listened to Billy Packer, who I like, and who I think likes me, and he said when Indiana was sending in Garrett and Smart, 'Well, here come the athletes into the game.' The word 'athletes.' I think that that's an unconscious statement concerning race. I don't like it.

"Magic and Michael Jordan and me, for example, we're playing on God-given talent, like we're animals, lions and tigers, who run around wild in a jungle, while Larry's success is due to intelligence and hard work.

"Blacks have been fighting that stereotype about playing on pure instinct for so long, and basically it still exists—regardless of whether people want to believe it or not."

I concluded that column with: "Thomas is on target in regard to his views of stereotyping blacks. When you hear 'athlete' these days, it often means 'black' in the context Thomas stated. . . .

"In the case of Larry Bird, though, his record—both personal and in regard to team performance—speaks with eloquence for him. Black, white or fuchsia, Larry Bird must be considered not just 'another good guy,' but one of the best players to ever tuck in a jersey. It says here, the best."

About a year later, in early May, Joe Vecchione called me at home.

"I have good news for you, and bad news," said Vecchione.

"Oh?" I said, not knowing what to expect.

"The good news is, you were a finalist for the Pulitzer Prize for commentary," he said.

"I was?" The *Times* has a policy of not telling its writers which of them has been submitted for prizes, so I had no idea I was even in the running. More emphatically, I had no idea I was anywhere *near* the running. The *Times* submits ten pieces of a writer's work for commentary—it's general, there is no sports category—and the one on top is generally the most compelling. The first one of my ten was the column I did on Isiah and Bird.

"What's the bad news?" I asked Joe. I couldn't imagine.

"The bad news is," said Vecchione, "you didn't win."

"That's not so bad," I said.

Strangely, in this moment in which I reached a peak in my profession, I felt a wave of disappointment suddenly come over me. I had been lifted up so suddenly, then just as quickly brought down. But my disappointment faded quickly. I had been one of three finalists, along with Michael Kinsley, whose insightful columns appeared in the *Washington Post,* and Molly Ivins, the firebrand columnist with the *Dallas Times-Herald.* The Pulitzer board, as it sometimes does, went over the head of the nominating judges and made its own selection, choosing Dave Barry, the humorist, for the Pulitzer for commentary. I was rather unfamiliar with Barry's work, but I found him to be a deserving choice. It took a while for me, though, to appreciate him. Envy can color one's views. In some way I think Isiah Thomas—for all the good points he made, and they were important points—and Dennis Rodman could understand.

I think, too, that my column opened some eyes about black players not being appreciated as much as whites for their work ethic and thought process during play. As time went on, I began to hear on television and read in the papers how this black player or that one used his wit and wisdom to achieve a desired result on the field or on the court. Others have told me that it changed perceptions. It was gratifying to think that, in ways large or small, one can make a difference, even on the sports page.

↙ My Chicago background also influenced my perspective in the case of Tonya Harding. On February 3, 1994, I wrote a column about Harding, whose former husband had admitted setting up an assault with a tire iron to break the knees of Nancy Kerrigan, Harding's chief rival, at the U.S. women's figure-skating championship in late December 1993. Kerrigan was also Harding's most formidable foe for a gold medal at the Olympics to be held in February 1994.

"This is a true story: In January 1957 there was a terrible murder in Chicago. Two teenage sisters, Barbara and Patricia Grimes, were found in a culvert in a park, their nude bodies frozen," I began the column. "A citywide search for the killer or killers was begun. Headlines screamed as suspects were rounded up. People were in panic. Who committed this dastardly deed, and why?

"Finally, a 21-year-old Skid Row illiterate bum and sometime dishwasher named Benny Bedwell, who wore long sideburns like Elvis Presley, was arrested. 'We got our man!' the sheriff gloated. [The bodies had been found in the county forest preserve, the sheriff's bailiwick.] Bedwell denied the charge but after more questioning, he confessed: 'Yes, I murdered the girls.'

"He said, among other things, that he had taken them out the night of the crime and fed them hot dogs. The coroner wondered about this, because there was no trace of hot dogs in their systems. Witnesses said Bedwell was at such and such a place when the murders were supposed to have occurred miles away.

"Soon after, a chagrined police department released Benny Bedwell from custody. Bedwell later made another confession: that he had said he committed the murders because, a lonely and forgotten man, he relished the attention.

"I've never forgotten this. I was 17 at the time and, like almost everyone else in Chicago, I had been convinced without a doubt that Bedwell had done it. It was a powerful lesson: something that seems black and white just may not be so. One must wait until all the facts are established."

My point was, in regard to the figure skaters, that it wasn't certain that Harding was guilty of complicity in the crime. At least in my mind. But a majority of the nation, if one could judge from letters to editors and discussions on television, felt otherwise. The U.S. Olympic Committee also rejected her application to be a part of the figure-skating team.

Harding, I wrote, "had denied being involved. There is no direct proof that she was."

In another column I wrote, "At this moment, the most anyone has been able to pin on her is guilt by association. If nothing else changes, it ought not to be enough to keep her from competing on the United States figure skating team in the Olympics next month in Norway. . . .

"At times like this, important officials, not bureaucratic satraps, must take a stand on what's right, not just what's politically correct, or 'easiest.'"

Harding had won first place in the U.S. nationals, with Kerrigan unable to compete. And so I added to end my column: "Harding ought to be assured by the Olympic Committee that, short of a confession by her or a judgment against her in court, she has earned the right to skate in the Olympics."

My stance was so contrary to most others in the media that I was asked to debate the point on shows from the "McNeil-Lehrer Report" to "Charlie Rose" to "Face the Nation," in which Bob

Schieffer moderated the head-to-head difference of opinion between Frank Deford of *Sports Illustrated* and me.

Shortly before the Olympic team was assembled to head for Lillehammer, a federal judge in Washington, Harding's home state and where she filed an appeal, said that she did not have enough time to marshal her defense, and so she must be allowed to compete in Norway.

I covered those Olympics, saw her arrive, saw her work out in an arena with Kerrigan, who had recuperated sufficiently to compete—they nearly brushed each other as they swirled through their practice routines—and saw Harding, in short sequined red dress and hair pulled back severely in a ponytail, lose her composure completely when she skated in the long competition and, partway through, a shoelace broke. I was seated just a few feet away when I saw her throw her leg up on the judge's table to show the snapped lace on her white skate.

The atmosphere of that event, in its buildup, suspense, and intrigue, rivaled only the first Ali-Frazier fight for intensity and drama. And it is still rated one of the top sports programs ever viewed on television.

Oksana Baiul of Ukraine won the women's figure-skating gold; Kerrigan came in a close second; Harding was tenth.

"I got out there and left my problems behind," Harding said later in the interview room, where I would write my story. "I did the best under all the circumstances because I think I was ready to have a nervous breakdown before I went out the first time."

A few years later Harding was convicted of having prior knowledge of the assault by her former husband, who, she said, had sworn that if she ever told anyone he would break her knees. She received a suspended sentence of three years. She has never confessed to being a part of the assault on Kerrigan; and, for all the world knows, she is telling the truth. And while it may seem far-fetched to some—sometimes to me as well—I remember how certain I was, and the rest of Chicago, that Benny Bedwell had slain the Grimes sisters.

⌒ I first met Pete Rose a few months after I arrived in New York, in the spring of 1968. He had already established himself as a premier ballplayer, a burly, take-no-prisoners second baseman for the Cincinnati Reds. I continued to write about him for the next four decades.

I have always felt, and written, that Pete Rose should be in the Baseball Hall of Fame. And I have always felt, and written, that the case against him is flawed—just as Rose himself is flawed, but that's another matter.

I came to know Rose and followed him through his best days and some of his worst. He could be charming and he could be crude. But he was a dedicated and extraordinary player. Among other remarkable achievements, Pete Rose was a team player who started in All-Star games at a record five different positions: first base, second base, third base, left field, and right field.

The general thought was that Rose was an overachiever, like Larry Bird in basketball, who wasn't as talented as some others. I never saw it that way. Rose and Bird were exceptional talents who worked diligently to hone their skills. People who make the big leagues in any sport are enormously talented. While they may not run as fast, say, as some others, or jump as high, I've come to understand that unusual hand-eye coordination and an uncanny understanding of the games and their gift give rise to their accomplishments.

I remember a conversation with Rose and some sportswriters during spring training in 1973. One of the writers said that black athletes could run faster and jump higher than whites. "They're built different," the writer said.

Rose said, "So how come the Russians run so fast and jump so high? They're all white."

There was silence from the writer. In fact, the previous summer at the Olympics in Munich, Valery Borzov of Russia had won the 100-meter and 200-meter races, and Juri Tarmak of Russia had won the high jump. One could always count on Rose to have an answer or an argument, and when it came to facts and figures on

I believe Pete Rose deserves to be in the Baseball Hall of Fame. Here I talked with him in Riverfront Stadium in 1985, when he was the Cincinnati Reds' player-manager, shortly before he broke Ty Cobb's all-time record for most hits in a major-league career with 4,192. [Photo by Dick Schaap]

sports and sports figures, he was invariably right. But gamblers, I knew, study such things. And while we all knew that Rose loved playing the horses, as many others in sports do, no one, not even the Reds' beat writers, ever considered that Rose might bet on baseball.

I was in Riverfront Stadium, home of the Cincinnati Reds, the night Rose broke the all-time hit record of 4,191 held by Ty Cobb. It took place 10 miles from the sandlots where he began playing baseball as a boy. Rose, then 44 and in his 23rd season in the major leagues, and now player-manager of the Reds, stepped to the plate in the first inning. It was September 12, 1985, a warm fall evening.

The sellout crowd of 47,237 that packed the stadium hoping to see Rose do it now stood and cheered under a twilight blue sky beribboned with orange clouds.

I was writing on deadline, and if Rose could get the hit now, just minutes before I had to file my copy, I'd have the story, which was scheduled for page one. So we had two dramas going at that moment, though no one else in the park could have cared about mine.

I was already writing my lead in anticipation of the hit, and then would fill in the necessary details.

"Now he eased into his distinctive crouch from the left side of the plate, wrapping his white-gloved hands around the handle of his poised black bat. His red batting helmet gleamed in the stadium lights. Everyone in the ballpark was standing. The chant 'Pete! Pete!' rose higher and higher. Flashbulbs popped.

"On the mound was the right-hander Eric Show of the San Diego Padres. Rose took the first pitch for a ball, fouled off the next pitch, took another ball. Show wound up, threw, and Rose swung and hit a line drive to left-center.

"The ball dropped in and the ballpark exploded. Fireworks being set off was one reason; the appreciative cries of the fans were another.

"Streamers and confetti came floating onto the field as though the skies were raining paper. . . ."

Rose, who was invariably cooperative with the press in his playing days, had helped me again.

I wrote that piece and then rewrote part of it, at the conclusion of the game, for the later editions. The Reds won 2-0, Rose getting another hit and scoring both runs.

"After the game," I wrote for the later editions, "in a celebration at home plate, Rose took a phone call from President Reagan that was relayed on the public address system.

"The President congratulated him and said that he had set 'the most enduring record in sports history.' He said that Rose's record might be broken, but 'your reputation and legacy will live for a long time.'

"'Thank you, Mr. President, for taking the time from your busy schedule,' Rose said. 'And you missed a good ball game.'"

Rose was being true to himself, as he often was, by bringing the discussion back to the joys of the game. And the president had no idea that his words about Rose's "reputation and legacy" would have a different connotation as time went on.

Just four years later Rose was banned from baseball by Commissioner Bart Giamatti for gambling on sports games, though, from an agreement worked out between the two sides, Giamatti did not say it was because Rose also bet on baseball. Rose denied he did until an autobiography was released in January 2004 in which Rose admitted that he bet on baseball as a manager. But in the 225 pages of the Dowd Report, commissioned by Giamatti to catalog Rose's gambling, there is not a word about him gambling on baseball as a player or player-manager. The report included seven volumes of 2,000 exhibits that presented, among other things, betting slips—some supposedly with Rose's fingerprints—as well as numerous and suspicious phone calls to bookmakers or those connected to bookmakers. All this documentation dealt only with the period after Rose retired as a player following the 1986 season. It concerned the period when he was, for another three seasons, strictly a manager.

When one is placed on the permanent ineligibility list by the commissioner, he may no longer have any direct connection with major league baseball, and he is removed from the ballot of nominees for the Baseball Hall of Fame. The eligible members of the Baseball Writers' Association of America vote for the Hall of Fame, but with Rose's name off the ballot, only a write-in vote for Rose would be effective. There have never been enough write-in votes to elect a player to the Hall. So Rose, who is more deserving of being in the Hall of Fame than many who have actually been inducted, is on the outside looking in.

The *Times*, virtually alone among newspapers, no longer allows its writers to participate in balloting for the Hall or the Emmys or the Oscars or such, the theory being that writers should report news, not make it. I think it's correct. But when I was voting, I wrote in Rose's name. This is why:

Pete Rose, nicknamed "Charlie Hustle" because of his desire to succeed on the baseball field, has never been accused of throwing a game as a player or playing less than his best. Again, all the exhibits in the Dowd Report cover only the years from 1987 to 1989, when Rose was field manager of the Reds.

No hard evidence exists that Rose gambled as a player, and Dowd, in a conversation with me, agreed, but said, "The only evidence is according to witnesses." There were three primary "witnesses," all of whom were themselves connected to illegal gambling with Rose in one form or another. Witnesses, as any lawyer can tell you, may or may not be reliable, depending perhaps on their own agendas.

If Pete Rose were to be eligible for election to the Hall of Fame, it would not be for managing but for performance as a player.

Indeed, his six-year record as a manager, 412 wins against 373 losses, and never a higher finish than second, is good but not up to Hall of Fame standards. His record as a player, however, is spectacular.

Some have insisted that Rose make a full confession before gaining eligibility to the Hall. This is contradictory reasoning. Even if he did confess to gambling on baseball–and he has, but opponents of Rose for the Hall of Fame still are not satisfied because he hasn't shown enough "penance"–that would not change the fact that he did it, that he committed baseball's capital crime. With that logic, he should never be named to the Hall of Fame, period.

Either he deserves to be in the Hall of Fame for his great twenty-four-year playing career in the major leagues, or he doesn't.

If the character issue were used broadly, numerous drunks, womanizers, racists, convicted tax evaders and drug users now immortalized with plaques in the Hall would be thrown out.

There is strong, documented evidence that Ty Cobb and Tris Speaker, two all-time greats, conspired to fix a game.

And still Rose is kept out by virtue of the current commissioner, Bud Selig, wringing his hands and "agonizing" over the decision to reinstate Rose. He doesn't have to reinstate him, of course, if he feels Rose's past—and maybe his present—will sully the game. But making Rose ineligible for Cooperstown is an entirely different issue, and one that is hypocritically defended.

It is Rose's "reputation and legacy" for playing the game that will remain forever unassailable. And what is a Hall of Fame if not for such a player?

This recalls a magazine article I once wrote on John Wayne. I interviewed him over a room-service breakfast in his suite in the Pierre Hotel in Manhattan. The discussion got around to heroes. He once said he had been in more battles than Napoleon, more wars than Germany, had captured Bataan, Corregidor, Fort Apache, and Maureen O'Hara. Although he had recently had a genuine battle with "The Big C," as he called it, his cancer was in remission. He had that larger-than-life frame, that craggy face and that craggy voice, but I found him to be thoughtful and without pretense. "Not in real life I'm no hero," he told me. "But I have tried to keep my word, and I've tried to maintain personal integrity. Sometimes it's been tough. Being a hero puts too much responsibility on you. You have to strain to live up to the image. I've lived up to the image a little better than some and a little worse than others.

"I've tried in films to portray the American way of life as it was. A great way of life. I've played different parts, from heavies to heroes. The only similarity in characters is that no matter how tough and rough I am, I've never been petty or mean.

"From what I see of the world today, the kids could use a few heroes. Someone to look up to, to try to emulate. It gives them something to reach for. But even your sports pages today are full of guys who refuse to report for practice or show up late or get busted or jump out of the bushes at little girls or do the damnedest things you ever heard of.

"I don't know where kids are going to turn for heroes. In the movies, you can always tell the bad guy. He's the one who works for a living."

Even though our politics were quite different–he being a widely known conservative Republican–I liked him. I hadn't thought I would. Shortly after, I was talking with my father on the phone and told him how I felt about John Wayne.

"So," my dad, the former Democratic precinct captain under Mayor Richard Daley, said, "you feel that America is big enough for the two of you."

I laughed. "Something like that," I said.

Along these lines, I'm reminded of the line from Red Smith that "writing is thinking." Without sound or thoughtful ideas, anyway, writing is shallow, and dull. If my views on Tonya Harding going to the Olympics because of insufficient evidence at the time, and Rose's credentials for election to the Hall of Fame on the merits of his playing career, go beyond the conventional wisdom, I'm not displeased.

And while America, as my father supposed, was big enough for both John Wayne and me, and the 1994 Olympics was big enough to allow Harding to enter the figure-skating competition, the Hall of Fame ought to be big enough to hang a plaque of Pete Rose on its walls.

9

~~~~~~~~~~~~~~

Full of the Devil

WHAT AM I DOING, and why am I doing it? This has been a continuing reflection of mine as a sportswriter. While such ruminations are hardly the sole province of practitioners of the writing and reporting of what Red Smith once termed "games that little children can play," they surely occur in the minds of a wide range of adult journalists. For me, more precisely, it is: What is, or ought to be, my place in the cosmos?

The question was brought back to me with a jolt in the spring of 2002. A story ran on the Associated Press wire and was picked up by the *New York Times*, where I read it, with the headline, "Islamic Charity Still Faces Charges." It began:

"CHICAGO, May 13—A judge refused today to dismiss perjury charges against an Islamic charity and its director accused of lying about ties to Osama Bin Laden and his network.

"Magistrate judge Ian Levin said evidence that the charity, the Benevolence International Foundation, had sent aid to rebels fighting the Russian Army in Chechnya warranted the charges.

"Lawyers for the charity had argued that the evidence of the ties was flimsy at best [and that the charity and the director] did not provide 'people or organizations known to engage in violence, terrorist activities or military operations of any nature.'

"But Judge Levin [ruled otherwise], and that there was probable cause to send the case to a federal grand jury. . . ."

It was a story I had been following for general interest but also for personal reasons.

Thirty years earlier, the summer of 1973 in downtown Chicago, I found myself in a small, staid Cook County Appeals courtroom, most likely along the lines of the federal courtroom in the Islamic charity case. Two black men had been convicted, possibly unjustly, of the rape and armed robbery of a white nun two years earlier. The men were not in the courtroom, but a tall, young, red-haired attorney was representing them.

The attorney, in a dark suit, stood before three black-robed judges. The convicted were behind bars serving twenty-five to thirty-five years. But the attorney had uncovered evidence that the prosecution had either withheld or ignored—perhaps willfully— and that might now serve to overturn the conviction. Regardless, this was conceivably the last chance for the accused.

The attorney was the head of the county public defender's office—defenders of the indigent. His name was Ian Levin—Ian Hersh Levin, my first cousin. We have been best friends as far back as we can remember, growing up in Chicago just six months apart, attending the same high school, playing as teammates on the school baseball and basketball teams, double-dating, sharing friends, relatives, and interests. We were named for the same grandfather, his first two names being Israel Hersh—I'm Ira Harvey. "We're like twins," Ian once said.

When Ian was speaking in behalf of the two black men, I had just flown to Chicago from New York to work on a sports assignment for NEA. As was often the case when I returned to my hometown, I had popped in on Ian to go to lunch and was told he was at trial.

As I entered the courtroom, I found the proceedings in session and located a seat in a back row. I saw Ian and heard the sound of his reasoned voice and began to listen to him argue the case with conviction. The judges listened without emotion. I was the only person in attendance other than a handful of court officials.

I noticed Ian's broad back and his red hair darker but thinner than in his youth. He turned a little to make a point and his profile came into view. I smiled at his full red mustache under a prominent nose. As he stood before the judges, I took in his still slightly concave left leg, set not perfectly after a high school softball injury. I always thought he risked life and limb–particularly limb–when he would slide–slide!–into the second-base manhole cover in long-ago games of stickball on Estes Avenue. (In those days, Ian's claim to decorum was: "At least I didn't slide head first." Sustained.) Now I was impressed with his bearing in the courtroom–professional, prepared, persuasive, dead serious.

But I had not been prepared for my own emotions in that courtroom. I felt proud of Ian fighting for–and doing so well–with so important an issue. But I was struck by feelings about myself.

While I was writing sports, Ian was dealing with the most monumental and noble of issues, a man's freedom. In other cases, then and perhaps in the future, there would also be matters of life and death. In 1973, though, we were both in our early thirties. I wondered then–and the thought would recur through the years–about the importance of what I do. I wrote about people involved in games that children play. Did I work, as someone once called it, in the newspaper's "toy department"–that is, the toy department of life?

Legal jargon and the citing of precedents thickened the air in this small courtroom. I recalled that I had once wanted to be like Clarence Darrow, a great lawyer for the defense, and, like Ian and me, a Chicagoan. But a quirk of fate, the entire experience at Miami and Dave Burgin, and, to be sure, Red Smith, led me to writing.

My cousin, federal judge Ian Levin (left), at a picnic with my brother Steve in the summer of 1994.

In high school, both Ian and I majored in eligibility, as it were. I finished in the lower quarter of my graduation class; Ian did a little better, finishing in the middle of his graduation class, a semester ahead of me.

Books were studiously neglected by us. But then, from the very beginning of college, something happened to both of us. Maybe it was an onset of maturity. Hard to say. But we both grew more serious toward the classroom. Ian was a leading student in undergraduate school, then enrolled in the DePaul law school, where he graduated valedictorian. He went into the practice of law, then the public defender's office, returned to private practice, was named a judge to the Cook County Circuit Court and finally to the federal bench.

Meanwhile, unlike lawyers and even judges, I was routinely dealing in miracles, as sportswriters do. That's the beautiful thing about sports and often about the writing of sports. Athletics, in the purest sense, do offer an oasis from the humdrum of the assembly line or the stove, or the incessant beat of political corruption. In sports we see men and women striving beyond their assumed capabilities, making an "impossible" catch, an "incredible" shot, an "unbelievable" kick. When we aren't ourselves performing such feats in our small duffer's way, we thrill vicariously.

A grace and beauty of description adds a valuable dimension to our appreciation of sports and to our own lives.

And yes, Yankee Stadium has been compared to the Roman Colosseum in its importance to a culture, and arenas in other parts of the nation draw people together to cheer, to argue vigorously but (in most cases) nonviolently, to share and pursue common interests that may extend beyond the playing fields. Even someone of the stature of Earl Warren, then chief justice of the United States Supreme Court, said that he turned first to the sports pages of the daily newspaper and only later to the front page, because "On the sports page I read about man's triumphs, and on the front page I read of his failures."

I interviewed Earl Warren in his office in the Supreme Court. It was May 1974, and my purpose was to get his reflections on the twentieth anniversary of the landmark *Brown v. Board of Education* decision, which declared that separate but equal education was unconstitutional. Warren was chief justice at the time, and spearheaded the unanimous decision. We also got around to talking sports, and he told me that, like President Clinton many years later, his hero was Henry Aaron, not only for his excellence as a baseball player and home-run slugger "but also for the dignified way he goes about his life."

More and more, however, one reads of man's failures in the sports section too. And it hasn't all happened just yesterday. Part of a sportswriter's job—the journalist's job—is to document the good, the bad, and the ugly that he or she has witnessed. It has been a concern—and, I have always believed, a professional responsibility—from the time I began in the business.

When I turned thirty, in 1970, I wrote a column for NEA about it. I said that to contemplate turning thirty is very much like contemplating a bad accident: you think it can't happen to you.

A sportswriter knows that thirty is a pivotal age in athletics. It is associated with the beginning of the atrophy of physical skills. It was somewhat comforting to know, however, that thirty, as far as we knew then, had no cause-and-effect relationship to senility. Not right away, anyway.

But I remember reading why Paul Gallico in the 1930s quit as the highest-paid sports columnist in New York, with the *Daily News*, to gamble on a career as a novelist (a successful gamble, it turned out). Gallico was covering a championship fight in Madison Square Garden. There was a knockdown, and Gallico leaped to his feet. A fan behind him screamed, "Siddown, you old sportswriter bum."

"I was a young man, then," said Gallico, "but I was afraid the guy might turn out to be right. I decided right then to quit."

And when Westbrook Pegler, a star sportswriter in the 1930s, transferred his talents to the editorial page, he said he had "gone global."

But there was another side. As time went on, I came to know Red Smith and asked him what it was that made Grantland Rice, once the dean of sportswriters, so special. "To Granny," said Smith, "every World Series was his first, every championship fight was his first. He saw everything through fresh eyes. He never grew old." Smith hoped to emulate Rice in that regard.

The world of sportswriting, meanwhile, has changed a great deal since the days of Grantland Rice and the "Gee Whiz" or cheerleader school of reporting. There was indeed an "Aw Nuts" or cynical school of sportswriting as well, but it had none of the virulence, none of the penetration of what was to come. Vietnam and Watergate helped immensely to turn the direction of all reporting onto a tougher road. After being lied to by the government in both those world-shaking events, and with attempts by the administrations at home to subvert the Constitution, coverage of all events took on a more cynical slant. It didn't stop in the A sections of the newspapers and carried over into the sports sections. It happened, to a great degree, on my watch, for I got my first newspaper job in 1965, with the *Minneapolis Tribune*, when America's participation in the Vietnam War–from a relative handful of "advisers" to thousands of combat troops–was only beginning to mushroom.

Sportswriters can help elevate the human spirit, no mean task. But they must also puncture myths, a task of at least equal significance.

In my view, if an atmosphere exists in which we confer unchallenged divinity on the kings of sport, this same mantle may be usurped, or the attempt made, by our politicians to be raised to such untouchable heights. And we see how they begin to rule with what they proclaim is divine right. A great home-run hitter and a president of the United States, alike, will have foul breath after eating onions. And recall: Cy Young won more games than any pitcher in baseball history–but he also lost more than any other pitcher.

"To be 30 in this day and age, and to be a sportswriter," I wrote in 1970, "is different from any time in history. There is the McLuhanesque threat that the printed word itself is passé, or rapidly getting that way. And with the cancer of Vietnam and America's race problems, the depersonalization of our lives by Big Brother, the escapism of sports becomes harder to justify as a profession.

"There are times when one feels guilty eating steak and drinking wine in the Waldorf-Astoria as the President"–Nixon at that time–"reminisces about football at a football banquet, and you know that outside there are people picketing for a more humane world. And so you must make a decision. . . .

"Sports today do mirror much of society," I continued. "I must write about the breakthrough (though often overrated–the battle has hardly been won) of blacks for equality, and the breaking of bondage of players from owners, and the drive for women to compete against men, and about athletes who believe they have something, and some influence, in telling the world how they feel about race, politics, and, in the case of Joe Willie Namath, the predilection for strawberry blondes."

My feelings have not changed a great deal in the thirty-five years since I wrote this. One can add drugs and steroid use and AIDS and spousal and sexual abuse and the threat of terrorism to the mix of problems in sports. And the war in Iraq has replaced, in most recent times, the many dangers and tensions we experienced with the war in Vietnam. Sportswriters deal with all of them. In fact, more and more sports stories appear on the front pages of newspapers and lead the nightly newscasts. The games, and the people who play them, increasingly touch us in ways well beyond the playing field.

I was asked by an editor on the sports desk at the *Times* to look into just such a story. In late May 2004 I was alerted to the plight of Specialist Danielle Green of the 571st Military Police Company stationed in Baghdad. Danielle Green had been a standout basketball player with a good left-handed outside shot at the University of Notre Dame in the late 1990s. I was told that she had been wounded in Iraq and transferred to a hospital in Germany. "We're trying to get the number in Germany for you," an editor said by telephone.

It turned out that Green was the unnamed female soldier in a dramatic front-page photograph in the *New York Times* the day after she was wounded. She was being transported on the hood of a Humvee to a hospital, flanked by nervous American soldiers, their weapons pointed warily.

While waiting for the number of the hospital in Germany, I called the sports information director at Notre Dame to get details on Green's life in basketball there. I mentioned that she was in Germany, but the SID corrected me. "She's at Walter Reed Hospital in Washington, D.C.," I was told.

So I called Walter Reed and asked for Specialist Danielle Green. I was put right through to her, and she answered from her fifth-floor bed. And this is the story as it unfolded for me:

In an apartment on the South Side of Chicago, at precisely five minutes to noon Chicago time on May 25, the phone rang. Willie Byrd, Danielle's husband, had been waiting for the call. It was Danielle, calling from Baghdad, but it was about two hours later than their prearranged phone calls were normally made.

"Honey?" she said.

"Yeah, baby," he replied. "How come you're calling so late?"

"I want you to be strong," she said.

"What's wrong? I know something's wrong."

"I'm okay," she said. "But—"

"But what?"

"I lost my left hand, but I'm okay."

"You're not okay!"

"I'm okay otherwise," she replied. "I promise you."

He shook his head, amazed that as strong a person as he knew her to be, she was still *this* strong.

"But I still have my wedding ring," she told him.

"You do? You said you lost your left hand."

"One of the guys in my unit found the hand. It was too late to try to get it sewn back on my arm. But he brought me the ring."

Danielle and Willie had been married for two months, about a year and a half after she had enlisted. She had always dreamed of being a soldier and decided after graduating from college with a degree in education, and after a few years as an assistant high school basketball coach, that she would try it.

"I grew up poor in Chicago, on the South and West Sides," she said. "And my father wasn't around at all, and my mother got messed up with drugs. And I remember as a small child loving the toy GI Joe. I thought, 'Oh, man, that's cool.'" She applied herself in school—and in the ROTC, where she attained the rank of lieutenant colonel—got a scholarship to college, and earned good grades as a psychology major, rising beyond the poverty of her youth.

"We have so much time in which we do nothing," Green recalled about her tour in Iraq, "and you stand outside, or, for me, sometimes sitting in the turret of a tank with your head exposed, and you're just waiting for something bad to happen."

When the attack occurred she was standing guard on the roof of a police station. She heard a burst of fire. Then a second blast, and a rocket from a homemade missile launcher in an apartment building next to the police station hit a water tank on the roof where she stood. The explosion ripped into her.

She screamed in pain. Her left arm had been hit, and shrapnel tore at her left leg and her face.

Within minutes, soldiers from her unit were up on the roof and covering her. She was quickly taken to the Humvee. She never lost consciousness.

"This is all part of war," she told me, "and you have to be brave. Good people get hurt. I was one of those people. I knew I was taking a risk in joining the army. I felt certain I'd be sent to Iraq. It's hard to imagine it's going to be you."

When she got to the hospital, Green said, she asked her sergeant, "Is my hand gone?"

"Yes," said the sergeant, whose last name, Harrelson, was all she could recall.

"And then I broke down," she said. "And I didn't cry again until yesterday"—five days after the incident occurred—"when Sergeant Pearce called and asked how I was doing. He was one of those who got me off the roof and onto the vehicle."

She thinks it was Sergeant Pearce who had recovered her ring.

As for her experience in Iraq, she said: "I thought we were going for humanitarian reasons, like building things and cleaning the neighborhoods up—it's filthy over there. But we hardly did any of it. We spent a lot of time just doing nothing."

"Looking back," she added, "I personally don't think we should have gone into Iraq. Not the way things have turned out. A lot more people are going to get hurt, and for what? It's like we walk around there as targets, with bull's-eyes on our backs."

When I visited Danielle Green in her room at Walter Reed, I saw that her left arm, which now ends just below the elbow, was swathed in bandages from surgery the day before for the insertion of a plate. It was her sixth operation, she estimated, since being wounded.

"I'm already learning to write with my right hand," she said. "It's not so pretty, but it'll get better. And worse things could have happened. It's happened to others over there. I'm just happy to be alive."

Willie Byrd said: "I've never known anyone like her, so strong-willed. You know, I had no intention of marrying anybody. And she told me: 'You need a good wife. I'm going to make you my husband, and make you happy.' And she did, and she has."

The story ran on June 3. It was originally scheduled for the front page of the sports section. But when the news department learned about it, it was decided to run it on page one of the paper. At the last moment, another story came in to bump it inside, but it remained in the front section.

On a Sunday morning following, I was sitting at home watching "Meet the Press" as the host, Tim Russert, interviewed Colin Powell. At one point, to my surprise, Russert said: "I saw this article in the *New York Times*. I want to ask you about it because of your involvement as a heroic military man and as secretary of state. This is Specialist Danielle Green, and here's her picture." I sat up. They were flashing my story on the screen. "She lost her left hand in war. She was known as 'D. Smooth' when she played basketball for Notre Dame, and she said this: . . ." And he repeated Danielle's remark about "'I personally don't think we should have gone into Iraq,'" and why.

Powell replied: "Well, I'm terribly sorry that she lost her hand. We regret all losses of that kind, loss of life, the injuries that our young men and women have suffered and those of the coalition forces and those of the Iraqi people as well. But I hope she will see in time that her sacrifice was worth it, that we are going to leave in place a nation that is better than the nation that we found when we went in, with the people that believe in the rule of law, that have defeated this insurgency, that are having democratic elections and will be a model for the rest of the region. And I don't think that's out of reach. These are difficult times."

And so they are. I was heartened to be a part of the dialogue of the war, which I believed to be ill-timed and ill-fated—that we were ill-prepared to fight it, and we were fooled by the Bush administration for going to war under false premises: Saddam Hussein had no weapons of mass destruction, there was no connection (as suggested by the administration) between Saddam and 9-11, and we were certainly not greeted universally with roses by the Iraqi people.

I thought Specialist Green was more right than Secretary Powell, who may or may not have fully believed what he told Russert, especially after his dramatic presentation to the United Nations General Assembly—with aerial photographs—arguing that Iraq possessed weapons of mass destruction, proved false.

~ As a sports reporter I've come in contact with people and found myself in situations that brought back memories from my earlier life in ways that I might never have imagined.

There are times, for example, when my very limited athletic career has proved helpful in my role as a sports journalist.

Once, after a basketball game in Miami, I wanted to talk with the Miami Heat's star guard, Tim Hardaway. He had not played a good game and was short with reporters who gathered around his locker. He dressed with his back to the writers and answered questions in monosyllables. When the others left, I said, "Tim." He said, "Yeah," I said, "Ira Berkow, *New York Times.*" He made no reply.

"Tim," I said, as he knotted his tie with his back still to me, "I'll bet that of the twenty thousand or so people in the stands here tonight, you and I were the only ones who either played for Carver or played against Carver."

He wheeled around. "You played for Carver?" he asked. He had gone to Carver High School on the South Side of Chicago.

"No," I said, "I played *against* Carver." Which was true. (I didn't find it necessary to go into the lousy game I had played.)

"You play against Cazzie?" he asked. Cazzie Russell had been a star at Carver–and later College Player of the Year at Michigan, and then an outstanding pro with the Knicks–and had been at Carver in the early 1960s, many years before Hardaway.

"I played before Cazzie was at Carver," I said.

Hardaway looked at me with what I perceived as newfound respect–curiosity may be closer to the point. And we went on to have a helpful conversation.

So it was with Danielle Green. When I first spoke with her on the phone, I asked what high school she had attended in Chicago.

"Roosevelt," she said.

"Roosevelt," I echoed. "You know, of course, I scored twenty-three points against Roosevelt."

"Ah, no," she said.

Of course not. It was in a freshman-sophomore game, and it was only some forty years before she became an all-state and all-American high school player. My so-called feats, on the other hand, had disappeared, except for my occasional recall. I asked if I might speak with her husband, and she gave me his cell phone number.

The phone conversation with Danielle was interrupted when an army officer walked into the room. He was from public information. He learned whom she was talking to–a reporter!–took the phone and said that I couldn't speak with Specialist Green unless it was cleared by his office. He gave me the phone number. I called and got a recorded voice message that said to leave a number and I would get a call back.

I called Willie Byrd. He arranged to see me the next day in the park adjacent to the hospital. Byrd, it turned out, knew some of the people I had played with and against all those years back in high school basketball.

I said I hadn't gotten a call back from the public information officer, and I wanted to be able to see her. He said rules were tight about that. I said I understood that. We talked some more, and I mentioned that I had told Danielle that I had had a good game against her high school alma mater.

"She told me," he said, with a laugh.

"Well," I said, "here it is."

I had made a copy of the clipping from my high school newspaper that confirmed the twenty-three points.

Willie Byrd smiled. I was indeed bona fide. Forget about credentials from such as the *New York Times*.

"You know," he said to me, "there's a back way to get to Danielle's room. C'mon, I'll take you there."

And that is how I met Specialist Danielle Green in person.

⌁ While stories like the one of Specialist Green transcend sports, covering the comings and goings of athletes in pursuit of baseballs and footballs and pucks and (for both two-legged and four-legged competitors) finish lines often remain a prerequisite of the job. And a pretty good job, to be sure. But periodically an identity crisis over what I do—even after forty years—does raise its head. Of course, this is not just the province of the writer.

"Sometimes I wonder what I'm doing, if I've wasted my time all these years in baseball," Al Kaline, the Hall of Fame Detroit Tiger outfielder, once said to me near the end of his playing career. "Sometimes I think I have. I would like to have done more to contribute to society. Maybe be a doctor. I don't know. Once in a while I'll sit in the dugout and look out on the field and wonder what good is all this. . . .

"So I have to think of myself as an entertainer, really. Maybe kids can draw an inspiration from what I can do. Maybe people who come out to the park can forget their problems for a while by watching me play."

Judge Levin too has wondered. When Ian was in the public defender's office: Should I not be earning more money for my family by being in private practice? When he was in private practice: Am I doing enough good, or am I too often helping out the fat cats of the world? And as a judge: Am I making the right decision, am I submerging my prejudices, am I being evenhanded? Will my decision hold up on appeal?

When I think about Ian in the courtroom in that case some thirty years ago, I recall his reasoned appeal to the three judges and the crucial uncovered fact that a shoe found at the scene of the crime and said by the prosecution to be worn by one of the convicted rapists was not the man's size shoe but one considerably smaller. (The size of the shoe had not been a point contested by the lawyer in the original trial.) Weeks went by as Ian and his clients waited anxiously for the decision to be handed down. Finally it was. Ian's clients would be released from prison within the next few days.

Not everyone can perform such important work. But over the years I, like many sportswriters, have had moments–from championing free speech, to exposing the ills of big-time college sports corruption, to giving voice to the underdog, to, as Dr. Samuel Johnson once phrased it, adding to the "gaiety of nations." In the end, one does what one can, or even what one was cut out for, and nothing less–for a writer, a sportswriter, a doctor, a plumber, a candlestick maker, an attorney for the defense.

In 1998 I was covering the Winter Olympics in Nagano, Japan, and standing in a pelting snow to write a story about snowboarders, who seem to be attempting with great joy to break their necks. I was trying to take notes and not succeeding very well, due to the wet notebook and the slippery pen point. It was freezing. I felt awful. And I was thinking, "What am I doing here? Ian is back in a courtroom in Chicago where it's warm, where people are bowing and scraping before him, and here I am doing this. Where did I go wrong?"

But the mood passed. Six months later I was covering the Big Apple women's golf tournament at the Wykagyl Country Club in New Rochelle, a New York City suburb. It was a gorgeous, sun-splashed July afternoon. I found a nice, shady tree somewhere along the lush fourteenth fairway, and sat down. I took a sip of lemonade from the bottle I had purchased from a vendor. Under the spreading leaves of the tree, there was just enough of a breeze to make it all perfect. I took some notes on the passing scene as the golfers, brightly attired, ambled by on this sparkling green golf course. And I thought, "Poor Ian. He's in a hot courtroom, sweating. People are arguing and yelling. And here I am in the lap of luxury. Where did Ian go wrong?"

10

~~~~~~~~~~

It Must Have Cost You a Fortune

SPORTSWRITERS don't normally lead dangerous lives. They do sometimes have to ask tough or uncomfortable questions. And yes, there's the occasional threat by a ballplayer who interprets— or misinterprets—something written about him and wants to rearrange the writer's nose as well as cripple his typing fingers. But that's rare. And yes, there's the fan who feels likewise, but only because you've written something that goes against the half-baked ruminations in his concrete-hard head. (My opinion.)

While we not infrequently deal with "heroes," we generally view them only in the context of winning or losing a baseball game, say, or a slalom race. We use the word "hero" relatively loosely, as we do the word "courage." Sometimes we look in the wrong place for a hero. And courage can take a variety of forms, some we may not even be aware of at the moment.

There was, for example, the earthquake.

I was in Candlestick Park in San Francisco for the *New York Times*, covering the third game of the World Series between the San Francisco Giants and the Oakland Athletics,

Tuesday evening, October 17, 1989. I was standing at my seat in the auxiliary press box in the upper deck behind home plate. It was about an hour before the game, the sun was beginning to set behind the stadium and creating shadows of the players in batting practice on the field when, at precisely 5:04, there was a rumble, as though an elevated train had decided to make a detour through the park.

I tottered. I'm not sure why, but I looked up at that instant and saw the tall light towers on the stadium roof, shimmering in the sunlight, swaying. I thought to myself, in those split seconds, something like: "I must be fainting. I've never fainted before. This must be what it's like to faint."

Then it stopped. "An earthquake, it's an earthquake!" people around me exclaimed. I heard one of the fans seated across the aisle from the press area say to his group, "Let's get out of here!"

I had never experienced an earthquake before–this one, we would learn, was 7.0 on the Richter scale, a devastatingly severe upheaval–but was oddly relieved that I hadn't actually been fainting. Quickly, however, I joined the rest of the crowd of some sixty thousand streaming for the exits–all of us surely feeling the same fears about not knowing if the ballpark was going to collapse at any moment and swallow us up.

Within minutes, it seemed, people with transistor radios and television sets were already spreading the word that part of the Bay Bridge had tumbled into San Francisco Bay, that fires were multiplying–all true, it turned out, along with a few dozen people killed, drowned in their cars in the Bay or crushed under toppling buildings.

I had packed up my laptop and the manuals and papers I needed for my work and, along with a friend, Tom Callahan, then the sports editor for *Time* magazine, hurried down the stairs and onto a runway behind the stands that led to a ramp. At that moment, coming in the opposite direction on the way to the ramp was, to my astonishment, a face from my past–I was positive it was him–a face I hadn't seen close-up in thirty-seven years.

He was a man I had sometimes thought about over the years, wondering what I might say to him if indeed I ever ran into him. Now he was obviously with three other people. Should I stop him, in the middle of an earthquake? This was Hank Sauer. As the saying goes, I would know that face anywhere.

As we drew closer, I noticed that he wore a name tag on his white sweater since he was a scout for the Giants. I had been a professional sportswriter for twenty-four years at that point, and had never crossed paths with him. I decided, earthquake or no earthquake, this was my chance. I whispered to Callahan that this was someone I had to speak to. He looked at me quizzically and said he'd wait.

From the time I was twelve years old I had wanted to confide to Hank Sauer how his glove had just happened to disappear one late morning during batting practice in Wrigley Field. Now, one dramatic day thirty-seven years after the larceny, I had the opportunity.

Sauer was the first man to be named most valuable player while on a team that finished in the second division—his Cubs finished fifth of eight National League teams. That was, yes, 1952. He had tied for the home-run lead in the major leagues with 37 and had led the majors with 121 runs batted in. He had a fine 15-year major league career with four teams, but he was so popular in Chicago, where he played seven seasons, that he was called the Mayor of Wrigley Field. He was as big as I remembered him— 6-foot-3 and maybe somewhat more than the 200 pounds of his playing days—still with that deeply lined face that struck fear in the hearts of pitchers but, up close, when I was seeking his autograph after games, a generous giant.

The face that I saw that late October evening was unmistakably Hank Sauer's, Mayor of Wrigley Field, even after all these years.

"Mr. Sauer," I said.

He stopped. "Yes," he replied, with raised eyebrows. Maybe he thought I wanted his autograph, even while a portion of northern California was being obliterated.

I introduced myself and then said, "Mr. Sauer, I've got something I'd like to say to you. In private, if you don't mind." He looked at me strangely but excused himself from his party—his wife, his son and daughter-in-law, it turned out. Callahan then introduced himself to them and, while they chatted, checking us out over their shoulders, Sauer and I moved over a few feet to a railing.

"It's something that happened in Chicago in 1952," I said.

"'52—that was my MVP year," he said.

"I know."

Then I told him how two kids from the West Side—one fourteen, the other twelve—had sneaked into Wrigley Field from a vendors' entrance early that day and made their way into the dugout and . . .

Hank Sauer listened intently.

"I–I was the twelve-year-old boy," I confessed, at long last.

Sauer reached out and placed his large hands around my throat. His hands were so big I later wondered how he could fit one into his baseball glove.

"You stole my glove," he said, his eyes narrowing.

"No, Hank"—when someone is throttling you it's remarkable how quickly you get on a first-name basis—"*I* didn't steal it. I won't say who did—I just wanted you to know what had happened."

Then Hank Sauer, still quite strong at seventy-one, withdrew his considerable hands from my neck.

"Thanks for telling me," he said. "I had always wondered. And I'm happy you got it off your chest."

And then we both left the ballpark, and soon we were in heavy traffic as darkness descended on San Francisco, the electricity went off, and citizens with flares came out to light the way along the thoroughfares. It was eerie, as was, in its way, my meeting Hank Sauer.

Everyone I've ever spoken to about Sauer has said he was a gentleman, besides being a good ballplayer and a good scout. I don't know what eventually happened to the glove, and it doesn't matter. I'm glad, though, that I told Hank Sauer the story when I did, for I never saw him again. Thirteen years later, after finishing the first hole on a golf course in Burlingame, California, near San Francisco, he suffered a heart attack and died.

When I learned of his death, I felt a sense of sadness because of the affection and admiration I had for Sauer, and unquestionably because of his generosity in understanding my long-held guilt.

↶ There are times like the one with Hank Sauer when a sportswriter has an opportunity, for good or ill, to catch up on a significant moment in his youth. This was another:

Shortly after the terrorists struck at the 1972 Munich Olympics, Eddie Waitkus, who had been shot by a deranged teenaged girl in Chicago when he was with the Phillies and I was a nine-year-old boy in Chicago, died. I wanted to write a column on him, one of my early baseball idols, and the impact that his being shot had on me—that even our greatest sports heroes are flesh and blood and not gods to be immortalized on pedestals. I called his sister, Stella Kasperwicz, who had been mentioned in the obituary. She told me Eddie had retained an interest in sports and had watched the Olympics. She said he had talked about the shooting of the Israelis.

"Eddie thought it was awful," Mrs. Kasperwicz recalled. "He said that none of us will ever be the same because of it."

I understood, I told her. I said I also felt that way about a similar incident that had occurred many years before, when I was a boy growing up in Chicago.

An odd thing happened after I wrote that column. I received a letter from a lawyer in Colorado Springs, Colorado, named Edward Waitkus, Jr.

Had Eddie Waitkus not been shot by Ruth Ann Steinhagen, he wrote, he wouldn't be here. After the shooting, Waitkus was transported to Florida where he underwent rehabilitation. A nurse who treated him became Mrs. Eddie Waitkus, and the mother of the lawyer in Colorado Springs, Edward Waitkus, Jr.

✎ After the earthquake in San Francisco, the World Series was delayed. It would be ten days before it resumed. Meanwhile the several sports reporters from the *Times*, as well as other newspapers, were summoned into action to report on the news events and occurrences around the devastated city. One of my jobs was to find a hero.

I set out in my search, feeling aftershock after aftershock. You'd be standing at a street corner waiting for traffic to abate—the city traffic lights still hadn't been turned back on, and the sidewalk would rise just a bit. "Feel that one?" a neighbor would say to another. "Sure did," came the response.

I asked around about any extraordinary escapes. When I spoke with firefighters on one street, they told me a remarkable story about a fireman who had saved a woman's life. Who was he? They didn't know. What fire company? They didn't know. I continued asking around. I got closer and closer. And then I found the firehouse. And the fireman.

His name was Gerry Shannon. When I arrived at the station house I was told he was sleeping. I informed the captain about my quest, and he said he'd see if he could rouse Gerry. A few minutes later a man in his mid-forties, hair rumpled, in slippers, fastening his suspenders around his shoulders, appeared.

I introduced myself, and Shannon and I sat down on the picnic bench in the middle of the station house where the firemen normally eat their meals. As he began to tell his stories, the other firefighters gathered around. They had known only the bare details. They were eager to hear it all.

It was perhaps an hour after the earthquake, at 5:04 Pacific time, tore through San Francisco. As they all knew, buildings and homes collapsed; some fell on cars and crushed them and those inside. One car, looking like a pancake, was found with only a finger recognizable. Some cars fell into the Bay when the bridge split apart. Fires raged. Shannon's unit was sent to the Marina District, a lovely area of San Francisco near the docks for the fishing boats. It was the area worst hit by the earthquake because the land mostly is dredged up from the Bay and, as some residents there describe it, shakes like Jell-O during a big quake.

As Shannon moved around a building on Beach Street, he heard a moan from within a collapsed house. It was a woman. When the earthquake struck, she was on the second floor. The floor had opened like a trapdoor, and she tumbled down, the rest of the building crashing down around her.

Her name was Sherra Cox, a fifty-five-year-old woman, and she lay trapped under a door and a doorjamb for what seemed an eternity for her. She smelled fire—the buildings around her were aflame—and felt the creaking of wood and stone. She feared she might be burned or crushed to death. She told herself, "Don't panic." She prayed.

Shannon, age forty-four, was a veteran of nineteen and a half years as a firefighter and had been involved in other earthquakes and other fires. But, he said, "never anything like this."

He was assigned to Hook and Ladder Engine No. 9 and had been helping fight a fire across the street when he heard someone was trapped in the other building. The first indication of this was the tapping inside heard by another firefighter. Someone still alive inside that building was obviously tapping something metal on wood. Shannon was closest to the spot and instinctively crawled through a space and began to dig his way toward the tapping.

He yelled, "Where are you? Where are you?"

He heard a woman's voice: "I'm here! I'm here!"

"Keep talking," he said, "so I can find you."

He would find that a wooden beam from the doorway had fallen across her body and that, by incredible good fortune, it had kept the rest of the building from burying her alive.

All around outside, sirens whirred, shouts were heard, but Shannon listened only for the woman's voice. The space was too small for him to maneuver with his fireman's helmet and turnout coat, so he removed them. Now, in blue T-shirt, he crawled through the debris and rubble, skinning his arms and knees as he clawed and wriggled through.

After about thirty minutes, as he continued to talk and reassure the woman, he was able to reach out and touch her.

"She grabbed my fingers," said Shannon, "and it was so tight I didn't think I could get loose."

"I've got to go back for equipment," he told her.

"Don't leave me," she said. "Don't leave me. I don't want to die in here."

He explained that he had to get a saw to cut through the wood beams.

"Promise you'll come back," she said.

"I promise," he said to her. "I promise I won't leave you. And when this is over, we'll have a cup of coffee."

Shannon recalled: "I knew I didn't have much time."

He left to get more equipment, and returned, and sawed and dug. He handed bits and pieces of wood and stone to the firefighter behind him, Bob Bodoures.

After another forty-five minutes, the saw he was using grew too dull to use, and he had to get another.

Sherra Cox groaned. "Be right back," said Shannon.

It was dark now, and getting cold. Shannon, on his return, gave Cox his coat and put it around her. He gave her his flashlight.

"She held it like in a death grip and she shined the light on her face," he said.

Meanwhile the fire from the building across the street had jumped to the building where Shannon was working to free the woman. The firefighters outside now began to pour water on the building.

"We only had about two and a half feet above us to work in," Shannon recalled, "and I saw the water from the hoses was making the wood above me heavy, and it looked like it was going to collapse. I hollered to them to stop pouring water.

"I thought 'We might not make it,'" he said. "But then I realized I couldn't think about that. And she saw the wood above her drop a few inches." The look in her eyes, recalled Shannon, was one of terror.

"And when I looked in her eyes," he said, "I knew there was no way I could leave her."

Finally, breaking the last beams with a hatchet, he was able to loosen Sherra Cox from the beams that had pinned her.

A stretcher was slid in, and she pushed with her feet and made it onto the stretcher.

Outside, in the glow of the fires, Sherra Cox, about to be put into an ambulance, reached up from her stretcher and grabbed the neck of Shannon, and pulled her to him and kissed him.

"You're my hero," she said.

"I owe you a cup of coffee," he said.

"I owe you more than that," she said.

And then she was taken to the emergency ward of San Francisco General Hospital. She would undergo surgery for a fractured pelvis.

Gerry Shannon, later, would tend to the "raspberries"–his scratches and bruises–that he received during business hours in the night.

When Shannon finished his story, the eyes of the other tough and gallant firefighters were moist with tears.

I visited Sherra Cox in her hospital room a few days after the quake. It turned out that she lived on the same street, Beach Street, as Joe DiMaggio, the former New York Yankee slugger. DiMaggio, then seventy-four years old, was seen in sport jacket and open-collared shirt the day following the quake, waiting in a long line at a shelter with other neighbors. He was there to learn whether his house would have to be demolished. He had been at the ball game the night of the quake and had escaped injury.

Three doors down from his two-story home—and directly across the street from Sherra Cox's—three people perished. DiMaggio's house suffered some damage but was saved. His sister was home and unharmed.

I mentioned to Sherra Cox how curious it was that one of America's most celebrated men, one who had been raised to hero status ("Where have you gone, Joe DiMaggio / A nation turns its lonely eyes to you," sang Simon and Garfunkel, in a paean to days when supposedly great men trod the earth), now elderly and white-haired, was, in the end, like everyone else, simply trying to survive. Meanwhile, all around, courageous acts by unsung fire-fighters, rescue workers, and everyday citizens were being performed in the aftermath of the earthquake.

"I wonder what the definition of hero is," Cox said. "I suppose it has to do with saving lives."

There are people like Gerry Shannon, and those who crawled through wreckage to find bodies flattened like license plates, who will never do a television commercial or be pictured on a bubble-gum card. This is no knock at those athletes upon whom we confer the title of role model or hero. It says more about the values of a nation that so prizes entertainers, including ballplayers.

I spoke with Rick Reuschel, pitcher for the San Francisco Giants, who said, "I've thought for a long time that ballplayers are elevated way too high. And when a disaster like this happens, we see how unimportant our job is in comparison to so many others."

"Life goes on," Cox said. "We pick up pieces. And I'm rooting for the Giants!"

Sports, for Cox and millions of others, even in disaster, does have the essential quality and potential of lifting spirits. And so it was with the woman whose life was saved by an unheralded working stiff.

Well, not quite. When the third game resumed, ten days after the quake, a dozen "heroes" of the disaster were honored by throwing out first balls before the game. Gerry Shannon was one of them. I sat in my seat and, like Cox, whom I spoke to later, was thrilled. My story on him had been read around the country, and from it, national television morning shows interviewed Shannon after the quake, and follow-up stories on him appeared in newspapers and magazines. In time I went back to writing sports, the Giants and A's went back to playing a kids' game, and Shannon went back to, whenever called upon, saving lives. In this regard, not much had changed.

✔ Some of our greatest so-called heroes, meanwhile, have not had the courage to stand up for issues of importance beyond the playing field, like Michael Jordan who, despite the facts, wouldn't raise his voice for Nike (his shoe sponsor) sweatshops in Vietnam; wouldn't raise his voice for gun control even after his father was murdered in a random shooting; wouldn't raise his voice against the right-wing Jesse Helms in the North Carolina Senate race against the black challenger, Harvey Gantt (Jordan was from North Carolina). Helms won in a close race; Jordan's endorsement might have made the difference. "Even Republicans buy shoes," said Jordan, excusing his inaction for the sake of business interests.

But Jordan had, to be sure, other compelling qualities, and hard work was one of them. I saw him shooting alone in the Bulls' practice facility the day before a playoff game against the Knicks in the mid-1980s. He was shooting jump shots from around the top of the key, and hitting them. Nothing unusual in that, except I soon realized that he was shooting them left-handed! At first I thought I was watching him in a mirror. Jordan was right-handed but had suffered a right shoulder injury, and there was a question of whether he could play. He was determined to play, even if he had to shoot jump shots left-handed. He did play, and played a characteristically terrific game, and did it shooting right-handed. It seemed he had willed his shoulder to heal.

Then there's someone like Jesse Barfield, a good though not spectacular outfielder who played for the Toronto Blue Jays in the 1980s. He stood up to do the right thing in a way that Jordan, in my view, did not. One day after a game, his teammate, George Bell, who was the star of the game, was naturally the center of attention with reporters in front of his locker.

A young woman radio reporter, Suzyn Waldman, new on the beat, held up her microphone along with others. Bell became irate, screaming that no woman should be in the locker room and that he would cut off the interview if she didn't leave. Abashed, Waldman turned and headed for the door, not wanting to ruin the interview for the others.

Barfield, who had never seen Waldman before, called out, "Hey, I got two hits today, don't you want to interview me?"

At first Waldman wasn't sure if he was joking, or adding a needle, but she walked over. And Barfield gave her the interview. It was an act of decency, of courage, of moral fiber by Barfield. He instinctively felt an injustice was being done, and decided to try to do the right thing. He risked alienating some teammates, risked being thought of as a wimp. He didn't care.

Women can generally take care of themselves. One example: when women in the locker room was a relatively new thing, Jenny Kellner, a reporter for the *New York Daily News*, was interviewing Mark Gastineau, the Jets' huge defensive end, who was sitting in front of his locker. He was naked except for the towel draped across his lap. At one point in the interview, Gastineau removed the towel and pointed to a spot between his legs.

"Do you know what this is?" he asked.

Kellner drew her gaze to the spot. "Looks like a penis," she said, "only smaller."

It took courage for Tom Paciorek, a former big-league outfielder and currently a sportscaster, to go public with the fact that he was molested by a Catholic priest when he was a boy in Michigan. He risked humiliation, but when he saw in the newspaper that that priest had gone to a new parish in the Upper Peninsula, Paciorek, a father of four, felt he had a moral duty to blow the whistle on the priest. The priest was suspended.

Arthur Ashe invariably demonstrated an innate sense of decency, humanity, and inner strength, from his outspoken convictions regarding apartheid in South Africa—he was the first black athlete to participate in an integrated sporting event in that country—to his becoming a spokesperson for educating people about AIDS after contracting the disease. I was with him when he was speaking to a group of students at a community college near Buffalo, New York. A student asked if he saw himself as a victim.

"No," said Ashe, "I see myself as a patient."

And then there was Muhammad Ali, to be sure, who stood up as a conscientious objector during the Vietnam War and had his world heavyweight boxing title stripped from him for his beliefs by spineless bureaucrats.

I followed Muhammad Ali's career for much of my professional life, wrote a great deal about him, and spent many hours with him. I witnessed the sad end to his fighting days, saw him slip into the impediments of Parkinson's Disease, saw him lose that facility for quick and lively speech.

Then, in April 1998, some forty years after I first interviewed him in that hotel room in Manhattan when he was first exiled from boxing, I met up with him again in a hotel lobby in Manhattan. He was with a small entourage that included his wife, Lonnie. He walked stiff-legged, and his face was puffy. A small boy in the lobby asked for his autograph, got it, then stood on tiptoe to kiss him.

"Ali is moved by people," Lonnie said, "and by human suffering." We were now in their suite and seated at a dining table. "What he does, he does from the heart. When we went into the Afghan relief village last year, Ali would find the dirtiest, most godforsaken kids, with sores and runny noses, and he'd pick 'em up on his lap and hug on 'em and kiss on 'em."

I said to him, "You sound like Mother Teresa."

Ali ran a thick, slow hand around his broad face. "Prettier," he said.

He had always been pretty, of course, though he was considerably slower in stride, at age fifty-six, and had put on more than a few pounds since he was the three-time world heavyweight champion. He reached for a bag of oatmeal cookies on the table.

"No other champs, not Sugar Ray Robinson, not Joe Louis, none of 'em did what I did," he said. "Sugar Ray was a beautiful fighter, and Joe, he brought pride to the black people. But I was controversial. I didn't believe in the Vietnam War—and I won that fight. I changed my name from Cassius Clay to Muslim—all that put together makes it different. And no one ever predicted the round he'd knock someone out in, and in poetry."

I recalled one example: "Moore will go in four." Which is when Archie Moore was in fact dispatched. But Ali, like most authors, felt that an excerpt left something to be desired. He recited: "When you come to the fight / Don't block the aisle / Don't block the door / Because Moore will fall in four."

Ali once told Joe Louis that if both were in their prime, Ali would beat him. Louis said, "You know, I had a Bum-of-the-Month Club."

Ali said, "I know."

Louis said, "You'da been one of the bums."

Ali smiled when this was recalled to him.

"Been no contest," he said. Then he pushed back his chair and rose.

"Joe shuffled," he said. His red tie dangling, Ali imitated Louis's crouch and stolid approach.

"I," Ali said with pride, "danced. He couldn't have touched me."

Suddenly Ali's fists were jabbing and hooking. And Ali, whose gait only a half-hour earlier was as stiff as that of a sleepwalker, was now doing the Ali Shuffle, with a funny, swift little jig in place. He put it into overdrive, his feet flying, his belly jiggling.

Enough. He grinned, slumped back into the chair. He was breathing about as hard as when he fought the Thrilla in Manila, the third and last classic fight with Frazier, which he won when Frazier couldn't answer the bell for the fifteenth round.

"The Shuffle," Ali said between nearly closed lips, "gonna make you scuffle."

The Champ laughed softly and reached for another cookie.

⌐ In writing, too, one aspires to be brave.

You try to lay it on the line. There are two ways to go: the "indirect way" that Walter Matthau liked or the no-nonsense punch between the eyes that Ann Landers approved.

Matthau, a great sports fan and chronic gambler on sports, was also an avid reader of the *New York Times*. We met and became friends. Sometimes he'd call me on the telephone: "I-ra," he'd say by way of greeting, the low, sonorous voice so familiar to moviegoers, "is anyone injured?"–thinking I might have an insight into a team he was planning to put a wager on. I invariably didn't know, which didn't dissuade him from calling a number of times and asking the same question. I think he just wanted to talk. But in writing he often liked what he called the "coming-in-from-the-side" approach.

"Wryness in humor is a quality I admire," he once told me. "When you look out from the backyard of my home in Pacific Palisades, you can see the ocean, and on Saturdays and Sundays there are thousands of sailboats out there. One day we had Charlie Chaplin over, and threw a party for him. He came out in the backyard and saw all the sailboats and said to me, 'It must have cost you a fortune.'

"One day Carol"–his wife–"and I were driving down the hill near our home and you could see the sailboats and she said, 'You hired those sailboats again.' I said, 'That's not good writing. That's on the nose writing–too direct. Chaplin came in on the diagonal. More subtle. That's good writing.'"

Another example was a story he told me that he said was true. Pia Zadora, the pretty young woman with, as was widely held, little talent, had been pushed hard for a career in show business by the rich, older man she had married. On stage in a Los Angeles theater she was playing Anne in *The Diary of Anne Frank*. Matthau said: "At the end of the play, when the Germans break into the store, the audience stood up and started shouting, 'She's in the attic! She's in the attic!'"

I thought that that one was pretty direct.

Eppie Lederer, the real name for Ann Landers, wrote to me about a column I did, and we developed a friendship. She wasn't a great sports fan, but she did have her interests. Football was not one of them, even though she had a correspondence with Bear Bryant, the gruff Alabama coach who, as unlikely as it might seem, read some of her columns to his players for inspiration. Eppie told me, "I can't hack football. I keep looking for the ball while everyone else is cheering."

She had written a column about how even great people fail at times. She had written that, for example, "Babe Ruth struck out 1,330 times—a major-league record." She wrote me that she had received a letter from a man in Honolulu telling her that Reggie Jackson, not Babe Ruth, held the strikeout record, with 2,597 whiffs. "Is this true?" she asked, writing on the margin of the man's letter. "I haven't had any other mail on it. Help! RSVP. Eppie."

I told her it was true. Shortly after, she wrote a correction in her column.

Eppie and I corresponded regularly. As is widely known, she was a pretty good letter writer. We were on such terms that she could be brutally honest with me when she was critical of something I wrote. She thought I was too soft on John Rocker, the Braves pitcher who made homophobic, anti–New York, anti–many things remarks. "Your column on John Rocker was OK, but no Pulitzer. You were much too easy on the momser [Yiddish for bastard]. Yes, you nailed him, but the nailing was too subtle."

I wrote a tribute column to her when she died, and used the word "momser." It didn't get past the desk at the *Times*. It was rightly considered "a pejorative," even if it was in Yiddish. The editors believed it would offend the sensibilities of some readers, and inserted outside the quote a euphemism: "an expression of, at best, contempt." The *New York Times* often has been a great place to work, but sometimes there is a softening of style that I find unnecessary, and even inconsistent and deflating for strong images and language. I once quoted Lawrence Taylor, the star New York Giants defensive end, as enjoying hitting an opponent so hard "the snot bubbles out of his nose."

Disgusting image, an editor thought, and it was expunged. I tried it again about a year later and it survived the cut. Times and tastes, I guess, change. Sometimes rapidly, from editor to editor.

✐ I lost some of my courage when Richard Nixon invited me to go to a baseball game with him. I declined, and now I'm sorry I did. After all, I'm a reporter. If there is an interesting person in the news, good or bad, it's to your benefit, and perhaps to your readers', to know as much about him or her as possible.

But at that time I thought I'd be mortified to walk into Yankee Stadium with Richard Nixon and have some of my colleagues in the press box see me with the man who I thought was a scourge on American politics. But then I got to know him, and, if not exactly come to like him, did come to comprehend the humanity of the man.

Nixon was a *Times* reader and a reader of the sports columns. I learned this when I received a note from him on June 25, 1982, when he commented positively on a piece I had done on Rod Carew, the batting star of the California Angels. He added: ". . . of the many ball players I have seen, Rod is by far the most graceful. Others are sometimes awkward; he is always fluid. . . .

"I met him for the first time in 1955 when I visited Panama as Vice President. When we met again at our home in San Clemente in 1979, he recalled that as a youngster he had seen me on that trip. . . . With warm regards, Richard Nixon."

I wondered about that recollection of Nixon's. Was this just a politician's remembrance, and one that had little to do with fact? How did Carew see him? Was he invited to the Panamanian president's mansion when he was ten years old? Highly unlikely.

I knew Carew, having helped him with his autobiography, *Carew*. I called and told him I was skeptical such an incident had occurred, and read him Nixon's letter.

"Oh, no," said Carew. "He was right. I was in the hospital in Panama City with rheumatic fever. He came by my bed on a visit to the hospital. I told him about it one time when he came into the locker room in Anaheim. He was good friends with our owner, Gene Autry."

So Tricky Dick was straight about that. You live and learn.

We struck up an acquaintanceship and, every year for several years, I received a birthday card from Richard Nixon. But it wasn't for *my* birthday, it was for his. I found that even a former President of the United States could be very odd, indeed. But with Nixon that was, of course, hardly news.

I first met Nixon shortly after that letter in a corridor at Yankee Stadium between the box of the team owner, George Steinbrenner (where Nixon sat as a guest), and the press box. This was around 1985, more than a decade after the Watergate scandal and his quitting the presidency in disgrace.

"I'm sure you lead a very interesting life," he said to me. I smiled. This was once the most powerful man on the planet. "Not as interesting as yours, Mr. President," I responded.

We were chatting on a wide range of subjects, including his telling me that only once in his life did he ever ask anyone for an autograph, and that was when he and his wife saw Babe Ruth in a New York restaurant in the early 1940s when Nixon was a naval officer. "I had Pat go over and ask him," said Nixon. "I was too embarrassed, and too awestruck."

A man whom I did not recognize came up to Nixon while we were talking and asked him to autograph the three baseballs he held in his hand. Nixon agreed amiably, the man gave Nixon his pen, Nixon signed the balls, and the man left. A few moments later, Nixon realized he still had the pen.

"Hey," he said to a Secret Service man beside him, "please return this pen to that guy. I don't want him to think I'm a crook."

Nixon invited me to his office in the Federal Building in Manhattan and I went there—it was private, being more comfortable for me to be sitting with him there than in a Yankee Stadium luxury box. We spent several hours talking about sports and world affairs. I saw him several times after that, and we exchanged letters as well. If nothing else, one had to admire Nixon's head-spinning ability to withstand personal disasters—and forge comeback after comeback.

About a year after I first met him, I was in the pressroom at Yankee Stadium with several other people, primarily journalists, at a table for lunch. Reporters trade stories, and I told about Nixon and the pen, and about the remark that he didn't want to be thought of as a crook.

"I was the guy with the baseballs," said a dark-haired fellow at the table, someone I didn't recognize. It was Barry Halper, who owned 2 percent of the Yankees and was perhaps the greatest memorabilia collector of all time.

"You were?" I said.

"Yes," he said, "and I never did get my pen back."

Halper, who also sat in the owner's box and was never short of brass, once approached Nixon there to autograph another baseball. He told Nixon that he was embarking on a project to have great players sign a baseball with their full name and their nickname: "Joseph Paul DiMaggio—the Yankee Clipper." "Theodore Samuel Williams—the Splendid Splinter." Halper asked Nixon if he'd sign a baseball that way. "I'd be happy to sign my full name"—Richard Milhouse Nixon—"but don't have a nickname," said Nixon.

Halper, who had a gentle but undaunted nature, said, "Uh, yes you do, Mr. President."

"What's that?"

"Tricky Dick."

"Oh no! I'm not signing that!"

"Well," said Halper, "how about 'The Trickster.'"

"What!" said Nixon.

He saw that Halper was actually waiting for an answer.

"I'll think about it," said Nixon.

Halper never got that request filled, but what persistence!

⌒ Courage may also apply in interviewing. One sometimes may avoid asking the hard or perhaps too personal question, for fear of not only ending the interview but ending the relationship with a good source or important figure in the world one covers.

At the end of April 2002 I traveled to Maui, Hawaii, where Mike Tyson was training to meet Lennox Lewis for the heavyweight championship. An interview with Tyson and several members of the media had been arranged. Tyson was staying at a hotel along the ocean, and we met in his suite, which was ground level and with a wonderful view of the beach. Tyson sat on a couch in a T-shirt, his muscles prominent. The several reporters stood and took notes or held tape recorders. Fearsome Mike was at his most mercurial, most nutty, most profane—among other things, he said he was currently reading a book titled *Machiavelli in Hell*. He answered questions sometimes with the politeness of a man who loves training pigeons, as he does, and sometimes with the ferocity of a bully, of a man who, among other bouts, knocked out Michael Spinks in ninety-one seconds of the first round in a title fight. Mike, though, was now thirty-five years old, well past his prime. Still, in his presence he remained a formidable figure.

Since I had been on the sports scene for quite a while, I had had occasion to interview Tyson several times in the past. But it was hardly a close relationship. At one point, as the interview was drawing to a close—and my notebook was filled up—I decided to ask Mike what might be considered a tough question. He had said that all the troubles he endured—two difficult marriages, a three-year prison sentence for rape, the disqualification for biting the ear of Evander Holyfield in a title fight, and so on—were because of the rough neighborhood and broken home he had had to deal with as a child and teenager, and that he was "a dog guy from the den of iniquity."

"But Mike," I offered, gently, "your brother, Rodney, dealt with the same issues, and he went on to have a successful career in the navy and now as a pharmacist in Los Angeles. In the end, don't you have to take responsibility for your own actions?"

He looked at me the way he might have looked at someone who was trying to steal his pigeons.

"You know," he said, "I could do anything I want with you. If we were in the slammer together, I could fuck you up the ass, and you couldn't do anything about it."

This was, to say the least, rather shocking. The other reporters stood stone quiet. I was standing next to a table lamp. The thought raced through my mind, if Tyson lunged at me—who knew what he might do?!—I'd grab the lamp, hit him over the head, and race right through the French doors. They were closed, but that wouldn't stop me. I wouldn't have to open them.

"Ah, Mike," I said, "I just can't see us crazy in love—so why don't we drop the whole thing."

He smiled a gold-toothed grin, and relaxed back on the couch.

In his bout against Lennox Lewis, Iron Mike was knocked out in the eighth round, bloody and badly beaten, his rump on the canvas and his arms draped helplessly on the ropes.

✍ I had come to know Joe DiMaggio when he was a coach with the Oakland A's in the late 1960s. He had a reputation for being difficult, but I always had good fortune with him. We talked baseball, of course, but we never spoke about Marilyn Monroe—until one day. It was widely believed that DiMaggio could turn off even the best of his friends forever if that subject, or any other that he deemed insensitive or intrusive, was posed to him. He could end an interview abruptly, turn on his heel, and walk away.

It happened that a judge in Baltimore had been a Marine sergeant when DiMaggio and Marilyn Monroe went on their honeymoon in 1954 to Tokyo. He took photographs of them and kept them for more than forty years. After I wrote a column on DiMaggio's seventy-fifth birthday, the judge sent the photographs to me. He said he had never known how to get them to DiMaggio, but he thought I knew him and could place them in his hands. He added that he wanted nothing from DiMaggio, not even an autograph.

On a Yankee old-timers' afternoon, I went to the Stadium and gave the pictures to a Yankee public relations man, asking him to give them to DiMaggio, which he did. I saw DiMaggio in the pressroom before the old-timers' ceremony, and I soon found myself alone with him. I decided to be forthright.

"Joe, I assume you got the pictures from when you were in Tokyo," I said.

"Yes," he said. "They were terrific. And that guy who took 'em an amateur photographer."

I said yes. DiMaggio also had the note from the judge, but DiMaggio said he'd have to drop him a thank-you note.

I ventured another remark. "Marilyn sure looked great in those pictures," I said.

"She was a beautiful woman," said DiMaggio, as though enlightening me on the subject of his former wife's attractiveness.

"Yes, yes she was," I agreed.

"But they killed her in Hollywood, they worked her too hard. She couldn't take it."

"Joe," I said, "there's a question I've always wanted to ask you, but didn't quite know how to say it."

"Oh," he said, eyeing me suspiciously, "what's that?"

"Well," I said, "there's one of the great sports anecdotes relating to you and Marilyn."

"And?" he said cautiously.

"It was when you two were on your honeymoon and Marilyn was asked by the army brass if she'd go over to Korea and entertain the troops. And she did and you stayed behind in Tokyo. And when she returned and came through the door of your hotel room she seemed excited. You supposedly asked her how it went, and she said, 'Joe, you never heard such cheering.'

"And you said, 'Yes I have.' Did that really happen?"

"Yes," he said, "it did."

Terse, but satisfyingly definitive.

⌒ In 2003 I traveled to San Francisco to interview Barry Bonds, a man noted not only for his ability to crush a baseball like none since Babe Ruth and Henry Aaron but also for his periodic surliness to members of the sporting press. I had called ahead to his public relations people and had been given the green light to see him. After batting practice one evening in Pacific Bell Park, I waited in the dugout while Bonds spoke with some people. When he finished, he rose and headed for the runway leading from the dugout to the clubhouse. As he did, I said, "Barry," and introduced myself. While I had been around him some in previous years, I held no illusion that he would recognize me. "Do you have a few minutes?" I asked.

"No," he said, and continued walking. Just as he was about to disappear into the tunnel, I said, "Barry." He turned around.

"I covered your father when he was a rookie," I said. It was true. I was in New York writing sports in 1968 when Bobby Bonds broke into the major leagues.

"You did?" said Barry.

"Yeah," I said, "with the Giants."

Perhaps out of respect for either my age or his father's youth, Barry paused and returned to the dugout and sat down. We had a nice chat for nearly half an hour. Then he left for the clubhouse.

I realized I had a question that I wanted to ask, but had forgotten.

Should I leave well enough alone, or should I bite the bullet and go up and ask him? I decided the question was of too much interest to me to let it go. So I went to the clubhouse. Bonds was removing his sweatshirt when he saw me. The look in his eyes said, "What is this, a fucking marathon?"

I steeled myself. "Barry," I said, "sorry, but there's one other question, and I forgot to ask it."

"What is it?" he said.

"You get walked so often, I wondered if you ever become lax or complacent at the plate."

He gave me one of those imperious looks of his. "If you've never been there," he said, "you wouldn't understand."

I raised the palm of my right hand. "Hold on, Barry," I said. "When I was a senior at Sullivan High School in Chicago in 1957, and playing first base, I batted .275." I looked at him square in the eye. "I've been there."

I'm not sure what I batted in high school, but .275 was the first thought that came to mind. And I'm not sure Bonds knew what to make of this. He stared at me as though I had just arrived via spaceship.

"That damn curveball," I added.

Barry Bonds smiled, and nodded.

"Ah," he said. "You have been there."

In a manner of speaking, yes. And he answered my question: "No."

Despite such obstacles, life for me at the *New York Times*, with its occasional and expected glitches, and unexpected earthquakes, was going relatively smoothly—without incident, as the saying goes. That is, until the other shoe dropped.

11

~~~~~~~~~~

It's Our Show Biz

FOR A REPORTER or an editor, even those working for a prestigious newspaper, as I was, life does not always go as smoothly as sailing a sled downhill. "The paper of record" is the *New York Times*'s well-deserved reputation, and indeed it has risen to the status of an important national resource. Perhaps more than any other institution, or any other news organization, it is relied on for the truth. It has hardly been perfect, by any means. The moans of reporters about the placement of their stories, for example, and the editing of such stories, is an everyday occurrence. But I believe—and seeing it from the inside for twenty-five years has underscored my view—that the *Times* has truly sought to live up to the worn adage, "All the News That's Fit to Print." In terms of thoroughness of coverage and of the considerable talents of its writers and editors, it may well be the best newspaper ever—the tragic Jayson Blair incident notwithstanding, nor my own conflicts at the paper.

Jayson Blair was a rising star at the *Times* who seemed harmless enough—short, quiet, nondescript apparel, friendly in an ingratiating manner, not particularly self-confident, soft smile, a young man eager, it seemed, to please. He was twenty-seven years old but looked younger. And for a young African-American man—for any young man—he had accumulated a large number of bylines, some six hundred in just under four years at the *Times* (and numerous front-page bylines, to boot). Who could have imagined, during those years of the early 2000s, that he would not only have a huge impact on the world of newsgathering and reporting in general but also, perhaps by extension, a significant and negative impact on my life at the *Times*?

Blair had been shifted from the national desk to the metropolitan desk to the sports department. Few of us, at the time, knew why. The fact is, he was terrible with facts. He'd get so many things wrong that some people wondered if he needed psychiatric help. The paper's senior editors felt that in sports they might be able to keep a closer eye on him. After all, if he got a score wrong, the desk could catch it. It turned out, he not only got a score wrong, more or less, but continued to interview phantom people—like a coach at Kent State, a man he had not spoken to, at a place to which he had never traveled. And for a while he was getting away with this in sports too.

Blair's desk was right by the pigeonholes that serve as the mailbox for sports department staff. I had not had a desk at the *Times* for years—for most of the twenty-plus years I had been writing a "Sports of the Times" column and feature stories. Since the columnists—Dave Anderson and George Vecsey in the earlier years, and Bill Rhoden and Harvey Araton and Selena Roberts and Robert Lipsyte later—rarely come into the office, to give any of us a desk was considered wasted space in a room already crowded with backfield editors, copyeditors, photo editors, layout people, clerks, and other office managers. (When we do come in and want a place to work, there's invariably an open desk because the occupant is either off or due in later.) There were times when I wanted to know if I had received a certain letter or package and called and got Jayson on the phone, and he quickly checked my mailbox for me. We were also cheek-by-jowl on the assignment schedule sent to all reporters every week. I was just above him in the alphabetical listing, "Berkow" then "Blair."

When the rash of sniper shootings began in Maryland and Virginia in 2002, the national desk brought Blair back to help with reporting. I was in the office one day and joked with him that they'd done him quite a favor, sending him from the safe environs of the sports office to be in the possible line of fire of a sniper.

He laughed, and said, "Well, I'm from the area, from Virginia. And I went to the University of Maryland. I guess the editors downstairs"—the general news department is on the third floor of the *Times* building, sports is on the fourth floor—"thought I could help in knowing the terrain."

The next time I saw Blair, the snipers, John Muhammad and his teenage accomplice, Lee Malvo, had been caught. He was at his desk in sports, which is where he returned when in the office and when taking a break from his sniper reporting.

I asked how the trial was going—he had also broken stories that made the front page of the *Times* but were hotly disputed by officials at the scene. "That Malvo is unbelievable," he told me. "He's a psycho."

"How so?" I asked, fascinated by this on-the-scene insight.

"Yeah, you should see him at the defense table," continued Blair. "When one of the officers who arrested or interrogated him comes in, he waves at them and practically throws them kisses. Yeah, he's nuts."

But not only had Jayson Blair got numerous facts wrong in his coverage of the snipers, he did likewise in other stories he covered—or allegedly covered. When he was supposed to be in Texas, for example, he was at his home in Brooklyn. With a "Los Fresnos, Tex." dateline, no less. And that one did him in.

Some time after his sniper coverage, Blair wrote a moving story about his purported interview with the family of a soldier missing in Iraq who later was found dead. When the *Times* was alerted by an editor at the *San Antonio Express-News* that parts of Blair's front-page article of Saturday, April 26, 2003, were nearly identical to the one they had run on April 18, the *Times* went immediately into red alert.

Blair was finally caught. On May 11 the *Times* did a phenomenal *mea culpa*. Following a ten-day investigation into his work, the paper wrote an unprecedented 7,397-word explanation—filling four pages of the Sunday paper—and went into gory detail about all of Blair's misstatements and blatant lies and fabrications and flagrant plagiarism in at least 36 stories that had appeared in the paper in just the preceding six months.

It rocked the *Times*, and it rocked the industry. I, along with every other member of the *Times*, I'm sure, felt a personal embarrassment. The *Times*, the pillar of integrity in the universe of newsgathering and reporting, had been conned by a virtual kid. Journalism had taken many hits in its long history, but there was little to compare to this. The publisher Arthur Sulzberger, Jr. called it "the low point in the 152-year history of the newspaper."

One day I was talking with one of the national editors about Blair, and told him how Blair had described Malvo in the courtroom for me.

"He did?" the editor said.

"Yeah," I said.

"He was never in the courtroom," the editor said.

↶ In recent years news agencies, particularly those dealing in print, had grown more cautious in their reporting. They were scarred first by the Vietnam War, when the government was found to be lying to the public about bombings and body bags after publication in the *New York Times* of the Pentagon Papers ("It stiffened the spines of all journalists," said Fred W. Friendly, the onetime president of CBS News); then by the Watergate scandal, in which the *Times*, especially, was slow to learn just how subversive and devious and potentially destructive to the nation the Nixon administration was.

All of us writing journalism were aware of this, or should have been. I know I was. You check facts and you check sources, and double-check them when need be. Yet, as human error would have it, some of our finest authors and journalists have made careless, if not stupid, mistakes. I remember Red Smith writing in his column in the *Times* in 1981 that Mickey Walker, a world welterweight and middleweight boxing champion in the 1920s and '30s, was "now in that speakeasy in the sky." When it was learned that Walker was indeed alive, Smith was mortified. "I could have sworn I remembered Mickey's death," said Smith. (The *Times* ran a correction the day after the column appeared, saying that Mickey Walker, age seventy-nine, "lives in Marlboro, New Jersey.")

One op-ed columnist for the *Times*, Tom Wicker, used to write a year-end column owning up to and clarifying mistakes he had made during the year.

Each day the *Times* prints "Corrections" on the second page of the first section. There are often as many as ten or fifteen of them. So many stories, so many words, so few errors, in actual fact—even though the ones that are caught are only the tip of the iceberg. But it is impossible to stamp them all out, as diligent as many of us are in this regard. And for writers, that's why there are editors. Memos from the reigning editors remind us regularly of the need for vigilance in the pursuit of facts. For every story I write in the *Times*, for example, a good seven editors read it, looking for mistakes or something that may be awry. This is not to mention the writer himself, who reads and rereads his stuff to make sure no cockroach, or squadron of roaches, has surreptitiously crawled into his copy. As it is said: "God knows we try."

In the wake of the *Times*'s investigation of his reporting, Jayson Blair was fired. The *Times* doesn't generally like to use that word. The term is often "dismissed" or "terminated." Perhaps "fired" is too much like slang, though I prefer it—it's the way people talk (the *Times* style book agrees, and says "fire" (v.) and "firing" (n.) are now "standard English," though it still prefers "dismissed"). There is a stiffness at the *Times* that, the hierarchy believes, correlates to its seriousness in getting accurately, as its logo suggests, "all the news that's fit to print." That is the environment. "It's our show biz," as one high-ranking editor explained to me. It's also, legitimately, their stock-in-trade.

In any event, Jayson Blair was no longer on the staff of the *New York Times*. And when I received my next schedule, the name "Blair" had disappeared from its previous line below "Berkow," replaced with "Broussard" (for Chris, one of our basketball writers).

The atmosphere at the paper was tense, and wary. The top editors—especially Howell Raines, the executive editor, and Gerald Boyd, the managing editor—came under intense scrutiny from people in the building as well as the rest of the nation. It was said the jobs of Raines and Boyd, in particular, might be in jeopardy. How could they not have seen what Blair was doing? What kind of managerial oversight was there, after all? Even when the metropolitan editor, Jonathan Landman, had sent a memo to the top editors saying, "We have to stop Jayson from writing for the *Times* immediately," Blair continued getting plum assignments.

I had been at the *Times* for just over twenty-two years when, in the late afternoon of April 25, 2003, the new sports editor (since February), Tom Jolly, called me into his office. My previous sports editors, Joe Vecchione, he had held the position for my first ten years at the *Times*, and Neil Amdur, who had been there the following twelve years, greatly supported me, and I greatly appreciated it. Vecchione hired me, gave me a great range of freedom to pursue and write what I was most comfortable doing, and promoted me to the "Sports of the Times" column. Amdur, an outstanding reporter in his time, had a seemingly endless supply of excellent ideas. Several of those ideas for me wound up being reprinted in the prestigious annual anthology *Best American Sports Writing*. He also retained my "Sports of the Times" column as well as suggesting me for the fifteen-part series "How Race Is Lived in America" (I wrote the lone sports story, "The Minority

Quarterback"), which won me a share of the Pulitzer Prize for national reporting. I had known Tom Jolly as weekend sports editor for a few years before he became an assistant news editor. We had had a good working relationship. Then he returned as sports editor, appointed by Raines.

Jolly informed me that an "Editors' Note" about a column I had written some two months earlier was to be printed in the *Times* on Sunday, two days hence. He had been given instructions that not a word should be changed. No one had discussed this with me earlier, and there was, I took it, nothing I could do about it. It was a *fait accompli*.

The "Editors' Note" referred to a column I had written about the institution of the death penalty. I have always been against capital punishment, believing, especially since DNA testing, that it is subject to inaccuracy, barbaric, administered unevenly (blacks and the poor get it in the neck because they generally can't afford the good lawyers that whites and the rich can), and hardly preventive of murder since most murders are committed either out of passion or without regard to penalty, the murderers invariably believing they can get away with it. And the states with the death penalty often have more murders per year than those without. Thinking I'd be interested in the subject, which I was, a friend of mine from Chicago, Dan Dorfman, had e-mailed me a very good feature story in the February 9, 2003, edition of the *Chicago Tribune*. It was written by Bonnie DeSimone. I had never read her work before and didn't know her. The story was about the retired University of North Carolina basketball coach Dean Smith's opposition on moral grounds to the death penalty.

The story sparked my recollection of reading Smith's autobiography, *A Coach's Life*, in which he discusses his feelings on the issue. I never followed up on it; perhaps at the time, four years earlier, I hadn't been as focused on the failures of the death penalty as I would become. But for a man in sports to come out strongly on such a controversial issue made me want to know more. I called Smith and spoke with him. I then pursued other avenues, looking for other people in sports who opposed the death penalty, with the anticipation of bringing greater awareness to a pernicious element in our judicial system. I found that Dale Brown, the former basketball coach at Louisiana State University, and Tom Osborne, now a congressman and former Nebraska football coach, were also opposed to the death penalty. While DeSimone had written only about Smith in her lengthy, 1,601-word article, I included Brown and Osborne in my 1,162-word column, headlined "A Stand on Death and Life," on February 12, 2003.

Jolly said Boyd had sent the "Editors' Note," though it had been written by one of the assistant managing editors at Boyd's suggestion. Boyd's role was to be in charge of issues like this one.

The last time I had received a note from Gerald Boyd was on December 19, 2001, when he sent to me—and the others who shared in the Pulitzer Prize–winning project in which he had been the editor in charge—a large, framed copy of the downsized front-page stories of "How Race Is Lived in America." That note on Boyd's stationery a year and a half earlier had read simply:

> Dear Ira,
> Your work was not just prize worthy, but journalism for the ages. Soma [Soma Behr Golden, the deputy editor in charge of the project] and I will always appreciate your talent, devotion, and hard work.
> Best,
> Gerald

(I feel certain Boyd sent a similar note to each of the other writers on the project, but it was appreciated by me nonetheless.)

Jolly handed me the piece of paper with the 463-word "Editors' Note" written on it.

This is it in full:

A Sports of the Times column on Feb. 12 discussed college coaches who have spoken out against the death penalty, in particular Dean Smith, former basketball coach at the University of North Carolina.

The column should have acknowledged that a central quotation from the coach appeared three days earlier in an article by Bonnie DeSimone of the *Chicago Tribune* and that several other passages closely reflected her words.

In a first draft, the *Times* column credited Ms. DeSimone for an anecdote in which Mr. Smith told a former governor of North Carolina, "The death penalty makes us all murderers."

The columnist, Ira Berkow, was told by his editors that a quotation so harsh should rightly be verified firsthand, so he telephoned Mr. Smith, who recounted the scene to him. Editors then deleted the attribution to Ms. DeSimone's article, though *Times* policy ordinarily calls for crediting news that originates exclusively elsewhere. (Coach Smith's activism had been reported in North Carolina publications, but not in detail comparable to the *Tribune*'s.) The *Times* column included two passages that were similar in language and concept to those in the *Tribune*:

The *Tribune*: "Sports figures, while often active in charitable causes, generally avoid taking sides in divisive, emotional national debates such as the one concerning the death penalty. Coaches for major Division I programs, as Smith was, recruit from a wide swath of the population and have an interest in not alienating people."

The *Times*: "Sports figures are often reluctant, at best, to go public with potentially divisive national issues, even when the issue is a matter of life and death. . . . For active coaches, coming forward on controversial issues could hamper recruiting if you take a side that may alienate, say, the family of a prospective point guard."

The *Tribune*: "Smith will not discuss whether he counseled his most famous protégé, Michael Jordan, during the 1996 trial of the two men who murdered Jordan's father three years before. The Jordan family never made its feelings known regarding punishment, according to Robeson County District Attorney Johnson Britt."

The *Times*: "Is it possible that Smith, meanwhile, had some influence over the decision of Michael Jordan and his family not to push for the death penalty for the two men who randomly murdered Jordan's father in 1996? Possibly. Smith said that he never spoke to Jordan about it."

The *Times* column also included this quotation from Mr. Smith about his religious views: "I do not condone any violence against any of God's children, and that is why I am opposed to the death penalty." Though Mr. Smith discussed those views in his *Times* interview, the exact quotation was taken from his autobiography, "A Coach's Life," and should have been attributed.

I was stunned, to be sure. I felt that none of what I wrote merited this kind of public flogging. I have no way of proving this, but the atmosphere, conceivably heightened by questions of Blair's reporting even before his story on April 26 that put the dagger into his journalistic coffin at the *Times*, was in there before his San Antonio story (recall Landman's admonition: "You have to stop Jayson Blair from writing for the *Times*, right now"). But there was certainly a greater sensitivity about accuracy industry-wide. And it was justified—after all, integrity and accuracy are the hallmarks of journalism, or ought to be. But had the *Times* lost some balance in my case? Had it overreacted? Should I, after more than two decades of positive work at the paper, have been called in, spoken with, perhaps a letter sent to the *Tribune* explaining the *Times*'s regret and action taken, and have the matter ended? Or maybe a one- or two-paragraph "Editors' Note" would have been in order without adding my name. In almost all cases before and after the Raines-Boyd administration, an "Editors' Note" does not contain the name of the writer (or the editor of the piece, or pieces, for that matter). At bottom, did the punishment fit this crime? I thought it emphatically did not.

I wrote a letter to Raines explaining my position, particularly the fact that *I* had not taken DeSimone's name off the article. Had it been left in the piece, the paraphrasing of those two references would not have been objectionable. The ideas were hardly original with Ms. DeSimone; I had touched upon them numerous times in my thousands of columns, and they were part of the general knowledge of anyone who covered sports. I said there was no intent on my part to conceal the fact that DeSimone had written about Smith, and that, as the "Editors' Note" stated, I had included it in the first draft of the column. Dropping it in the second draft was simply an accident. I also said I could not understand how the paper could print something like this without even conferring with the writer. Criticism of the sort contained in the "Editors' Note" had never happened to me in my thirty-eight years of journalism—twenty-two of them at the *New York Times*—and I hoped and anticipated that this would pass. I expected it never to occur again.

I spoke to Boyd about my letter and expressed the hope that my side of the issue would also be printed. Boyd seemed preoccupied, if not completely disinterested. "I've got other problems," he said. Which was true. Unknown to me, and most people on the staff, the paper was in the midst of its investigations into the incredible and insufferable activities of Jayson Blair. The jobs of both Raines and Boyd, as it turned out, were indeed hanging in the balance.

I added to Raines: "I have a thorough history of using attributions whenever they are warranted. I enclose one example, of my Sports of the Times column written 20 years ago nearly to the day that my death-penalty column was published. It is also a prime example of my addressing the matter of an important sports figure evading, in this case, a public stance on a major social or cultural issue." And: "DeSimone writes about the reluctance of sports figures to come forward on important social issues. If one has been in sports writing for nearly four decades, as I have, one knows that this is not news. It is common knowledge, a universal truth. It is a concept that I have dealt with in print on numerous occasions. While there was some similarity of expression with DeSimone, I believed that my twist on it made it mine. The subsequent suggestion of duplication has never happened to me before. It won't happen again." It was defensive, yes, but, after all, I was defending myself, and properly, I thought.

Raines wrote back:

"Thank you for your letter concerning the Editors' Note in the paper of April 27. It seems to me that it appropriately covered a situation that the readers needed to be brought up to date on. However, it was a lapse on the part of the editors handling the note that the content was not discussed with you before publication.

"I'm pleased to hear of your expectation never to be in this kind of situation again. The precise attribution of quotes, including their sources, is essential to maintaining our readers' trust.

"I've heard reports that your hip surgery went well"–I had had a double hip replacement the previous December–"and I'm glad to see that you are back in the paper.

"All best regards

"(signed) Howell."

As it happened, the column I enclosed, from February 2, 1983, was titled "Alabama's Bryant and Racial Issue." It began, "'Throughout the 1960's and 1970's, these two men were the dominant figures of public life in Alabama and the state's main representatives to the nation,' wrote Howell Raines, referring to George Wallace and Bear Bryant in the Jan. 24 issue of *The New Republic* magazine....'" Raines was then a reporter in the *Times*'s Washington bureau and had written this freelance piece. The attribution was an example of what has been commonplace for me in my writing.

Later in that piece I quoted Raines as saying that Bryant had conceivably not shared Wallace's racial views. "But Bryant, according to Mr. Raines, 'was big enough to have taken on Wallace. . . . If he had offered one clear-cut public gesture of condemnation, who knows what might have been spared that benighted state?' . . .

"Curious as to Bryant's opinion, I sent him the article and asked if he'd comment on it. He never replied. He died Jan. 26.

The questions posed in Mr. Raines's introspective article remain. Why wasn't Alabama football integrated until 1970? Why did Bryant not speak out in a time of seething racial turmoil in his state and at his university? If he was in fact a saint or a hero, then what is the stuff of such saints and heroes?"

It was a topic, as I said, that I had long been interested in, and had written about not for the first time.

If "Editors' Notes" appear only periodically in the *Times* and rarely, if ever, include the writer's or any relevant editor's name—the idea being that the subject matter is at issue, not the person involved—why was it done in my case? Some twelve months later, when the *Times* admitted that its reporting on Saddam Hussein's weapons of mass destruction had been totally inaccurate, no writers or editors were mentioned. Whether the atmosphere at the paper because of Jayson Blair, even before the eruption of his egregious reporting, influenced the editors to act against me, I don't know. I believe it is a strong possibility.

In the nine months that I worked, off and on, on "How Race Is Lived in America," I didn't always see eye-to-eye with Gerald Boyd. Could there also have been a personality conflict between him and me that resulted in the "Editors' Note" being handled the way it was? Possibly, but I'd like to think not. I don't believe I'll ever know.

The "Editors' Note," besides meeting with my anger and mortification, also drew a great response from other writers, and readers generally. "What," said one *Times* writer, whom I had never met and had never heard from before, in an e-mail to me, "is the Times doing? That Editors' Note was outrageous, unnecessary and stupid." And that's how it went.

While all writers and editors make mistakes—some excusable, some less so—the most responsible unquestionably seek to go about their business with the utmost integrity. And even the greatest of writers can occasionally say the same thing in virtually the same way. Dylan Thomas, a poet and storyteller I've read with delight, said it beautifully: "There is only one position for an artist

At home: Writing is easy, Red Smith said, "you just open a vein."

anywhere: and that is upright." He wrote that in an essay, "Artists in Wales," in his book *Quite Early One Morning*, first published in 1954. And E. B. White, in his essay, "Bedfellows," published in 1956 in the *New Yorker* and included in his collection *The Points of My Compass*, wrote a similar sentiment: "All writing slants the way a writer leans, and no man is born perpendicular, although many men are born upright."

Along with getting it right comes the *struggle* to get it right—and make it good. Gene Fowler, a widely read Hearst journalist in the early twentieth century, wrote that "Writing is easy; all you do is sit staring at a blank sheet of paper until the drops of blood form on your forehead." Red Smith later was often quoted as saying something similar, but shorter.

But maybe all these admonitions are so well known they don't bear repeating. "It is tedious to tell again tales already plainly told," wrote Homer. And Shakespeare later added: "Life is as tedious as a twice-told tale."

⤶ Some six weeks after the Blair episode became public, Raines and Boyd, unable to withstand the continuing problems and aftershocks, were asked to step down. After each had served some twenty-five years at the *Times*, and risen to its editorial heights, they left the paper. This was a tragedy in itself, since no executive editor or managing editor of the *Times* had ever been dismissed, or terminated, or "fired." I held no animosity toward either of them, though many others at the paper believed the two of them to be arrogant and dictatorial. They were, in the end, part of the corporate structure, a structure that could be heartless and heedless of a human being's feelings. They were, while all was well, given their head to do what they believed was in the best interests of putting out the best newspaper in the world. And though they had been the top guys in the newsroom, they ended up fall guys. Some of it, it has to be said, was their own doing.

Oddly enough, on the very day the "Editors' Note" about me ran on page two of the sports section, on page five was a column by me across the top half of the page. It was about the Cubs, and it took a necessarily wry look at the team that I followed as a kid in Chicago. At one point I dealt with the theory that day baseball–until 1988 the Cubs were the only team in the big leagues not to have lights for night games, and they still played relatively few in the evenings–had hurt the Cubs' chances over the years.

"If the heat supposedly wilts the Cubs," I wrote, "then why didn't it wilt others, like Greg Maddux, who left the Cubs as a free agent after a Cy Young award season, or Bill Madlock, who led the National League in batting two straight seasons, then was traded? And how was it that Ferguson Jenkins and Ernie Banks and Billy Williams didn't disappear in a puddle of sweat under the summer sun?

"It is evident that over the years it has been poor management, not the lack of lights at night, that has done in the Cubs. Other teams have folded at various points of the season, but none other than the Cubs have copped a plea using sunstroke as a defense."

In the end, the *Times*, during that critical time I described above, was, not unlike the Cubs—though with a vastly different level of gravity—suffering from a management crisis. Indeed, the reputation of the *Times* took a considerable blow from the scandal. But, contrary to the ever-languishing Cubbies, the *Times* quickly made salient changes in the top echelons of the news department that have—in my view and by a general consensus as I interpret it—now sutured the wounds in morale and oversight and restored the paper to its historic prominence in journalism.

12

~~~~~~~~~~~~~~

Me and Koufax

WHEN I BEGAN as a sportswriter, in 1965, baseball teams were no longer taking trains—the old writers talked about the lengthy rides on trains in the twenties, thirties, and forties, when players and writers played cards and had conversations well into the night. But by the 1960s teams were flying chartered planes.

In the summer of 1969, still a relatively new face in New York, I made a trip to Pittsburgh with the Mets by commercial airline. I sat in a coach seat by the window. I was twenty-nine years old, about the same age, height, and weight as some of the ballplayers, though, needless to say, without the hand-eye coordination, the steely concentration, the gifts of powerful arm, speedy legs, and gritty determination that many of them needed and possessed to make and stay in the major leagues.

Dick Young, then the esteemed and highly opinionated sports columnist of the *New York Daily News* and generally considered the premier baseball writer of the day, got on the plane, looked at me—I remember his piercing eyes and jutting jaw—and sat down in the aisle seat in my row.

"I'm Dick Young," he said, putting out his hand to shake mine. "Were you just called up?"

"Well, in a manner of speaking," I said. "From Minneapolis. But it's been more than a year."

He stared at me. How could I be with the Mets for over a year and he had not noticed me?

"Are you a ballplayer?"

"No, I'm with NEA, writing about the Mets."

And that's how it was when a writer could get to know a player on a plane ride, as I did on many occasions. Not anymore. Does this impede coverage? Yes and no.

Yes in that it's always better to know more than less. And in such cozy situations the writer can relax with a subject and casually plumb his thoughts and background. On the other hand, becoming too friendly with a subject can make objective reporting more difficult. One could have the normal tendency to protect the player in some way.

But the good reporter can still get good stories, and the intrepid and tireless reporter can still get great stories. And ballplayers—some, anyway—can be responsive and forthcoming.

I was chatting in the Yankee clubhouse one day with the left-handed relief pitcher Dave Righetti. I had done a story on Righetti when he was in the minor leagues; a bond of sorts is often established when you spend time with a player in the minors. It's as though you cared when he was "nobody." Now I asked Righetti a question. He said, "I'd like to answer it, but if I do"—and he looked around the locker room—"these guys will get pissed off when they read it." I don't remember what the question was, but in a moment he turned back to me and said, "These guys don't read the *New York Times*. I'll tell you." And he did. It was fairly innocuous, as I recall, but he did answer my question. And he remained unharmed by his teammates.

Are ballplayers, considering their wealth and status on pedestals, nastier with the press than ever before? Is this something possibly new? There's the famous line by the *New York*

Journal sports columnist Frank Graham, when the taciturn Long Bob Meusel, a Yankee outfielder, was finishing his career and was now suddenly greeting people with a smile. "He's saying hello," Graham wrote, "when it's time to say goodbye." That was in 1930. Others of his time were like that, others were not—like today. In some instances players today can be difficult, sure. I've always felt, however, that their reactions with the press and others often depend on how they were brought up.

I've always liked the response to a surly ballplayer by Jerome Holtzman of the *Chicago Tribune*, one of the best baseball writers ever. He approached George Bell, a Toronto outfielder, in the dugout. (Holtzman was smoking a cigar, as he often did, except when typing his stories. Then he hummed. I've sat next to him in a press box when we were writing and, given the lesser of two evils, I prefer the cigar smoke.) "George," Holtzman said, "got a minute?"

"Not today," Bell said.

Holtzman took a drag on his cigar and blew out the smoke.

"That's okay," he responded. "Maybe I'll catch you next year. Or the year after that."

Then there's the reverse. I was in the Mets' clubhouse talking with catcher Mike Piazza. He was open and congenial. The locker next to his belonged to the pitcher Al Leiter. Leiter was not at his locker. So I pulled up his chair to talk with the seated Piazza. After a few minutes, I felt a tap on my shoulder. It was Leiter.

"You're sitting in my chair," he said. "Sorry," I said. I really didn't know Leiter and didn't think he knew me. And I stood up. "But I brought you a chair," he said. And he placed a chair he was holding for me beside Piazza. That was a first. I once told the veteran sports columnists Dave Anderson, of the *Times*, and Jerry Izenberg, of the *Newark Star-Ledger*, what Leiter had done and asked if, in their combined nearly one hundred years on the beat, that had ever happened to them. "No," was the mutual response, "never." I contend that Leiter's parents did a good job with Al.

⤳ The complaint is not uncommon among fans that the ballplayers of today are so different from the ballplayers of the past. The contention often is that money is the difference. The players make so much money now—in baseball, for one example, the average salary of a major leaguer in 2005 was more than $2.3 million, with a minimum of $300,000. When I began as a professional sportswriter, in 1965, the average ballplayer's salary was $19,000, with a minimum of $6,000 (my reporter's starting salary was even higher than that, $6,240!). The highest salary in major league baseball then was the $105,000 paid to Willie Mays. The current highest salary as I write this is earned by Alex Rodriguez, the Yankee third baseman, who makes an average of $25 million a year on a ten-year contract of $252 million. Fans have always resented the money ballplayers make—never resenting how much owners make, or movie stars, for that matter—thinking why should that second baseman make more than me when he's only playing a game and I'm digging ditches?

Joe DiMaggio was booed in the 1930s when he returned to the Yankees early in the season after holding out for more money. And before him, the revered pitcher Walter Johnson had a contract dispute with his club, the Washington Senators, who had paid him $14,000 in 1914. He was vilified in this headline: "Almighty Dollar Johnson's Ideal."

I've never resented athletes making as much money as they could. Is this not an essential part of American capitalism? It is stupid, to be sure, when a basketball player like Latrell Sprewell, who was making $14.625 million a year, says he won't play hard for his team, the Minnesota Timberwolves, because he wants a contract extension. "I need it," he said, "to feed my family." It may have come as a surprise to him that some breadwinners make a great deal less and are still able to put food on the table for their broods.

And you look askance as some of the players who, seemingly without a brain in their heads, get hooked on drugs. But then the old-timers got hooked on alcohol, which could be equally deleterious to trying to master the spin on a ninety-mile-an-hour curveball.

Steroids are a different matter. Athletes take steroids to "get an edge." Making themselves bigger and stronger and with greater stamina provides, for them, that edge. It is no secret that the competitive urges of some, if not many, athletes are more important to them than the harmful effects that steroids may cause to their bodies—and, in the famous case of the all-pro football player Lyle Alzado, death at a young age. (He was forty-two and the poster boy for steroid abuse. He admitted taking steroids heavily from the time he was twenty-seven.) To win the gold medal, to come in first—or just to make the team—and take ten or fifteen or twenty years off their lives is worth it to those athletes. But such risks for others aren't worth it, and so the playing field is rendered uneven. Which is why steroids should be ruled out of the games, as the authorities in various sports have attempted to do—some with muscle, some halfheartedly, depending on how much money may be in it for them if their athletes succeed. Better teams, in most cases, will draw greater crowds.

And there are the young guys oozing with talent who take it all for granted, especially with the luxury of a long-term contract. Like Darryl Strawberry, who was touted as the next Ted Williams when he came up, a tall, power-hitting left-handed batter like the great Williams. But Strawberry, who became a drug addict, pathetic and tragic, was already on the way to oblivion as a young player. One of the Mets' coaches, in the early 1980s when Strawberry came up to the team, was Jim Frey. Frey was assigned to work on Strawberry's fielding in right field. Every day Strawberry was expected to come to Shea Stadium early, and Frey would hit balls to him in the outfield. One day Strawberry showed up late. "Where've you been?" asked Frey. "C'mon, let's get to work." "I'm not going out there anymore," said Strawberry, "I don't need it." He was wrong, of course. Strawberry often covered so little ground in right field that the area he generally planted himself in was called by writers "the Strawberry patch."

The reserve clause bound a player to his team for as long as the owner wished. But when it ended in the 1970s, player salaries exploded. The money that players make today—and the money the clubs make—has indeed drawn a greater chasm between the two than ever before. Once, you could arrange to meet a player for lunch when he had a night game. Or dinner if there was a day game. The player was happy to have someone pick up the tab since his meal money from the club was meager. Rarely is that done anymore. Invariably, interviews are conducted at the player's locker, or in the dugout, or behind the batting cage during batting practice. And the teams fly charter jets, with no writers allowed.

✎ I have never been able to boo a professional ballplayer, though I may look askance at someone who is obviously going at partial speed. I have a clear understanding and respect for their talents and how hard it is to make the big time in any sport, having played with and against two baseball players in particular, Jimmy Nelson and Jim Woods. Both were about my size, my height and weight. It helped me identify with them. Both were, in our youth, outstanding players as boys and young men, head and shoulders above most of the rest of us who played with or against them.

Jimmy Nelson was a semester behind me at Bryant Elementary School. We were friends and teammates on a championship West Side Pony League team when we were thirteen, he starring at shortstop, me laboring at third base and first base. Jimmy would make all-city in baseball at Farragut High School (the school that produced not only Kevin Garnett, the star NBA forward, but Kim Novak too), and then Jimmy went on to start at shortstop for three seasons at Northwestern University, was captain in his senior year, 1961, and, at one point in that season, when I checked on his progress, he was the second leading hitter in the Big Ten. He wound up with a .333 average and was then signed by the Minnesota Twins. It appeared he might have a bright baseball future. He could hit, he could run, he had a terrific arm and covered a lot of ground.

Jimmy played one season of Class A ball, hitting only a little better than .200 with a few home runs and a handful of runs batted in. He was released at the end of the season and not picked up by any other team. After his brief baseball career ended, he got a teaching degree and eventually became a junior high school principal on the South Side of Chicago. I once visited him there. We embraced, after not having seen each other in years. At one point in our conversation, I asked what happened to his pro career. "It's hard to believe just how good these guys are," he said. "The twenty-fifth guy at the end of the bench on a major league team is an immensely talented athlete. You have no idea."

When an athlete as proficient as Jimmy Nelson hardly got a leg up on the rung of professional sports, I got the idea of how skilled are the others who make it, and the hundreds of thousands who sweat and struggle but miss by the difference between safe and out on an infield ground ball: perhaps a half-step or so.

But for me the classic case to explain the levels of the game is Jim Woods. I played against him in Little League and Pony League (a North Side Pony League, played in a handsome little ballpark called Thillens Stadium, when I was fourteen) and high school. I pitched against Woods in the Pony League, and he hit a home run off me that was hit so hard, and went so far, that some fifty years later I can still see it in my mind's eye soaring over the high left-field fence and over some trees behind it. I am still amazed by it.

In high school, in a championship game played at Comiskey Park, Woods, then a junior, hit a home run into the left-field stands. As a junior he pitched his high school, Lane Tech, to the Chicago Public League championship and then the Illinois state championship, mowing down batters with his fastball (he struck out eighteen of twenty-one batters in the state semifinals) and at bat—he also played third base—spraying base hits and smashing home runs.

Full Swing

The last time I'd seen James Jerome "Woody" Woods, as the listing in the *Baseball Encyclopedia* has it, was on a dusty baseball field on a warm late afternoon at Winnemac Park on the North Side of Chicago. It was early June 1957, and my high school, Sullivan, was playing Lane. I was then a first baseman for Sullivan. When I was in the batter's box facing him, Woods didn't look much different from any of the rest of the teenage boys on either side of the diamond. In his green-and-grey uniform, he stood about six feet tall and appeared to weigh 165 pounds or so. He was a redhead, with high, almost gaunt cheekbones, and, though the bill of his green cap was pulled low, shading his intense eyes, he gave the impression that he'd be as comfortable in a 7-Up ad as he was on the spike-scarred mound at Winnemac Park. A righthander, he threw hard, to be sure, but he seemed to be standing unfairly closer than the 60-foot-6-inch regulation distance from the rubber to home plate.

Some three weeks after that game in Winnemac Park, both of us, at seventeen, were graduated from high school. While I went to work on a garbage truck for the summer, Jim Woods, incredibly, was not only signed immediately by the Cubs but went *directly* to the major leagues, to Wrigley Field, and became a member of the Chicago Cubs! Wrigley Field was only a few miles from Winnemac Park, but it was worlds apart. Woods's swift ascension to the big leagues was unheard of. No one from the sandlots of Chicago—or any other sandlot, for that matter—goes straight to the big leagues. But there he was, Jim Woods in the National League with Willie Mays and Stan Musial and Hank Aaron. He was signed as an infielder. He played in two games at the end of the season, both as a pinch runner. In the first, he was picked off third base. Later I would learn that it wasn't his fault, that it had been a botched squeeze play.

Woods was sent down to the minors for "seasoning," then traded by the Cubs to the Phillies along with Alvin Dark, for Richie Ashburn. Woods played all of thirty-four games over two seasons for the Phillies in 1960 and 1961, years in which they fin-

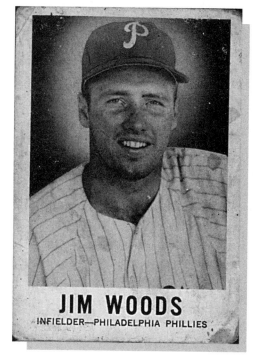

The 1962 baseball card of Phillies third baseman Jim Woods, my "connection" to the major leagues—I had competed with him in Little League, Pony League, and high school baseball.

JIM WOODS
INFIELDER—PHILADELPHIA PHILLIES

ished last. He hit a total of three home runs and batted in twelve runs. He struck out twenty-eight times in eighty-two at-bats and finished with a .207 batting average. One of the highlights of his quick major league career, however, was hitting a long double off Sandy Koufax, the Dodgers' left-handed star.

Soon after, though, Woods was sent back to the minors and seemed to disappear from sight. I had followed his journeys in the minor leagues in the *Sporting News*, but now he was gone. For years I wondered what had happened to him. Sometimes I'd ask someone who either knew him or might have known what happened to him, and came up empty. In my column in the *Times* in August 1986, I had occasion to write about him:

"Most of us have had some connection, however distant, with someone who reached a particular height. And we followed that person's career, knowing that there but for just a little more talent, a little more courage and/or a little more brains, go I."

I concluded: "I think about Woods sometimes, think of the homer he hit off me (in a Pony League game) that may still be going, think of him as my link to the major leagues, and that he realized that boy's dream that so many of us once shared.

"And I wonder, Where have you gone, Jim Woods?"

I found Jim Woods in 2004, some eighteen years after that column appeared. He was living in Modesto, California, retired from the airlines where he worked as a baggage handler and reservations clerk. He was married for the second time and had three children, all now adults, a son and two daughters. I went to see him to write a magazine story about him, having found my long-lost connection to the big leagues.

When he picked me up in his car at my motel, he was also wearing a retro Cubs cap, circa 1957. Other than that, I wouldn't have recognized him. He wore glasses, had a white mustache, a bit of a paunch, and walked slightly unsteadily, having had a hip replacement. He had a genial confidence, not overbearing.

As for his professional baseball career, he said he was called up by the Phillies from the Class AAA Indianapolis team of the International League—where he had made the all-star team—when he was twenty-one years old, at the end of the 1960 season. He started the next season with Philadelphia, but, despite hitting two homers in the span of five days, was sent down in May, never to return to the big leagues. He was traded to the Cincinnati Reds organization, where he drifted for a few more years in the minors. Then, while playing for Macon, Georgia, in the Class AA Southern League, he quit. He was twenty-four years old.

He was playing third base at Macon behind a young Cuban, Tony Perez, who later became a Hall of Fame player with the Reds. With the Phillies, Dick Allen, who became an outstanding major leaguer, was their choice for a future third baseman. And with the Cubs, his competition for Chicago's third-base future was the young Ron Santo, a Hall of Fame candidate.

"I didn't get lucky," said Woods. "And I was raw. I could have used more instruction. But in those days even the big-league organizations were skimpy on instruction. They kinda left you on your own." He said he never offered to try pitching, despite his sensational high school pitching record, and no one in baseball asked him to try it. Overall he said he had few regrets, but he still thinks he could have been a contributing big-leaguer for several years. But, he said, he was content with his memories. After all, how many of us made the major leagues at all—even for thirty-six games?

And he recalled that hit against Koufax. "It was in the Los Angeles Coliseum, and I pinch-hit and I crushed one—a real shot—that hit the top of the high screen in left-center, a double," he said, with a small smile of satisfaction. "If the screen hadn't been so high—it was forty-two feet high—it would've been out of there. I was looking for a fastball, and I got it."

When I left Jim Woods I thought about all the dreams of all the kids who fantasize making the major leagues. I had been one of them until I came to realize—maybe when I was twelve or thirteen, and saw how Jimmy Nelson played, and then how Jim Woods played—that it was truly nothing more than fantasy for me.

And I recalled that towering home run Jim Woods hit off me in the Thillens Pony League. So he had crushed a pitch off both Sandy Koufax and me. Yes, I thought, yes, despite never having made it past high school baseball, I was indeed in very good company.

13

~~~~~~~~~~~~

The Comedy Poorhouse

IN CONVERSATION one day with Red Holzman, the Knicks' coach, I brought up a point, probably obscure, about something or other. "You know, writers are like coaches," he said, "you're always filing things away, consciously or subconsciously. Never know when you're going to use any of it."

I still don't. What has intrigued me as much as anything else in the study of writing are the people who do it. Or are involved in it in one way or another. Invariably, they—and sometimes their subjects—provide the humor that lends perspective—for without humor it's a long, uphill climb to a view of, pardon the expression, the human condition.

I thought P. G. Wodehouse was as funny a writer as I've ever read. I've laughed out loud on airplanes reading of the exploits of the inimitable butler Jeeves and his "man" Bertie Wooster, causing those seated nearby to shoot menacing looks my way. Wodehouse was also a sports fan, particularly, a golf lover, and one afternoon in 1969 I traveled to Remsenberg, a town on Long Island, to interview Wodehouse.

"Plummy," as people close to him called Pelham Grenville Wodehouse, lived in a modest-sized house on Basket Neck Lane. He was eighty-seven years old at the time and still writing regularly—that is, several hours every day. He was a tall, baldish man with horn-rimmed glasses and, having been born and having lived much of his life in England, still had a decided British accent.

He credited his golf game for much of his writing success. "I think it is rather a good thing to be a poor golfer," he told me. "You get comic ideas."

One of his characters, for example, "The Oldest Member" of the golf club, comments on "love" and "golf": "Love is an emotion which your true golfer should always treat with suspicion. Do not misunderstand me. I am not saying that love is a bad thing, only that it is an unknown quantity. I have known cases where marriage improved a man's game, and other cases where it seemed to put him right off his stroke. . . .

"There are higher, nobler things than love. A woman is only a woman, but a hefty drive is a slosh."

Wodehouse had taken a widely quoted line by Rudyard Kipling, "woman is only a woman, but a good cigar is a smoke," and made it his own.

"How I loved the game," Wodehouse told me. "I have sometimes wondered if we of the riffraff don't get more pleasure out of it than the topnotchers. For an untouchable like myself, two perfect drives in a round would wipe out all memory of sliced approach shots and foozled putts, whereas if Jack Nicklaus does a 64 he goes home and thinks morosely that if he had not just missed that eagle on the seventh, he would have had a 63."

At one point in our interview, which was conducted in his backyard, he tried to light his pipe, and had, as Bertie might have said, "a deuce of a time." Wodehouse shook his head. "There's always just enough wind to blow out my match."

And while Wodehouse was disheartened at the moment for his lack of success with his fire, I found that a comic, or a comic writer, actually looks for or remembers such incidents with a kind of goofy glee. Their antennae are always up for the zany, and if it's not there, their mind may simply see it as skewed, or wish it so. It is the nature of the humorist.

Case in point: I had lunch one day with Jackie Mason, the renowned comic, at a small restaurant in Manhattan. He was with a woman friend. She ordered a tuna plate. When it arrived she looked at the food heaped on the dish and said, "My God, look at all that food. I can't eat all that food."

And Mason said: "Why do people always say something like that when food comes in a restaurant? Just because the food's there, doesn't mean you have to eat it. If you go into someone's home, you don't say, 'Look at all those chairs. There are so many chairs, how can I sit down?'"

Another example: I was standing with Jimmy Cannon on a sunny Sunday morning in January 1971, in Miami Beach, waiting for the press bus to take us from the hotel to the Orange Bowl for Super Bowl V, Baltimore versus Dallas. Cannon and Red Smith were considered the best sports columnists of the mid-century. The warm morning was taking its toll on Jimmy's reddish, roundish face, speckled now with spots of sweat. The sun gleamed off his sunglasses, his baldish head, his brown loafers.

Coming up Collins Avenue, I noticed about thirty people, adults and children, on bicycles pedaling in our direction. They looked like several families going to a picnic. There were little pennants on the handlebars and lunch bags in the bike baskets. Some sight.

I turned to Jimmy. "See that?" I said.

He looked toward the cyclists, and squinted. "Jee-sus Christ," he said in his side-of-the-mouth New York style, "look what inflation has done to the Hell's Angels." Skewed. Wonderful.

✓ In 1974 I sent Wodehouse a copy of my recently published book, *Rockin' Steady*. In a letter dated February 15 that year, Wodehouse, then ninety-two, wrote: "I hope you have been going

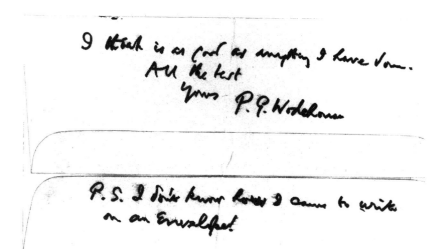

P. G. Wodehouse, in a letter to me, wondered "how I came to write on an envelope!"

strong since I last saw you. I am in great form as regards my brain and am just finishing a Jeeves and Bertie novel which I think is as cool as anything I have done. All the best, Yours, P. G. Wodehouse.

"P.S. I don't know how I came to write on an envelope!"

It was indeed an envelope on which he had composed that letter to me. He had folded it, placed it in another envelope, and mailed it off.

It reminded me of a phone call I once returned to Sammy Cahn, the beloved lyricist who wrote scores of standards, including "I Walk Alone" and "Call Me Irresponsible." He had been interested in producing a movie based on my book *The Man Who Robbed the Pierre*. It never came about, but I remember that when he answered the phone he politely asked if I could call back. "I'm working," he said—and indeed I could hear him tinkling with the keys of his piano. He was then in his late seventies.

I thought, How wonderful to be so absorbed in work even at that age. I hoped I could be in such a state of mind when I was that old. Or ninety-two, like Wodehouse. And it wouldn't matter if I was writing on an envelope or not.

〜 I've read that the Marx Brothers, before embarking on one of their movies, would play the entire show at a live theater and have a laugh meter with them. If a joke didn't hit a certain mark on the meter, it was taken out of the show. I know the Marx Brothers had writers writing some of their stuff, but I also understood that the brothers themselves, particularly Groucho, inserted and ad-libbed material.

One afternoon I experienced just such off-the-cuff stuff from Groucho himself. It gave me a chance to observe the cut of his mind, such as it was. It was May 1971, when he had come to New York to do a one-man show in Carnegie Hall. He was then in his early eighties. I met him in the elegant lobby of the Regency Hotel where he was staying. He was resplendent in blue blazer, jeans, and beret. Even without the famous greasepaint black eyebrows and mustache, he was still recognizable with grey eyebrows and 'stache. He introduced me to the redhead on his arm, who appeared some forty years younger. "This is Erin Fleming," he said. "She's my secretary," and added a stage wink.

The rather formal manager of the hotel introduced himself to Groucho and asked how he liked his room.

"It's all right," Groucho rasped, "except for the dog in there. Get the dog out."

The stiff fellow blinked, then struggled on with decorum.

"Did you enjoy the wine we sent up?" he asked.

"Of course not," replied Groucho, "the dog drank it all."

The manager smiled wanly and departed, perhaps to double-check about a dog in a room.

Groucho and I talked about the movie *Horse Feathers*, a spoof on higher education in America that he made with his brothers. Groucho played Professor Quincy Adams Wagstaff, hired by "Huxley College" as president in order to produce a winning football team. I told him I memorized some of the lines, like "The trouble is, we're neglecting football for education." And to members of the faculty: "Where would this college be without football? Have we got a stadium?" "Yes." "Have we got a college?" "Yes." "Well, we can't support both. Tomorrow we start tearing down the college."

Groucho nodded: "You memorized that?"

"Yes," I replied. "I think it still says a lot about segments of higher education in America."

"All I can tell you," he said, "is that mine was pretty low. I quit school when I was thirteen. Chico was the only one of the brothers to finish public school. He got high marks, but it held no interest for him. He'd rather play the horses, play pool, and play poker. If there was no action around, he would play solitaire—and bet against himself."

Groucho, of course, built part of his reputation on being a comic rake—even his lope seemed leering—and so I asked him a fairly prosaic question, but a legitimate one I thought, given the feminist movement.

"Groucho," I said, "What do you think of women's rights?"

"I like both sides of them," he replied.

Hard to argue with that, even if, I felt certain, it wasn't the first time he had used that line. But after all those maniacally wonderful years of splitting the sides of millions of fans, he was entitled.

〜 I've had a periodic correspondence with Saul Bellow. It began when I called him in 1974 while researching my book on Maxwell Street. In a *Life* magazine story on him, he had been pictured shopping on Maxwell Street and said he enjoyed the color and action of the marketplace. I called him when he was a professor on the Committee on Social Thought at the University of Chicago. I considered including him in the book. He said, "When I'm done with my book"—possibly *Humboldt's Gift*, published in 1975—"I'd be glad to go down there with you. Actually,

I'm not a good informant, although I loved the street in my youth. If you like I can give you the names of some people who grew up there." He did, and they did, though we never took that walk down Maxwell Street.

On occasion I would contact him about one matter or another, and he was always generous with responses.

I admired his technique as a writer, his unusual turn of mind and phrase. In a letter to me written from his apartment in Chicago in 1982, for example, he demonstrated in a most casual and succinct manner how to take two disparate thoughts and weave them into a subtle and humorous but firm conviction:

"I am at this moment looking over Lake Michigan, a gray sky, wet on wet, waves carrying yellow sand; the smelt season is over and the gulls are cleaning up on the last of the alewives. In this morning's *Trib* (to bring you up to date) Jane B's press guy"—Jane Byrne was then mayor of Chicago, and Bellow was referring to the *Chicago Tribune*—"told reporters, 'Let's not hear any more of this crap about the First Amendment and the public's right to know.' Life is still amusing here but the seagulls are doing better than the rest of us."

In a letter dated July 10, 1992, I wrote to him:

"It happened that I was with Jackie Mason last night, and in the course of events I told him that I had just read a joke in a short story of yours. I said that the joke was new to me, and I wondered if he had heard it before. I told the joke, about the restaurant that had no menus and you ordered your meal by pointing to a spot on the stained tablecloth ('What's this? Tzimmes? Bring me some,' and so on, and the waiter writes no check. The customer goes straight to the cashier. She picks up his necktie and says, 'You ate tzimmes.' But then the customer belches and she says, 'Ah, you had radishes, too.'). When I finished Jackie looked at me strangely. 'To tell the truth,' he said, 'if I never heard it again I wouldn't be upset.'

"It must have been the way I told it, because when I read the joke in 'Cousins'"—it was included in Bellow's short-story collection *Him with His Foot in His Mouth*—"I got a good laugh out of it."

Bellow responded: "I am acquainted with Jackie Mason, so it was a disappointment to me that he failed to laugh at the tablecloth joke (which I particularly hold in respect because it was one of my late father's favorites). Stand-up comedians are always under strain. Offstage, Myron Cohen was, I remember, very tense. They do not readily laugh at the jokes of amateurs. So don't take it to heart. . . .

"Thanks for your kind letter. And tell Jackie Mason that he should not despise the offerings of us kids from the comedy poorhouse."

Bellow also provided an insight for me into the difference between politics and sports in America.

In a call to Bellow in March 1999 I mentioned to him the curious fact that there were just one hundred members of the press in the Senate for the start of the impeachment proceedings for President Clinton, and five times as many for Michael Jordan's retirement announcement.

"What does that say to you, if anything, about the country?"

"That they've given up on politics," he replied. "As they should. They know it's a low, lousy game, and they just sort of turned their backs on it. When the chips are down they'd rather watch a good basketball game."

⌐ Of the teams I have followed, the Cubs remain dearest to my heart. And if you don't take them seriously (if you do, you might want to walk into the sea with rocks in your pockets), they do provide a large dollop of humor. Once you root for a team as a child, it seems to stay with you, for better or worse, the rest of your life. I've also contended that rooting for the Cubs disqualifies you as a fan, since there is no point in continually having expectations for a team that forever disappoints. The last time they won a World Series was in 1908; the last time they won a National League pennant was 1945. (Not news, but ever amazing.)

When yet another new manager had been named to try to plug the overflowing dike of failure, Tom Trebelhorn in 1994—naming a new manager was a virtual annual rite for the Cubs—the club held the traditional press conference to introduce this new hope in double-knit knickers and billed cap.

"What's it like taking over a team that hasn't won a World Series since 1908?" one of the reporters asked.

He seemed to take umbrage. "Hey," he said, "anyone can have a bad century."

And so, since there is the well-deserved adage of "no cheering in the press box"—the title, by the way, of a superb book about sportswriting by Jerome Holtzman—I covered whatever stories about the Cubs I had to with proper if not solemn professionalism.

In New York, meanwhile, where fans consider one year away from a championship a disaster—I've always thought that losing like the Cubs, but eternally trying, teaches more about life than nonstop winning—I was moved to write a column about a particular home run that is part of Cubs lore.

I wrote the column in the spring of 1991, which in New York was a time when the "Shot Heard 'Round the World,'" forty years earlier, was being recalled. That was when Bobby Thomson of the New York Giants, in the third and final playoff game with the Brooklyn Dodgers for the National League pennant, hit a game-winning home run in the bottom of the ninth inning. Of course, since it happened in New York, it was felt there that nothing like it could compare to drama and excitement.

I wrote a column begging to differ. I recalled that summer afternoon in 1951 when Phil Cavarretta, the longtime first-base star for the Cubs, had been named player-manager. In a critical moment in a game that meant nothing in the standings—it rarely did for the Cubs—Cavarretta, the newly hatched skipper, looked down his bench for a pinch hitter and decided that *he* should be the likely suspect.

The bases were loaded as Cavarretta stepped to the plate. The other team, the Phillies, brought in their ace pitcher, Robin

Roberts, to face Cavarretta, and Cavarretta, in non-Cub tradition, hit a home run to win the game. I saw the game on television at home on the West Side. I was eleven years old and was beside myself. I jumped and screamed. The neighbors below us, the Heifetz family with the father the chiropractor, hit a broom handle against his ceiling to quiet the commotion over his head. Maybe he missed a bone in someone's back because of it, I don't know.

Shortly after my column appeared, I received a letter from Mike Royko of the *Chicago Tribune*. I had a great regard for Royko, whom I—along with a legion of his fans—considered as good a general columnist as there was in the country. And one who, skewering the local politicians with a wonderfully unerring acerbic pen, made me laugh out loud. He added his own memory of that moment:

" . . . I remember the day. I was 18 and triple-dating at the Indiana Dunes. One of the guys was Cavarretta's nephew and we heard his heroics on a portable radio. I went even goofier than the nephew.

"I once had the pleasure of meeting Cavarretta. I was 15 and a student at Montefiore, sort of a day-school for delinquents. (I was railroaded; a teacher shoved me so I punched him.) Cavarretta came to Montefiore to hand out Christmas gifts. Most of the kids were kind of wild and didn't know who he was. They were almost mugging him for the gifts until he yelled 'Siddown, ya' little fuckers, it's Christmas.'

"Of course, nobody is perfect, and it still bothers me that he tried to spike Jackie Robinson's foot during Robinson's first game at Cubs Park. . . ."

I wrote back: "I've told people for years that I discovered you. I'll never forget reading stories in the summer of 1963 (or thereabouts) of guys with weird nicknames getting blown up every time they started their cars. These were front-page pieces in the *Daily News*"—Royko wrote for the *Chicago Daily News* before going on to the *Sun-Times* and then the *Tribune*—"and they broke me up. I began looking for the reporter's byline: Mike

Royko. I told everyone about them. Then you got the column, and I've never stopped reading you. . . . "

And it was true, right up until his sudden death at age sixty-four in April 1997 from a brain aneurysm.

✍ Of the athletes I've covered over forty years, none stands out for me more than Muhammad Ali.

Ali was called, often by those who wished to disparage him, "The Mouth." But there was substance as well as humor. He could not only fight, not only stand up for what he believed, but he was also a poet, in spirit if not altogether in iambic pentameter. Perhaps he wasn't T. S. Eliot, but he had his moments beyond "Moore will fall in four."

In 1971 Ali was training in Chicago for a fight with Jimmy Ellis. Before leaving New York to interview Ali, I was asked by a woman acquaintance if I'd get his autograph for her two small boys, age nine and eleven.

I said no, that it simply wasn't professional. She persisted. "Okay, if the occasion arises, I'll do it," I said. "But please, don't expect it."

I spent the day with Ali, and before departing, I said, "Champ, I hate to ask you this, but would you mind signing an autograph for two small boys?"

"No problem," he said. He asked me what the names of the boys were. I told him, and for some reason I added, "Their mother has trouble making them clean their room."

Ali wrote: "For Timmy and Ricky, from Muhammad Ali. Clean that room or I will seal your doom."

✍ I've been to the White House twice, both times for reasons of sports. While one doesn't normally think of the White House as a place for belly laughs, there have been moments.

The first time was in February 1986 when President Reagan invited the Super Bowl champion New York Giants and a handful of reporters. Reagan, his hair darker than I'd imagine that of a man in his eighties, and with hearing aids, was surprisingly and impressively quick on his feet. Looking back, I think he was even more impressive considering the Alzheimer's disease he suffered in coming years. One of Reagan's best friends was Ambassador Walter Annenberg, another *Times* sports-section reader, whom I came to know and visited on his estate in Palm Springs, California. In the mid-1990s he told me he played golf with Reagan at the exclusive Los Angeles Country Club. "I'm not sure he knew who I was anymore," said Annenberg. "His mind was pretty well gone. What was remarkable, though, was that at least he knew when he hit a bad shot. Then he'd swear like a sailor."

Speaking of presidential disabilities, Joe Louis once told me that not long after America's entry into World War II he was invited to the White House to meet President Roosevelt, who suffered from polio and was relegated to a wheelchair. Louis, then the heavyweight boxing champion of the world, recalled: "The president felt my muscle and said, 'This is the kind of strength we need to win the war.' But what was surprising to me was that the president's grip was stronger than mine." Louis surmised that the power came from Roosevelt's years of rolling his wheelchair.

Louis had another kind of strength: the way to deal with an uncomfortable situation. He did it, as he did most things, with a sense of dignity.

I was riding in a taxi with Tom Seaver, then the Mets' ace pitcher; Curt Blefary, a run-of-the-mill outfielder for the Orioles; and Louis. We had left a sports dinner at a midtown Manhattan hotel and were headed to Penn Station for a train to take us to Rochester, where we all had been invited for a sports presentation the following night.

Seaver, Blefary, and I sat in the back seat, Louis was in the passenger seat. The cab driver was a young man with a long ponytail. Music played from the car radio. This was 1970, and ballplayers, usually conservative, still had short-cropped haircuts. Blefary, who had been drinking, began to make disparaging remarks to the driver, needling him about, among other things, his "hippie" hair. I know I was uncomfortable with this. I didn't know if Seaver or Louis were as well. Then Blefary said, "Hey, turn off that hippie music." Louis, silent until now, looking straight ahead, said, "That's Greek music."

The music remained, and Blefary said not another word.

When I was invited to the Clinton White House the night after Monica Lewinsky appeared on the "Barbara Walters Show," Hillary wasn't talking to the president. But I spoke with her about her playing basketball in high school at Maine Township in suburban Chicago in the 1960s. "We were allowed only to play half-court," she recalled. "The feeling at the time was that it would be too strenuous for girls to play full court. We might fall down in a faint from overexhaustion." She laughed. "How times have changed."

I met George W. Bush when he was president, but not President of the United States. He was president of the Texas Rangers baseball team. He was standing behind the batting cage at the ballpark in Arlington, Texas, wearing jeans and cowboy boots. He was very youthful looking—this was in the early 1980s, when he was about forty-five years old.

I told him that not long before seeing him I was in the "morgue" of the *New York Times*, where clips and photographs could be obtained for use by reporters and editors, when I overheard one of the black employees behind the desk saying to another person, "Did you ever see pictures of Barbara Bush when she was young? She was a feet-stoppin' fox!"

George W.'s furry eyebrows rose. "Really?" he said, obviously very pleased. "I can't wait to tell mother."

As a "conservative," he supposedly tries to save taxpayers' money. But doing the reverse made him rich. He and his baseball partners had threatened to move the team from the Dallas–Fort Worth area unless Texas citizens paid for a new ballpark. So a tax was levied on goods that were shared by rich and poor alike. There being more poor people in the area than rich, the tax was absorbed more by those who could less afford to pay it. With this money, the private entrepreneurs built the new ballpark, then sold the team for millions—the team being worth more because of the new stadium—and George W. became rich. His original investment in the team was $600,000, money he obtained from friends of his father. When the team was sold, his share came to $14 million.

I had heard stories about Bush when he ran the Rangers. When he came to owners' meetings he'd sit with his cowboy boots up on a table and his face hidden as he read *USA Today*. Periodically he'd lower the paper when someone was speaking and say, "That's a bunch of bullshit," and raise the paper to his face again. Other times, to amuse himself, he threw spitballs. His level of concentration did not seem high.

Years later I asked a fellow baseball owner, "Did you ever think, at those league meetings, that Bush would become president?" This was on a ball field at the start of a World Series, and other reporters were milling around.

The fellow owner looked around to see if anyone else was listening, decided no one else was, and bent over and whispered in my ear, "Never!"

But Bush was hardly the callow young man he seemed. The bulge in his wallet when he left baseball told a different story. He had made himself a multi-millionaire.

⌒ I celebrated one Father's Day with my father by going out to play golf with him. I don't remember ever playing catch with a baseball with my father, as many fathers and sons historically did. We never went out to play tennis, or even shuffleboard. But my father had taken up golf in his retirement. He said that previously he had made excuses of being otherwise occupied when friends asked him to play. He didn't think he was very good. Then one day, after he retired, he stopped by a golf course where some of his friends played and watched them swing at the first tee.

"Lot of them were duffers," he said. "But they all looked like they were having fun."

Tentatively he began to play. Soon he was hooked. "Hooked" in his case meant playing once or twice a week, reading some golf manuals, and in the living room demonstrating to my mother, who has never touched a golf club in her life—cards for poker, or Kaluki, yes, but not a golf club—demonstrating how he used a 2-iron on the dogleg on the eighth hole. She'd nod and then return to her newspaper, happy for him and happy for herself that his swing was with an imaginary club and didn't imperil her nearby vase.

While my father became entranced with golf, I had rarely played. But when my dad suggested that we go a round, I said, Sure.

We went to the public course where my father knew the people working there, and where some of his friends in politics played. My dad went out to the first tee, rolled up the cuffs of his pants, smoothed the baseball cap on his head, and was set, almost.

"Last week," he told me, "they dragged a lady away from here in an ambulance."

I looked around. The fairways were exceedingly narrow. My dad explained how the ball that was hit from one fairway wound up not only in the adjoining fairway but smack in the middle of a woman golfer's forehead. "Got her right between the eyes," he told me. "Laid her out flat."

"You've got to keep your head up around here—except when you're about to hit the ball," he added. "They're coming at you from all directions."

I teed up and the ball fell off the tee. Then the tee fell. Then the ball and the tee. The image of the woman with the golf ball in her forehead was still on my mind. My father came and set up the ball and tee for me, and we were off.

It was a well-tended, tree-studded course, bright and green on this sunny June morning. And while my father and I were in the woods looking for one of my wayward shots, the foursome behind us were already taking dead aim at us. Plop. Plop. Two balls landed nearby. "Two weeks ago," my father said, "a ball whizzed right past my nose."

"What did you do?" I asked.

"Ducked," he said.

As we went along, driving a motorized golf cart, I heard a lot of "Fore!"

At one juncture I saw so many people in the fairway from other parts of the course searching for their balls that it looked like a hunt for Easter eggs.

A ball cracked off a tree trunk. Another ball clanged off a nearby golf cart.

It was hard to concentrate on hitting the golf ball. My father seemed relatively unperturbed. He was having a grand time. Oh, he had his share of muffed shots, but he was good. Once, on a dogleg, he hit one right over the trees. He watched it soar and land in perfect position for a chip to the green. "Oh, man!" he said with unabashed delight.

And when I'd muff another shot, he said, "Hey, Nicklaus and Palmer aren't perfect, either." He suggested, "Take an easy swipe at the ball. Let the club do the work for you."

"You know," he said at one point, "the old guys'll beat the young ones every day in the week. The old guys hit it short, but they're consistent down the fairway. The young guys hit it eight miles, but then they can't find the ball."

We played nine holes. It was a great day, a great time—and now we were safe from rocketing golf balls. I took pleasure in my father's pleasure. One moment seemed to sum it up.

He had chipped his ball onto the green, and it rolled to within a few feet of the hole.

"I never take a 'gimme' putt," he said, lining up the shot. "I like to hear the ball drop in the hole."

∽ In December 2001 I returned to Chicago on another matter, a grave one. My father, who was eighty-seven, was dying.

14

~~~~~~~~~~~~~~~~~

Blue Skies

MY FATHER was opposed to selling the two-bedroom condominium in which he and my mother lived on the North Side of Chicago—he thought that if he moved to a senior citizens' home he'd lose his independence, and perhaps a part of his sense of manhood. But I urged him to sell. Both of them, now in their late eighties, were becoming frail, and I thought that such a living situation, one that would provide meals and medical attention on the spot, would be best for them. My mother thought it was a good idea—"And they've got Bingo too," she said—and finally my father, ever reluctantly, agreed.

I had suggested their moving to New York, but both thought that, having lived all their lives in Chicago, this was where they wanted to stay. "Why don't you move back to Chicago?" my mother asked.

"He's got a job in New York," my father explained. "He's got a life there. He just can't up and move."

"We did," my mother said.

"It's different for us, Shirley," he replied.

With my parents, Shirley and Harold Berkow, in 2000, when they were residents of the Lincolnwood Place retirement home, just outside Chicago.

In the summer of 2000 we found a well-appointed, well-organized living quarter, Lincolnwood Place, in Lincolnwood, just across the city line from Chicago and about a mile and a half from where they lived. I thought it would be good for them to be in the relatively same neighborhood as the one they had lived in, and with the same friends and family close by. But those worlds, as my father noted, were shrinking.

"All my friends," my dad said to me once, "are either dead or out of their minds."

When he walked into Lincolnwood Place for the first time as a resident, after their furniture had been put in place in their one-bedroom apartment in the independent-living area, he looked around the very nice lobby, with its chandeliers and thick carpet and a reading room with leather couches and stacked book-shelves. He also noted the several grey-haired men and women with walkers, others being carted about in wheelchairs. My father smiled wanly and, almost to himself, said, "This is the end of the road, isn't it?"

"Dad," I said, taken slightly aback, "it doesn't have to be. There's entertainment every night. First-run movies. A piano player comes in, a magician, singers—you can sing with them. They've got different functions. Outings. They go to museums. They've got speakers—current-affairs discussions. You'll love that stuff."

In fact he became friendly with the current-affairs speaker who also held a question-and-answer session after her talk. And sometimes she'd ask questions as though in a quiz show. He did like that. My father, before going off to sleep every night that I can remember, listened to serious talk shows on the radio beside his bed.

One day I asked how the session the day before had gone. "I answered for the first two questions," he said. "I answered them right off the bat. Then I stopped answering questions."

"Why?" I asked.

"I didn't want to look like a show-off," he explained.

And he still had his car, which he drove more and more slowly. Sometimes I'd follow him someplace and he'd forget to turn the turn signal off, and it would be blinking continually. He'd forget some directions to places he'd been going to for years. It was getting harder for him to count. He worried about money. I told him he was okay, and wrote out for him all the particulars of what he had in banks. He and my mother, while enjoying life and not being particularly frugal, had been careful with their money nonetheless, and my father was wise enough, with pensions and Social Security and small investments, to wind up financially comfortable.

"Didn't do so bad," he once said to me. The implication was that he did just fine, especially coming from a background with little means and a broken home. "Could've done better. Little more education. But what's the use of talking."

Another time, walking through the corridor of Lincolnwood Place, he saw old men and women seated and dozing, heads on chests. "If you ever see me in a situation like that, nodding off all day," he said, "shoot me."

They had been living there for several months and had made friends. They ran into people they had known years before who were living there. One was the son of a man who owned a surgical supply store that specialized in trusses. The store was located across Roosevelt Road from my father's cleaning store, at the corner of Springfield Avenue.

My father recalled to the man that his father used to have a sign up in the truss store that my dad loved. It read, in Yiddish, "Dine Killa Es Mine Godilla." Translated into English, it meant, roughly, "Your hernia is my happiness."

"I still have the sign," the man said. "It's upstairs!"

↙ My father, meanwhile, was adjusting to Lincolnwood Place. But he remained realistic and was never as happy there as I had hoped.

One day my mother was telling him a story about a woman in the residence.

"Who is she?" my father asked.

"You know," my mother said, "the old lady."

"That," said my father, "describes every woman in the joint."

I still was working in New York, and still traveling. But through my work with the *Times* and by dint of invitations to visit Chicago for various speaking engagements, I was able to drop by to see them at least once a month.

In the latter part of 2001 my father had become very sick. He was suffering from congestive heart failure. Some ten years earlier he had undergone a quadruple bypass of the heart. He told me over the phone now that it had taken him two hours to dress that morning. He was also looking after my mother, who suffered from arthritis and diabetes as well as "a mild form of dementia" (the doctor's description). He was her primary caregiver, watching over her with the love and care he had always shown. "Your father," their internist David Levine told me, "is keeping your mother alive."

On the day before Christmas 2001, I called their home early that evening. My father sounded so tired he could hardly get words out of his mouth.

"I'm coming to Chicago," I said. He said, "It's not necessary, I can take care of things." He always had, but I didn't think he could now—I was sure he couldn't.

I caught perhaps the last plane out to Chicago that night. I had a key to their apartment, and when I came into their bedroom I saw him lying partially on the bed with his legs hanging over the side. He was fully clothed. He had tried to undress and didn't have the energy. I helped him get into bed.

My mother, lying beside him, didn't know what to do and had virtually forgotten even how to make a telephone call.

"I'm going to have to call the paramedics," I said.

"No," he said, "don't. I'll be okay, I'll get better." Then he added, "I don't want to go through that lobby on a stretcher and everyone around there looking at me." He was too proud to be sick. But that didn't change his medical condition.

"You can't lie here like this," I said. "You need help."

I phoned the paramedics and, despite my father's wishes, they took him to the hospital. It was late. There were few people in the lobby of the residence, but my father wasn't about to look around to see who, if anyone, was there. Now wearing an oxygen mask, he stared straight up to the ceiling as he was carried to the ambulance. In the emergency room at St. Francis Hospital in Evanston, I stayed with my father for several hours. His blood count was nearly zero. He was given transfusions and eventually color returned to his face. When attendants came to remove him to a room they had cleared, I kissed him on the forehead and told him I was going to leave.

He looked at me through his glasses. "Thank you," he said softly.

"Thank *you*," I replied.

"For what?" he said.

"For everything," I said.

On the way back to their apartment–I had been able to get a caregiver to stay with my mother in their bedroom while I slept on their couch–I thought about my dad, thought how much he had meant to me.

He was in the hospital for a week when the doctor pulled me aside outside his room and said he didn't think my father had long to live. "A few weeks, not much more," he said. "There's not much left of his heart."

And then, with my assent, the doctor told him the dire report. When the doctor, Edwin Smolovitz, left, that's when I asked my father how he felt, and he said he wasn't scared or depressed, and then I began to tear up, and my dad looked at me and said, "Don't cry for me . . . Argentina." And that's when I broke down laughing and crying at the same time.

Within a few days my father returned home and was under hospice care. I also hired a twenty-four-hour-a-day caregiver, a Filipino woman named Althea Miranda Abellanosa, whom everyone called Lee. My father seemed to rebound to a degree, and I thought I could go back to New York and work again, giving the caregiver instructions that if there were an emergency, to call me– I bought a cell phone for this purpose–and I'd come immediately.

On the afternoon of January 23, 2002, I was in a hotel room in Toronto, planning to write a column on that night's Knicks-Raptors game, when the call came. "Your dad's breathing is labored," Lee said. "The hospice nurse is here, and it looks like he doesn't have long."

I told her I'd come right away. I raced out of the hotel, grabbed a cab, and jumped on a plane. Thoughts of my father flooded back to me.

⌒ Although I had been a starting guard for my high school and college teams, my father was too busy to attend games (which didn't bother me; most of the parents of our players didn't come). In 1984, however, I was invited back to Chicago to play in a charity basketball game between the Chicago Bears–including wide receiver Willie Gault, a world-class sprinter–and a group charitably called the Former Chicago North Shore All-Stars.

I was considerably less than our name suggested, at any time, but that's what the organizers chose to call us (a few of my teammates had been legitimate high school and college standouts). My parents and Steve were at the game. I hit several shots and was rather proud of myself. Afterward my dad acknowledged the shooting and said, "But I was thinking as you ran down the court that you were a little slow. Then I realized–you're forty-four years old!"

I said, "Dad, I *am* slow–nothing's new–and I *am* forty-four years old. But just about everyone else in the world looks slow next to people like Willie Gault!" He laughed in agreement.

I remembered the time when he was struggling after selling his cleaning business, and someone offered him a secret recipe for soap in which you didn't need soap. My father bought the "secret recipe" for a nominal sum–under a hundred dollars, I seem to remember. It was pure sand, to my estimation. My father loaded it all into the bathtub and had family and friends experiment with it. You rubbed your hands with it and then wiped them on a towel. The towel got sandy. I don't remember my hands getting any cleaner, just stickier. My father was pretty good about phonies, but he wasn't, obviously, perfect.

He had a way of making a point with me. In high school I'd sometimes come home late and undress in the dining room, for some reason. When I'd wake up in the morning, I'd find that he'd thrown my clothes on my head.

My father once wrote a short story. It was the only story I ever remember him writing. It was about a crippled boy. He read the story to me at the kitchen table when I was five years old. I don't remember many other details, other than that it was such a sad story that I cried. But the boy was able, despite a reliance on crutches, to make something of himself.

When I was a young child, my father would come to my bedside and tell me stories. They were invariably about the Lone Ranger and Tonto "riding down the range." They too saw a small boy crying. His house had been burned down; his parents were gone. I don't remember where. But the boy was alone. The Lone Ranger and Tonto rode up to comfort him and take care of him. I don't remember how any of it ever turned out because by then I was generally fast asleep. While there was pathos in these stories, there was also something positive about them. Not in a saccharine way but in a real way, as I perceived it.

He once told me a story about a tailor named Berkowitz—no relation to us—who had a shop near our apartment on the West Side. "He was a little guy," my father recalled, "and people used to say, 'You know that SOB tailor, he's got his lights on every night. Look at the big money he's making.' They were jealous of him. One day I had to get a pair of pants cuffed and went to him. We began talking. He was aware of what people were saying about him. 'I know, they say I have more money than Carter has liver pills. I'm not rich. I'm a tailor. Who's going to get rich sewing up patches? But I'd rather they envy me than pity me. I'd rather they say what they say rather than, "That poor man, he can't make a living."'

"I was reminded of when I was a kid without parents. People would say, 'Poor kid, just doesn't have anything. An orphan.' I always hated it. And you know, when I got in the cleaning business, people began to say I was making big money too. I wasn't, but I didn't mind. I was like that little tailor. I understood completely. Better to be envied than pitied."

There was something else about my father's youth that he rarely spoke about. And that was his brother Henry, and my father's scare when he went to visit Henry. The family never spoke about Henry. And it was only when one of my father's sisters, Lillie, died, and my other aunt, Sylvia, gave the names of the eight brothers and sisters at the memorial service and, out of nervousness, added "Henry." It ran in the newspaper. I read it and asked my father who "Henry" was.

And he told me. Henry had a health problem. Had an operation and somehow it affected his brain. He was relegated to a mental institution in a Chicago suburb. One day, when my father was a teenager, he visited Henry. He heard screams and blabbering from the people around Henry. Henry himself, my father recalled, was quiet, though with a vacant stare. At the end of the day, my father prepared to leave. And the doors began to shut before he was able to exit.

"I got so frightened," he said. "I thought they might keep me in there. I wasn't sure I would ever get out. But pretty soon one of the guards found me and opened a door and let me out onto the street. I began getting headaches after that. I don't know if that visit was the sole reason, but I've had a headache almost every day of my life since then."

My father was the baby of the family and yet felt a responsibility for his siblings. They often looked to him for help, as successful as some of them became, and while none were wildly wealthy, they were able, as my father said, "to make ends meet."

One of my father's sisters, Ella, was eccentric. The rest of the family called her a "gypsy" because of the way she moved from apartment to apartment. She was argumentative and demanding. But when my father was on the streets as a boy, he could always count on Ella to feed him and provide a place for him to stay. She was married twice and divorced twice.

Ella had two sons, both of them backward—nice but backward. The younger one, Herbie, was gotten job after job by my father, often in easy labor, like cutting grass for the Park District. But somehow Ella always felt he was going to get a hernia and managed to get him on disability until he lost the job completely.

Marvin, the elder boy, was just a few years younger than my father. He was drafted into the army for the Second World War and discharged after a short stay at a military base in Texas. The family story was that he became "shell-shocked." But from what I learned, he was "shell-shocked" before he ever got into the army.

He was sent to the veterans' hospital at Great Lakes, just north of Chicago. Periodically he would run away to his mother's apartment. She was unable to care for all his psychological and medical needs and had to have him returned. She always called my father to drive Marvin back to Great Lakes. My father, not always happily, would nonetheless drop everything and do this.

One time, Marvin said to my father, as he was about to get in the car, "I want a woman." Marvin, then in his thirties, had never been with a woman.

My father, who delivered cleaning and knew the neighborhood, drove Marvin to a brothel. He parked the car and told Marvin to stay seated. My father knocked on the door. The madam answered. My father explained the situation. He went back to the car, got Marvin, led him up the stairs to the waiting woman. My father returned to the car and waited for Marvin to conclude his tryst, the first of his life.

When Marvin reappeared at the door, my father went to get him, then drove him back to the base.

While Marvin had been drafted for duty in the war, my father had been rejected. He was declared 4-F by his draft board. He had flat feet, bad eyes, and a family. He had wanted to do something to help our war effort, and while volunteering for home-front activities, as did my mother, he also placed a big sign in the window of his cleaning store: "Free Dry Cleaning for Military Personnel."

A friend of my father's once made a disparaging remark to him about his not having served in the war. My father took great umbrage at that. He said he had done what was asked of him. Not everyone was needed in the trenches. From that point forward, my father never had anything to do with that man.

Sometimes, when I was at my parents' apartment, I'd write a column with my laptop on the dining-room table. I'd look up to see my father watching me. I knew that my father took pleasure in my writing, though he was never effusive. That wasn't his nature.

"Finished?" my father would say.

"I think so, until the editors see it," I said, with a smile.

"Read it to me," he said.

He listened quietly.

"Good," he might say.

"Yeah, good," my mother might say. "Kinda long."

Under the glass on his bedstand he had inserted a few family pictures as well as, one time, a small clip from the *Chicago Tribune* that had picked up a quote from a story I had written. "If Bowie Kuhn were a carpenter," I wrote, "he'd always have a sore thumb." My father liked that. I don't think he had any opinion about Kuhn, then the commissioner of baseball, but he liked the line, I guess. I think he may also have been proud that the local paper thought it clever enough to republish.

On the other hand, he didn't like a review in the daily *New York Times* of *Hank Greenberg: The Story of My Life*, a book I had put together from the late home-run hitter's tape recordings to himself, as well as research I did into his life. One of the criticisms the reviewer had was that there wasn't enough about Greenberg's sex life.

My father's response to this was, "If the guy wants to read about more sex, he should buy *Playboy* magazine."

Throughout my entire writing career, my father had been my close friend, someone I could confide in, someone I'd bounce ideas off. The same went for Ian, his nephew, who not infrequently called my father for advice. Sometimes my father agreed with an opinion I was writing, sometimes he didn't. "You aren't going to write that, are you?" he might say. "Yes," I'd reply. One in particular concerned Bruce Kimball, a twenty-five-year-old Olympic silver medalist in diving, who was a candidate for the U.S. team trials for the Seoul Olympics in 1988. While driving drunk, he killed two teenage girls, but a judge let him out on bail. I thought he should continue to earn his living–diving is what he did with his life. Anyone else out on bail could resume normal activities, so I didn't think being on the commercialized and politicized Olympic team was any different.

My father didn't go so far as to say he was canceling his subscription to the *Times*–I had insisted on paying for it anyway–but he clearly could not fathom my position. There are times when, no matter how beloved one is in one's life, he must strike out on his own. And be struck out too, if it comes to that. It goes under the age-old rubric: sink or swim.

Looking back now, as I imagine my father's last breaths, I think of the long, long road he traveled–the long road both of us traveled, separately and together. I was proud of his achievements, of his business success and the respect he engendered, having done all of it, often alone, as a boy and young man during the depression. But I was even prouder of the man that I knew, the courageous and loving and wise–if somewhat understated, from his own avoidance of the spotlight–father and husband and brother and uncle and friend. I have hoped, in my best hours, to emulate the man my father was. I know that his words and his actions were often on my mind, a guide, and it was up to me to follow his lead by my own lights. Whatever strengths I might have been given, and whatever energy I might have summoned, it was up to me to get the most out of them, however I could, as I believe my father did.

While we talked on the phone often when I was not in Chicago, my dad, as it happens, wasn't big on writing notes or letters. He was always rather brief and concise when he did. My mother wrote longer missives. But my father, besides his penchant for singing, had a creative bent to him. On the last Valentine's Day of his life, for example, in 2001, it was snowing too hard for him to leave the apartment to buy my mother a card. So with pen and paper he drew a heart for her, arrow and all, and wrote her a short poem. The poem is now lost.

My father and I didn't discuss religion very much. I believe he was an agnostic, though I'm certain he never would have put a label on his beliefs. "I'm not sure what happens afterward," he said. "How can anyone know?" My father's religious beliefs might be summed up in the Yiddish proverb he periodically quoted, "Mensch tracht und Gott lacht," which, as he translated for me, meant "Man plans and God laughs."

⌒ My plane from Toronto landed in Chicago around 8:30. I rented a car—why I didn't just take a cab I still don't understand—and was at my parents' apartment within the hour. Lee, as she later told me, had been kneading my father's chest and telling him, "Hang on, Harold, Ira's coming, hang on."

He hung on. He might have been surprised at my speed, I don't know. He was still alive, though comatose, when I got there. I sat by his bedside, in the semidarkness of the bedroom, the only light coming from the living room where my mother, not fully aware of the seriousness of the situation—she knew for certain that "Daddy was very sick"—sat staring at the television set on low volume. I don't how much she absorbed of what she saw.

My father's eyes were closed, his eyeglasses were on the nightstand beside him, and he was breathing heavily, trying with difficulty, it seemed, to swallow each breath. I held his hand, which felt slightly cold and very weak.

I asked him, the words catching in my throat, if he was aware that I was there. After a pause, slowly he fluttered his eyelids. He died an hour later, with me still holding his hand.

I then went into the living room and put my around my mother.

"How's Daddy?" she asked.

"Ma," I said gently, "Daddy's gone."

Her eyes widened. "Gone? He's dead?" she said.

"Yes, Ma."

She began to sob. I held her tight. After a moment, she straightened up. She wiped her tears.

"How's Daddy?" she asked.

﹏ At my father's funeral, with perhaps a hundred people in attendance, I delivered a eulogy. I told about how subtle but wise he was in being supportive of me, even when I might be least aware of it.

Like handing me *30 Days to a Powerful Vocabulary* in high school, when all I was interested in was anything other than academics. But he knew I would profit by it.

And I recalled a particular time of trial for me, shortly after I had graduated grammar school in June 1953. The family had moved from the West Side of Chicago to the North Side. For much of that summer I returned to the West Side to see old friends—I missed them and was lonely. I took one bus and transferred to two others in the twelve-mile journey. My father thought I should try to make friends in the new neighborhood. I wasn't interested. Without my knowing, he scouted the area and found Green Briar Park about a half-mile from our new home. One Saturday morning he suggested we shoot some baskets at the nearby park. I said yes.

This was the first time I'd ever shot baskets with my father. He hadn't played much sports as a boy because of his bad eyesight and because he had to work. But he managed to become a very graceful swimmer. (And a strong one. When he took the family on vacation to Miami Beach after selling his cleaning business in 1953, when I was thirteen and my brother Steve was seven, at the beach my brother got caught in an undertow. He was hollering for help and going down. I was also in the water and went out to get him, and then *I* got caught in the undertow. I was going down! My father was on the beach with my mother. Seeing that we were in trouble, he raced to the edge of the beach, dived into the water, and swiftly swam out and brought us both back to shore. Years later, recalling that incident—I don't remember mentioning it before—I asked my father how he was able to swim back with two kids under his arms. "You were my boys," he said. That was all.)

At Green Briar Park now he exhibited an ancient—I'd say 1920s—two-hand underhand set shot from anywhere on the court.

He was, to say the least, a bit rusty. This was the age when the jump shot was just becoming popular, and I was able to shoot it. In short-sleeve shirt, slacks, and leather shoes—somewhat less than full-court apparel—my father bent his knees as though about to plop onto a stool, his glasses glittering in the sunlight, and let the ball fly. I suppressed a laugh at his attempts.

Shortly, a few boys came to the court, and then more. They asked if I wanted to get in the game. I agreed. My dad went to sit on a nearby bench. I played a game, and another, and another. I would make lifelong friends with some of those boys. But what I remember most distinctly is that at one point in the games, I looked over to where my father had been sitting. The bench was vacant.

My father was gone. But he had, as was his intention, sent me on my way, in more ways than one.

When I finished the eulogy, I turned on a tape recorder that I had brought to the lectern. I played two songs that my father had recorded of himself singing two of his favorite songs, a cappella. One was "Pennies from Heaven," the depression-era tune that held out hope in those dark days, and the other was "Blue Skies" ("Blue skies smilin' at me / Nothin' but blue skies do I see . . ."). The voice was resonant and tuneful and carried clearly through the chapel.

It was blue skies that he sought for me, and my mother and brother, and himself too, and he did all he could, on that winding and inevitably unpredictable journey from cradle to grave, to achieve that aim.

And then there were the words to that other song that he had mentioned to me shortly before his death: "Don't cry for me . . . Argentina."

Well, maybe only now and then.

Acknowledgments

IN ACKNOWLEDGING gratitude, appreciation, or simply a boost in a book of this nature—the story of one's life—one ought to begin at the beginning. And I do. So my parents at the earliest stage get their proper, founding due—first paragraph of the prologue.

After that it gets hard, because so many people have contributed in so many ways to my travels through, as the saying goes, the vagaries and vicissitudes of life. As well as to the making of this book.

Many of them are found in the contents of the book. Some are not. My apologies to those who know they should be in it, who know I know it, but either by my wispy memory or a descent between cracks, have not been included.

As for the work of putting a life onto the printed page, there are several who were, in this case, indispensable.

My literary agent, David Black, who has been an ever-welcome creative mind and backbone for me;

Larry Klein, who helped in the earliest writing stages with the structure of the book;

Acknowledgments

Richard Frederick, who read with care and astuteness the several drafts of the manuscript;

Drs. Peter Berczeller and Marc Siegel, intimates whom I have happily and gratefully entrusted with my life—and the reading of my manuscript—and both of whom have responded with uncommon sensitivity and brilliance;

Charles Miron, who always had a novel idea for a contribution; Ginny Hoitsma and David Fox, and Shelley and Loren Ross, who made important suggestions on the page proofs;

Ivan R. Dee, friend and editor and publisher of this book, whose guidance from the time he offered to take the book on to his personal, artful editing of the manuscript has made all the difference.

And to Dolly, with love everlasting.

Index

Aaron, Henry, 5, 84, 181, 215, 240
Abellanosa, Althea Miranda, 265, 272
Across the River and into the Trees (Hemingway), 70
Adventures of Augie March (Bellow), 142
AIDS, 205
Albion College, 54
Aleichem, Sholom, 44
Ali, Lonnie, 205
Ali, Muhammad, 114, 116, 141, 169, 206, 207; comeback of, 117; as conscientious objector, 115, 205; against Frazier, 117, 118, 119; as poet, 254
Allen, Dick, 152, 242
Allen, Richie. *See* Allen, Dick.
Allen, Wally, 107

Alzado, Lyle, 237
Amdur, Neil, 222
American Revolution, 67
Anderson, Dave, 218, 235
Andretti, Mario, 104
Angell, Roger, 12
Annenberg, Walter, 255
Anti-Semitism, 78, 79, 101
Araton, Harvey, 218
Arcaro, Eddie, 75
Ashburn, Richie, 240
Ashe, Arthur, 205
Athletes: genius and, 136
Atlanta Hawks, 123
Atlas, James, 81, 82
Auerbach, Red, 130
Augusta (Ga.), 62
Auschwitz, 101
Auto racing, 104
Autry, Gene, 210

Index

Baiul, Oksana, 169
Ballplayers: drugs and, 236; press and, 234; reserve clause and, 238; salaries and, 236, 238; steroids and, 237
Baltimore Colts, 246
Banks, Ernie, 231
"Barbara Walters Show," 5, 256
Barfield, Jesse, 204
Barnett, Dick, 123
Barry, Dave, 166
Baseball, 3; team expansion and, 11; writing and, 120
Baseball Encyclopedia, 240
Baseball Hall of Fame, 173, 176; character issue and, 174, 175; hypocrisy and, 175; Pete Rose and, 174, 175, 176
Baseball teams: commercial flights and, 233
Baseball time, 12
Baseball Writers' Association of America, 10, 173; membership, decline in, 11
Basketball, 125, 130, 131
Basketball Hall of Fame, 144
Baylor, Elgin, 143
Bedwell, Benny, 167, 168, 169
Bell, George, 204, 235
Bellamy, Walt, 128
Bellow, Saul, 5, 81, 82, 142, 249, 250, 251
Benevolence International Foundation, 177, 178
Berkovitz, Joe (grandfather), 38
Berkow, Eddie (uncle), 41
Berkow, Ella (aunt), 268

Berkow, Harold (father), 13, 18, 40, 147, 176, 257, 259, 260, 261, 262, 266; background of, 38; as confidant, 270; creative bent in, 271; death of, 272; draft board, rejected by, 269; funeral of, 273, 274; golf, fascination with, 258; illness of, 263, 264, 265; personality of, 37; politics, entry into, 42; as precinct captain, 42, 43, 44; religious beliefs of, 271, 272; responsibility, sense of, 268, 269; self-improvement of, 42; as storyteller, 267; as trustworthy, 39; work history of, 29, 39, 41, 48
Berkow, Henry (uncle), 267, 268
Berkow, Judy (sister-in-law), 50
Berkow, Lillie (aunt), 267
Berkow, Max (uncle), 38
Berkow, Max (grandfather), 47
Berkow, Rose (aunt), 47
Berkow, Shayne (niece), 50
Berkow, Shirley (mother), 46, 260, 261, 264, 266, 272; illness of, 263; personality of, 45, 48; reading habits of, 18
Berkow, Steve (brother), 46, 49, 266, 273; death of, 50, 51; as schoolteacher, 50
Berkow, Sylvia (aunt), 267
Berlin Crisis, 75
Beyond the Dream (Berkow), 139, 161
Bin Laden, Osama, 177
Bird, Larry, 164–165, 166, 170
Black Sox scandal, 144

Index

Blair, Jayson, 217, 218, 219, 220, 226, 227; firing of, 221, 222
Blefary, Curt, 255, 256
Bodoures, Bob, 200
Bonds, Barry, 216; surliness of, 215
Bonds, Bobby, 215
Book of Knowledge, The, 18–19
Borzov, Valery, 170
Boston Celtics, 130, 164
Boxing, 119
Boyd, Gerald, 222, 224, 226, 227, 229, 231
Bradley, Bill, 123, 124, 128
Bradley University, 143
Branch, Edgar, 65
Braves, 135
Bretts, Lenny, 17
Britt, Johnson, 225
Brooklyn Dodgers, 120, 241, 252
Bronzeville, 32
Broussard, Chris, 222
Brown, Dale, 224
Brown, Sweet Charlie, 143
Brown v. Topeka (Kansas) Board of Education, 144, 181
Brundage, Avery, 5, 6
Bryant, Bear, 208, 228, 229
Bryant, Kobe, 130
Bryant *Snoops*, 17
Burgin, Dave, 68, 69, 111, 112, 161, 179
Bush, Barbara, 256
Bush, George W., 256, 257; administration of, 188
Byrd, Willie, 185, 187, 189, 190
Byrne, Jane, 250

Cahn, Sammy, 247
Caldwell, Joe, 123
Calessi, Fiori, 39–40, 41
California Angels, 209
Callahan, Tom, 194, 195, 196
Camus, Albert, 66
Candlestick Park, 29, 193
Cannon, Jimmy, 246
Capital punishment, 223, 224
Capone, Al, 45
Cardinals, 20
Carew (Carew), 210
Carew, Rod, 209, 210
Carnegie, Dale, 42
Carver High School, 188, 189
Case, Dolly (wife), 148, 149, 150, 160
Castro, Fidel, 99
Catcher in the Rye, The (Salinger), 8
Cavarretta, Phil, 252, 253
CBS News, 220
Celestino, Yonkers Joe, 151
Chaplin, Charlie, 207
Chechnya, 177
Chicago, 113; description of, 27; as diverse, 19; racism in, 63; West Side of, 3, 15, 20, 28, 38, 63, 94, 273
Chicago American, 81
Chicago Bears, 20, 266
Chicago Bulls, 130, 203
Chicago Cubs, 20, 21, 22, 28, 195, 240, 251, 252; day baseball and, 231, 232
Chicago Daily News, 253
Chicago Stadium, 27

Chicago Sun-Times, 18, 70, 253
Chicago Tribune, 223, 225, 226, 250, 253
Chicago White Sox, 20, 152, 158
Chones, Jim, 164
Churchill Downs, 90, 93, 94
Churchill, Winston, 70
Cicero (Ill.), 63
Cincinnati Enquirer, 70, 75, 127
Cincinnati Reds, 71, 170, 171, 174, 242
Citation, 103
Civilian Conservation Corps, 39
Clay, Cassius. *See* Ali, Muhammad.
Cleveland Art Museum, 66
Clinton, Bill, 5, 6, 7, 181, 251, 256
Clinton, Hillary, 256
A Coach's Life (Smith), 223, 226
Cobb, Ty, 171, 175
Cochnar, Bob, 139, 140, 141
Cohen, Myron, 251
Cole, Nat King, 33
Columbia (S.C.), 63
Comfort, Bobby, 151, 152, 155, 156, 159; as charming, 153; death of, 157; as lazy, 154; as sociopath, 154
Comfort, Millie, 152, 153
Comiskey Park, 27, 55
Conn, Billy, 99
Cooperstown (N.Y.), 12
Copy desk, 90, 91
Cosby, Bill, 117
Cox, Sherra, 199, 200, 201, 202, 203
Crosby, Joan, 125
Crosley Field, 71

Crusade in Europe (Eisenhower), 58
Cuba, 99

Daley, Richard J., 29, 42, 55, 176
Daley, Richard M., 55
Dallas Cowboys, 246
Dallas Times-Herald, 166
Damascus, 92
"Dare to Compete" (documentary), 5
Dark, Alvin, 240
Darrow, Clarence, 68, 106, 179
Davies, Bob, 130
Davis, Miles, 33
DeBusschere, Dave, 123, 124, 128
Dempsey, Jack, 163
DeVarona, Donna, 5
Dayton Daily News, 70
Death penalty. *See* capital punishment.
Deford, Frank, 169
DeSimone, Bonnie, 223, 224, 225, 226, 227
Detroit Pistons, 143, 164, 165
Detroit Tigers, 190
Diary of Anne Frank, The, 208
Dickson, Bob, 102
DiMaggio, Joe, 13, 201, 202, 211; Marilyn Monroe and, 213, 214, 215; reputation of, 213
Dirksen, Everett, 84
Discrimination, 95; stereotyping and, 96
Disraeli, Benjamin, 79
Donahue, Phil, 154
"Don't Be Cruel," 56

Index

Dorman, Dan, 223
Dowd Report, 173, 174
Drugs, 27
Durham, Yank, 118
DuSable High School basketball
team, 143; as historic, 144; racial
barriers, breaking of, 144
*DuSable Panthers, The: The
Greatest, Blackest, Saddest
Team from the Meanest Street
in Chicago* (Berkow), 143

Edgewater Beach Hotel, 22
"The Ed Sullivan Show," 56
Einstein, Alfred, 67
Eisenhower, Dwight, 58
Elements of Style, The (Strunk
and White), 124
Elias Sports Bureau, 136
Ellis Island, 9, 38
Ellis, Jimmy, 254
Ellison, Ralph, 31
Embry, Wayne, 65
Eskew, Willee (wife), 79, 80, 82,
84, 86, 89, 100, 101, 109, 110, 111,
113, 147, 150; parents of, 85
Europe, 87, 101

Farragut High School, 238
Feldmeier, Daryle, 101, 107
Financial Times, 96
Finnegans Wake (Joyce), 66
Fleming, Erin, 248
Florida Times-Union, 116, 139
Flynt, Larry, 142
Focsani (Romania), 38
Football: discrimination in, 96

Ford, Tennessee Ernie, 16
Former Chicago North Shore All-
Stars, 266
Fort Gordon (Ga.), 60, 62, 63
Fort Leonard Wood (Mo.), 60
Fort Meade (Md.), 76
Fowler, Gene, 230
Franks, Bobby, 106
Frazier, Joe, 169, 207; against Ali,
117, 118, 119
Frazier, Walt (Clyde), 123, 124, 125,
127, 131, 145
Frey, Jim, 237
Friendly, Fred W., 220

Gallico, Paul, 182
Gambling, 26, 27
Gannt, Harvey, 203
Garnett, Kevin, 238
Garr, Ralph, 136
Gastineau, Mark, 204
Gault, Willie, 266
Genius: athletes and, 136
Gardner, Bruce, 157, 161; suicide
of, 158, 159
Gardner, Erle Stanley, 66
"Garfield," 131
Garrett, Wayne, 136
Gerber, Ann, 80, 81
Germany, 101
Gertz, Elmer, 106
Giamatti, Bart, 173
Glasgow Celtic, 97
Glasgow Rangers, 97
Glasgow (Scotland), 97
Goldberg, Arthur, 23
Golden, Soma Behr, 224

Index

Golf, 101, 245
Goodfellas (film), 154
Goodman, Benny, 23
*Gospel According to Casey, The:
Casey Stengel's Inimitable,
Instructional, Historical
Baseball Book* (Berkow and
Kaplan), 146
Grace, Mark, 21
Graham, Frank, 235
Granat, Mrs., 47
Green, Danielle, 184, 185, 186, 187,
188, 189, 190
Greene, Bob, 50, 51
Greene, Lou, 98, 99, 100, 101
Greenwich Village, 113
Grimes, Barbara and Patricia, 167,
169
Grodno (Russia), 47
Groves, Donald, 30, 31, 32
Gulfstream Race Track, 4
Gun control, 203

Hairston, Jack, 116
Halper, Barry, 211, 212
Halperin, Errol (cousin), 46
Halperin, Jerry, 46
Halperin, Lil, 46
Halperin, Julius (uncle): arrest of,
44, 45
Halperin, Molly (grandmother), 44
A Handful of Clients (Gertz), 106
*Hank Greenberg: The Story of My
Life* (Berkow), 270
Hardaway, Tim, 188, 189
Harding, Tonya, 167, 168, 169, 176
Harlem Globetrotters, 143

Hartman, Sid, 99, 100, 101, 102,
103, 107
Hawthorne, Bower, 91
Hearst, Patricia, 115
Helms, Jesse, 203
Hemingway, Ernest, 36, 70
Henry V (Shakespeare), 68
Heroes, 203; definition of, 202;
image and, 175, 176; as mortal,
22, 197; during San Francisco
earthquake, 198, 199, 200, 201,
202, 203
Him with His Foot in His Mouth
(Bellow), 251
Hitler, Adolf, 132
Hoch, Paul, 115
Holiday, Billie, 33
Holm, Eleanor, 5, 6, 7
Holman, Nat, 130
Holocaust, 101
Holt, Barry, 53
Holtzman, Jerome, 235, 252
Holyfield, Evander, 213
Holzman, Selma, 121
Holzman, William (Red), 121, 122,
123, 124, 129, 244; background of,
130; genius of, 128; influence of,
130; spotlight, shunning of, 127,
128
Horse racing, 91
"How Race Is Lived in America"
series, 222, 224, 229
Hoyt, Waite, 13
Humboldt Park, 50
Humboldt's Gift (Bellow), 249
Humorist: nature of, 246
Humphrey, Hubert, 105, 106

Index

Hunter, Catfish, 12–13
Hupper, Jerome, 42
Hussein, Saddam: September 11
  and, 188; weapons of mass
  destruction and, 229
Hypocrisy: Baseball Hall of Fame
  and, 175

Ice fishing, 89, 90
Indianapolis 500, 104
Indiana University, 143, 163
Inside Kasrilevke (Aleichem), 44
Inside Sports magazine, 157
Iooss, Walter, 124
Iraq: war in, 184, 185, 186, 187, 188,
  219
Ivins, Molly, 166
Izenberg, Jerry, 235

Jackson, Jesse, 93
Jackson, Phil, 123, 124, 130
Jackson, Reggie, 208
Jacobson, Steve, 114
James, Jesse, 9
Jenkins, Ferguson, 231
Jews, 85
Johnson, Dennis, 165
Johnson, Lyndon, 57, 106
Johnson, Magic, 165
Jolly, Tom, 222, 223, 224
Jones, Brucie, 77, 78
Jones, Sarah, 108
Jordan, Michael, 130, 165, 203, 204,
  225, 226, 251
Journalism: accuracy, sensitivity
  about, 226; fact checking and,
  221; objective reporting and,

234; office politics in, 162. *See
  also* Sportswriting.
Joyce, James, 71
Jungle Princess, The (film), 126

Kafka, Franz, 66
Kaline, Al, 190
Kaplan, Jim, 146
Kasperwicz, Stella, 197
Kellner, Jenny, 204
Kennedy, 2nd Lt., 61
Kennedy Airport: Lufthansa
  robbery at, 154
Kentucky Derby, 90, 91, 103;
  Derby Day and, 93, 94;
  protesters at, 92, 93
Kerrigan, Nancy, 167, 168, 169
Kimball, Bruce, 270
King, A. D. Williams, 92
King James Bible, 124
King, Martin Luther, Jr., 90, 92,
  93; assassination of, 94
Kinsley, Michael, 166
Kipling, Rudyard, 245
Knight, Bobby, 163
Koufax, Sandy, 241, 243
Krakow, Harris. *See* Levinsky,
  Kingfish.
Krakow, Louis, 55
Kroan, Morrie, 26
Kuhn, Bowie, 270

Lamey, Mike, 101, 102
Lamour, Dorothy, 125, 126, 127
Lancaster, Burt, 118
Landers, Ann, 207, 208, 209
Landman, Jonathan, 222, 226

Index

Lane, John, 124
Lane Technical High School, 239, 240
Lang, Jack, 11
Lawndale, 19
Lederer, Eppie. *See* Landers, Ann.
Leiter, Al, 235
Leopold, Nathan, 68, 106
Levin, Ian, 56, 57, 177, 178, 179, 180, 190, 191, 192, 270
Levin, Lou, 57
Levine, David, 264
Levinsky, Kingfish, 55
Lewinsky, Monica, 5, 256
Lewis, Lennox, 212, 213
Lillehammer (Norway), 168, 169
Lincoln, Abraham, 124
Lipsyte, Robert, 218
Livingston, Bob, 161
Loeb, Richard, 68, 106
Los Angeles Lakers, 130, 164
Louis, Joe, 55, 99, 206; dignity of, 255, 256
Louisville (Ky.), 90; demonstrations in, 92
Lucas, Jerry, 123
Lumpkin, Paxton, 143

Macbeth (Shakespeare), 68
Machiavelli in Hell, 212
Maddux, Greg, 231
Madlock, Bill, 231
Major League Baseball, 4, 136
Malamud, Bernard, 18
Malden (Mass.) *Evening News*, 141
Malvo, Lee, 219, 220
Manfredonia, Johnny (Peanuts), 151

Mann, Thomas, 66
Mantle, Mickey, 12, 83
Man Who Robbed the Pierre, The (Berkow), 247
Margolis, Ralph, 16
Margolis, Ted, 75, 76
Marjorie Morningstar (Wouk), 18
Marquette University, 163
Marx Brothers, 248
Marx, Chico, 249
Marx, Groucho, 248, 249
Marx, Harpo, 3
Maryland: sniper shootings in, 219
Mason, Jackie, 246, 250, 251
Matthau, Walter, 207
Maule, Tex, 133
Maxwell Street, 22, 23, 25, 44, 45, 56, 65, 249, 250; corruption at, 54, 55; description of, 24, 26
Mays, Willie, 114, 134, 135, 136, 137, 236, 240
McGuire, Al, 163, 164
McMillon, Shellie, 143
McNeil, Neil, 82, 84
McNulty, John, 125
Mele, Miss, 16
Metz, Bob, 139, 140
Miami Heat, 188
Miami Student, 68, 69, 70, 75, 111
Michelangelo, 87
Millan, Felix, 136
Minneapolis-St. Paul (Minn.), 89
Minneapolis Star, 108
Minneapolis Tribune, 11, 87–88, 90, 96, 98, 100, 101, 102, 103, 106, 108, 162, 183; atmosphere at, as stifling, 132

Minnesota Timberwolves, 236
Minnesota Twins, 97, 99, 100
Moby Dick (Melville), 65
Monroe, Earl, 123, 124
Monroe, Marilyn, 58, 213, 214, 215
Moody, Miss, 16, 17
Moore, Archie, 206
Moore, Marianne, 119; on
  baseball, 120; on sports, 120
Mora (Sweden), 91
Moran, Frank, 97
"Morris B. Sachs Amateur Hour,"
  24
Morrison Hotel, 41
Muhammad, Elijah, 114
Muhammad, John, 219
Murphy, Bob, 102
Musial, Stan, 240
Muslims, 114
Myrtle Beach (S.C.), 64

Namath, Joe, 184
National Football League, 133
National Guard, 60, 75
Natural, The (Malamud), 18
Navy Pier, 56
Neff, Janet Annenberg, 154
Nelson, Jimmy, 238
Newman, Paul, 67
News agencies: cautious reporting
  of, 220
Newsday, 113
Newspaper Enterprise Association
  (NEA), 7, 8, 111, 114, 115, 116, 125,
  139, 162, 234; comic strips of, 131;
  cost-cutting measures at, 140
New York, 113

New York Daily News, 233
New York Giants, 209, 252, 254
New York Jets, 204
New York Knickerbockers, 121,
  122, 127, 128, 129, 189, 203, 244;
  championship of, 123
New York Mets, 233, 234, 235, 237
New York Times, 160, 161, 162, 166,
  173, 221, 225, 226, 227, 241, 256,
  270, 271; Jayson Blair incident
  and, 217–220; management crisis
  of, 231, 232; Pentagon Papers
  and, 220; reputation of, 217, 232;
  stiffness at, 222; tension at, 222;
  weapons of mass destruction,
  reporting on, 229
New York Yankees, 17, 71, 211
Nicklaus, Jack, 245
Nike, 203
Nixon, Pat, 210
Nixon, Richard, 7, 106, 183, 209, 210,
  211, 212; administration of, 220
North Carolina, 203
Northwestern University, 82
Nortown News, 80
Novak, Kim, 238

Oakland Athletics, 193, 203, 213
Oates, Johnny, 135, 137
O'Hara, Maureen, 175
Olderman, Murray, 111, 112, 114,
  116, 118, 119, 133, 137, 140, 141, 157,
  161; uniqueness of, 132
O'Neal, Shaquille, 130
One Man's Meat (White), 126
On Writing Well (Zinsser), 124
Osborne, Tom, 224

Index

Paciorek, Tom, 204, 205
Packer, Billy, 165
Padwe, Sandy, 112, 116, 160, 161
Paine, Thomas, 67
Paley, William, 23
"Peanuts," 131
Pegler, Westbrook, 182
Pentagon Papers, 220
Perez, Tony, 242
Philadelphia Inquirer, 112, 161
Philadelphia Phillies, 22, 240, 242, 252
Piazza, Mike, 235
Pierre Hotel: robbery of, 150, 151, 154
Pimlico Race Course, 137
Podres, Johnny, 17
Points of My Compass, The (White), 230
Poland, 101
Politics: sports and, 251
Pony League, 238, 239, 242, 243
Popowcer, Red, 23
Powell, Colin, 187, 188
Poynter, Mike, 140
Pratt, Nancy (wife), 146, 148, 150
Pratt, Tim, 147
Preakness, 137
Presley, Elvis, 56
Professional Golf Association, 95
Proud Clarion, 92, 94

Quarry, Jerry, 117
Quite Early One Morning (Thomas), 230

Raines, Howell, 222, 223, 226, 227, 228, 229, 231

Reagan, Ronald, 172, 173, 254, 255
Redford, Robert, 67
Reed, Willis, 123, 124
Regency Hotel: robbery at, 151
Reuschel, Rick, 202
Reusse, Pat, 102, 103
Rhoden, Bill, 218
Rice, Grantland, 182
Richards, Bob, 133
Rickover, Hyman, 23
Righetti, Dave, 234
Rip Off the Big Game: The Exploitation of Sports by the Power Elite (Hoch), 115
Roberts, Robin, 253
Roberts, Selena, 218
Robinson, Jackie, 253
Robinson, Sugar Ray, 206
Rochester Royals, 130
Rocker, John, 208
Rockett, Willie, 94, 95
Rockin' Steady: A Guide to Basketball and Cool (Berkow and Frazier), 124, 125, 127, 145, 246
Rodman, Dennis, 165, 167
Rodriguez, Alex, 236
Rogovoi, Sam, 81
Rollins, Mack, 78
Rolvaag, Karl, 105
Romania, 8, 19
Romanoff, Harry, 81, 82
Romeo and Juliet (Shakespeare), 67, 68
Roosevelt, Franklin, 39, 255
Roosevelt High School, 189

Index

Roosevelt Road, 19, 45
Roosevelt University, 59, 64, 131
Rose, Pete, 142, 170, 171, 172, 176;
    baseball, banned from, 173, 175;
    gambling and, 173, 174; record
    of, 174
Ross, Barney, 23
Ross, Sayre, 152
Royko, Mike, 253–254
Rubinstein, Richard, 58, 59
Ruby, Jack, 23
Ruken, 92
Russell, Cazzie, 123, 189
Russert, Tim, 187, 188
Russia, 8, 19
Ruth, Babe, 84, 208, 210, 215
Rutherford, Johnny, 104

Sachs, Eddie, 104
San Antonio Express-News, 219
San Diego Padres, 172
San Francisco: earthquake in, 193,
    194, 198
San Francisco Giants, 134, 193,
    203, 215
Santo, Ron, 242
Satterfield, Bob, 33
Sauer, Hank, 28, 29, 195, 196;
    death of, 197
Savona, Freda and Olympia, 108
Schecter, Leonard, 115–116
Schieffer, Bob, 168–169
School segregation, 144
Scopes "Monkey Trial," 68
Scott, Jack, 115
Seagren, Bob, 132
Seattle University, 143

Seaver, Tom, 255, 256
Selig, Bud, 175
September 11: Saddam Hussein
    and, 188
Shakespeare, William, 67, 231
Shannon, Gerry, 198, 199, 200, 201,
    202, 203
Shea Stadium, 135
Sherry Netherland hotel: robbery
    of, 151
Show, Eric, 172
Sid! (Hartman and Reusse), 102
Sinatra, Frank, 118
Sirica, John, 7, 8
Sirott, Herb, 113
Smith, Bob, 102
Smith, Dean, 223, 224, 225, 227
Smith, Lou, 75
Smith, Red, 44, 71, 72, 74, 81, 106,
    107, 112, 124, 137, 138, 139, 160,
    161, 163, 177, 179, 182, 221, 246;
    death of, 162; as literary figure,
    70; work of, 73, 75; on writing,
    176, 230
Smolovitz, Edwin J., 14, 265
Soldier Field, 27
South: life in, 62; racism in, 63
South Africa: apartheid and, 205
Soviet Union, 57, 75
Speaker, Tris, 175
Speer, Albert, 132
Spinks, Michael, 212
Spinoza, 73
Sports, 3, 22, 180, 181; escapism of,
    183; politics and, 251; society, as
    mirror of, 183, 184; spirits, lifting
    of, 202

Index

Sportswriting, 107, 180, 193; cynical school of, 182; human spirit, elevation of, 183; job of, 181

Sprewell, Latrell, 236

Sputnik, 57

Stefansson, Janne, 91

Steinbrenner, George, 210

Steinhagen, Ruth Ann, 22, 197

Stengel, Casey, 13, 83, 84, 145; death of, 146

Stereotyping, 96; of blacks, 165, 167

Steroids, 237

Sting, The (film), 67

St. Louis Hawks, 122

Storytelling, 66, 74

St. Paul Pioneer Press, 101

Strawberry, Darryl, 237

Strunk, William, 124

Successor, 92

Sullivan High School, 16, 20, 52, 57, 216, 240

Sulzberger, Arthur, Jr., 220

Super Bowl V, 246

Sutton, Willie, 9, 10

Swanson, Merrill, 107

Tarmak, Juri, 170

Tarzan's Revenge (film), 5

Taylor, Lawrence, 209

Texas Rangers, 256, 257

Thillens Stadium, 239, 243

30 Days to a More Powerful Vocabulary, 53, 58

Thomas, Dylan, 66, 70, 229, 230

Thomas, Isiah, 163, 164, 165, 166

Thomson, Bobby, 252

Thorpe, Jim, 120

Tiede, Tom, 140

Toronto Blue Jays, 204

Trans-Mississippi Amateur Golf Championship, 101

Trebelhorn, Tom, 252

Turner, Edwin, 60

Twain, Mark, 14, 84

Tyson, Mike, 212, 213

Tyson, Rodney, 213

Ulysses (Joyce), 65

United Nations, 188

United States, 57

University of Chicago, 249

University of Illinois (Champaign), 57

University of Illinois (Chicago), 56, 59

University of Miami of Ohio, 65, 132

Upper Iowa University, 53

U.S. Olympic Committee, 168

Ussery, Bobby, 94

Vass Loppet, 91

Vecchione, Joe, 161, 162, 163, 166, 222

Vecsey, George, 218

Versailles, Zoilo, 99

Vietnam War, 106, 114, 182, 183, 184, 205, 220; sweatshops in, 203

Virginia: sniper shootings in, 219

Waitkus, Eddie, 21; death of, 197; shooting of, 22

Index

Waitkus, Eddie, Jr., 197, 198
Waldman, Suzyn, 204
Walker, Mickey, 221
Wallace, George, 228
Walsh, John, 157
Wanzer, Bobby, 130
Warren, Earl, 181
Warsaw Uprising, 85
Washington Post, 166
Watergate scandal, 7, 182, 220
Wayne, John, 175, 176
Weigel, John, 65, 66, 127
Weil, Joe (Yellow Kid), 67
Wertz, Vic, 135
West Rogers Park, 20
When We Were Kings (film), 117
White, E. B., 109, 124, 125, 126, 127;
    on writing, 94, 230
Wicker, Tom, 221
Wiechers, Jim, 102
William Cullen Bryant
    Elementary School, 15, 238
Williams, Billy, 232
Williams, Ted, 9, 211, 237
Wodehouse, P. G., 244, 245, 246,
    247, 248
Wolff, Leo, 39

Women: in locker room, 204
Woods, Jim, 238, 239, 240, 241, 242,
    243
Woolf, Virginia, 66
Words: beauty of, 53
World Series: of 1954, 135; of 1955,
    17; of 1961, 71; of 1989, 193, 198
Wouk, Herman, 18
Wright, Ben, 96, 97
Wright, Richard, 31
Wrigley Field, 27, 28, 240
Writing, 10, 94, 230; art of, 73;
    baseball and, 120; craft of, 4;
    humor and, 244; nuance,
    observation of, 44; sports and,
    131; as thinking, 176; typing and,
    52, 53

Xavier College, 69

Yankee Stadium, 181, 210
Yates Elementary School, 50
Young, Dick, 233, 234

Zadora, Pia, 208
Ziegfeld Follies, 5
Zinsser, William, 124

A NOTE ON THE AUTHOR

Ira Berkow has been a sports columnist and feature
writer for the *New York Times* for twenty-five years.
In 2001 he shared the Pulitzer Prize for National
Reporting with his article on "The Minority
Quarterback," later published in *The Minority
Quarterback and Other Lives in Sports*. Mr.
Berkow's work has appeared in numerous sports
and literacy anthologies, and he is the author of
more than a dozen books. Born in Chicago, he
graduated from Miami (Ohio) University and
Northwestern University's Medill Graduate School
of Journalism. Before coming to the *New York
Times* he worked for the *Minneapolis Tribune* and
Newspaper Enterprise Association. He lives with
his wife, Dolly, in New York City.